Feminists Doing Ethics

Feminist Constructions
Series Editors: Hilde Lindemann Nelson and Sara Ruddick

Feminists Doing Ethics
    edited by Peggy DesAutels and Joanne Waugh

Forthcoming Books in the Series by

Bat Ami Bar On, Sandra Lee Bartky, Anita Allen, Amy Baehr, Nancy Potter, Joan Mason-Grant, Eva Kittay, and Ellen K. Feder

Feminists Doing Ethics

Peggy DesAutels and Joanne Waugh

ROWMAN & LITTLEFIELD PUBLISHERS, INC.
Lanham • *Boulder* • *New York* • *Oxford*

ROWMAN & LITTLEFIELD PUBLISHERS, INC.

Published in the United States of America
by Rowman & Littlefield Publishers, Inc.
4720 Boston Way, Lanham, Maryland 20706
www.rowmanlittlefield.com

12 Hid's Copse Road
Cumnor Hill, Oxford OX2 9JJ, England

British Library Cataloguing-in-Publication Information Available

Library of Congress Cataloging-in-Publication Data

DesAutels, Peggy, 1955–
    Feminists doing ethics / Peggy DesAutels and Joanne Waugh.
        p. cm. — (Feminist constructions series)
    Includes bibliographical references and index.
    ISBN 0-7425-1210-X (alk. paper) — ISBN 0-7425-1211-8 (pbk. : alk. paper)
        1. Feminist ethics. I. Waugh, Joanne, 1951– II. Title. III. Series.
BJ1395 .D47 2001
170'.82—dc21

                                                                2001019407

Printed in the United States of America

♾™ The paper used in this publication meets the minimum requirements of
American National Standard for Information Sciences—Permanence of Paper
for Printed Library Materials, ANSI/NISO Z39.48-1992.

Contents

Acknowledgments

There are many people who had a hand in bringing out this volume, and we hope, memory permitting, to acknowledge all of them. First we would like to thank Hilde Lindemann Nelson and Sara Ruddick for including this book in their Feminist Constructions Series at Rowman & Littlefield and for their enthusiasm and support in seeing the project to completion. We also wish to thank the contributors for their original and thoughtful essays, which continue the lively and timely discussion of recent advances in feminist ethics that began at the Feminist Ethics Revisited Conference in Florida in October 1999. This conference was sponsored by the Department of Philosophy and the Ethics Center at the University of South Florida (USF), and we are grateful to Peter French, who was chair of the Department of Philosophy and director of the Ethics Center when the conference was held. We are also grateful to David Schenck, current director of the USF Ethics Center, for supporting the publication of this volume. Kathy Agne, who served as office manager of the Ethics Center until September 2000, was indispensable both in organizing the conference that inspired this volume and in preparing the resulting manuscript for publication. We do not know how we would have managed without her or without the many USF graduate students—too many to name—who helped us in so many ways. A special thanks also goes to Eileen Kahl, who applied great skill and care in preparing the index of the volume. Last, we want to thank Robert Richardson and Butler Waugh for their help and support.

Introduction

Peggy DesAutels and Joanne Waugh

We offer this volume as a contribution to the ongoing conversation that goes under the name of "feminist ethics." This conversation took an exciting and interesting turn recently at the Feminist Ethics Revisited Conference; many of the essays in this volume articulate ideas and analyses first presented there.[1] The term *feminist ethics* was used broadly at this conference—as it is again here—to refer to the perspectives on women's experience that come into view at the intersections of ethics, politics, philosophy, and literature. Earlier generations of philosophers—both male and female—have found that the experiences of women fit neither easily nor neatly into the categories favored by traditional, mainstream philosophy. That the dominant discourse of philosophy still strains to accommodate women's experiences has prompted feminist philosophers to go beyond the usual boundaries, especially in ethics. In her contribution to this volume, "Seeing Power in Morality: A Proposal for Feminist Naturalism in Ethics," Margaret Urban Walker succinctly summarizes feminists' achievements in ethics. "Feminist ethics," Walker writes, "is inevitably, and fundamentally, a discourse about morality and power" (4). Our volume emphasizes this essential insight of feminist ethics.

Philosophical ethics typically neglects power, taking its subject to be the ideal or transcendent nature of morality—something finer and higher than mere power. When attention is paid to questions of power, it is typically seen as standing in opposition to morality. Walker decries this neglect and denies this opposition at the same time that she insists that the concept of morality should be neither reduced to power nor eliminated in its favor. Walker insists on the importance of morality for challenging the legitimacy of distributions of power, for those who are powerless have neither grounds nor means for challenging existing power relations without appealing to morality. Indeed, this is one reason why feminist moral discourse asks whether and how power is distributed equally and unequally, whether and how it gains legitimacy or sustains itself illegitimately, and whether and when people having power over others is, in Walker's words, "morally necessary, arbitrary, or catastrophic" (5). To answer such questions Walker suggests that we recognize that morality "*is a disposition of powers through an arrangement of responsibilities*," that these responsibilities and powers are both social and distinctively moral, and that they are no less "natural" for being either or both (6). Indeed, such powers and responsibilities are "natural" *because* they are necessary in order for human societies to function, and human life naturally perpetuates itself through human societies.

Moral concepts can be abstracted from social practices only at the risk of missing the part of their meaning—typically the largest part—that is embedded in the social practices that generate the concepts. This is not to deny the *moral* authority of morality; rather, it is to insist that there is a specifically moral understanding of social practices, an understanding that we might, following Walker, call the *moral structure* of these practices. Walker sees this moral structure in practices of responsibility; and with the understanding of responsibility comes the understanding of agency and the values, positive and negative, that attach to those agents to whom we differentially ascribe responsibility. It is our understanding of these practices and the concepts embedded in them that grounds the trust that is recognized in the very notion of the moral authority of morality. Of course, these practices may be sustained by power and authority that is not moral, a fact that is often more transparent to those who have a lesser share of power and responsibility and are accordingly valued—or devalued—by those with a greater share.

Walker provides an example of how a concept like the social contract—as a contract between equals—when analyzed in terms of the social practices that make sense of it, defines itself in terms of the powers that white male equals have *over* those who are neither male nor white and thus are *not* equals.[2] As Walker puts it, "Equals do not just have different and greater powers and entitlements *relative* to those below: they are defined *as equal* by their shared entitlements *to* and powers *over* those below" (12). Indeed, the logic of equality that allegedly structures the Enlightenment project of moral universalism may also be what renders the project impossible. There is still another problem with this project of building an ethics and politics on consensual equality, for as feminist philosophers have insisted, within the scope of our moral concern we find those who are not equal because of their immaturity, disability, incapacity, vulnerability, and dependence. Such inequality, as Walker notes, describes or will describe all of us at some point in our lives—whatever our rational agency at this time. Questions about our responsibilities to those with whom we have unequal power relationships thus move us to undertake *political* analyses that invoke concepts other than a social contract between and among equals, analyses in which questions must be asked about the exercise of power, the same questions that those working in feminist ethics ask.

These political analyses also provide us with occasions on which to develop the solidarity necessary for feminist politics and ethics, as Uma Narayan suggests in "The Scope of Our Concerns: Reflections on 'Woman' as the Subject of Feminist Politics." Such occasions for developing solidarity are crucial in Narayan's analysis because she finds the suggestion that feminist politics groups together all experiences of those who identify themselves as women to be a nonstarter. Indeed, Narayan takes this to be the question that currently faces feminist ethics: "Can the scope of feminist analyses, and the agenda of feminist moral and political engagement, be justifiably restricted to 'issues pertaining to the interests of women'?" (15). That feminist politics should take its project as fighting for the interests of *all* women had been the conclusion of radical feminists, who took "women" as the name of a group whose members had been systematically oppressed *because* they were women. But the analyses presented by radical feminists were themselves contested by poor women, women of color, and women of differing sexual orientation(s) as not taking *their* experiences into account. One response to these objections, which Narayan labels the "Differences Critique," is to include the interests of these neglected groups, expanding the view of women's interests to form what Narayan calls the "Jigsaw Puzzle Picture Model of Women's Interests." But if all of women's interests do not fit together as this model suggests, then feminist politics (and feminist ethics) may not entail advancing the interests of *all* women. What *should* drive feminist politics and feminist ethics, Narayan suggests, is solidarity based on shared *political* analyses and not necessarily the experience of being oppressed by patriarchy. Solidarity based on shared politics can lead to privileged women—and men—working against their own privileged interests and with and for women whose oppression results from some combination of gender, race, class, and sexual orientation. Gender is not merely added to these other factors; the relevant metaphor for this combination is chemical, not mechanical. Because one cannot cut off the effects of gender from those of race, class, and sexuality, Narayan suggests that the "Oppressed Identity–Based Cutoff Model" of political membership may deprive feminists of theoretical insights and practical strategies for dealing with oppression.

Questions about how analyses of inequality and oppression affect conceptions of agency have received a good deal of attention from feminist philosophers, and there has been some concern that the very notion of agency as it has been formulated in traditional ethics is fatally compromised insofar as it assumes, first, that moral agents are *equal* in power(s) and, second, that autonomy should be identified with those who are *depended on* rather than *dependent*. Not only is this notion of the equality of moral agents defined, as Walker observes, in terms of their sharing entitlements *to* and powers *over* unequals, the concepts of dependence and independence invoked in such a notion themselves depend on distinguishing—artificially— between the public and the private spheres and on identifying morality with public behavior. Feminist ethics is left with a host of problems to address, not the least of them being whether and how moral damage is done to oppressed people by diminishing their conception of themselves as moral agents. Especially pressing are questions of how the concept of moral agency may be admitted into feminist ethics: What formulation(s) and what metaphors are and should be used to introduce the concept? And how will certain formulations and metaphors affect the moral structure(s) of the social practices of which they are a part?

Diana Tietjens Meyers takes up the question of how social categories of gender affect women's conceptions of themselves in "Social Groups and Individual Identities—Individuality, Agency, and Theory." Meyers argues for a conception of identity that recognizes the power that social constructs of gender exercise in individual identity, despite individual choice. The conflict that may ensue between a socially mandated conception of identity, in which one is a member of a subordinated group, and a sense of a self that belies this social identification may result in a sense of alienation, but it is a sense of alienation that Meyers regards as desirable insofar as it provokes moral reflection and emancipatory social criticism. Reflection on the ways in which gender identities do and do not affect an individual's sense of personal identity makes an individual self-conscious in a way that enables social critique. That some feminists have rejected theories of gender because they seem incompatible with individualized identities results, Meyers suggests, from a tendency to see gender theories as essentialist, that is, as conforming to a social-scientific epistemic model based on inductive generalizations about women. As universal generalizations about women, gender theories are easily disconfirmed by empirical data, despite the fact that elements of these theories resonate with the experiences of many women. Inspired by Marilyn Frye's suggestion that we regard gender theories as metaphors that provide insight and understanding without asserting identity or equivalence between things,[3] Meyers suggests that we can do justice to gender theories that, in turn, do justice to some women's experience by viewing them as we do literary texts. Just as interpretations of literary texts seek support in passages from the texts and address seeming inconsistencies between the interpretation and other parts of the text, theories of how social constructions of gender affect individual identity provide different perspectives on the ways in which gender—as well as class, race, and sexuality—is constitutive of an identity that is nonetheless *personal and individual*. In reading gender theories of identity describing other socially subordinated groups as we would literary texts, we must pay attention to the rhetorical value of the universalist tone of these theories, for this tone functions in a way similar to hyperbole and shouting: it quells disagreement and dissent. The goal, then, must be to generate theories of gender—and social practices that employ them—that allow members of subordinated groups to find their voices.

In "Identity and Free Agency," Hilde Lindemann Nelson looks at the power that some texts—ones she refers to as master narratives—have in structuring the identities of members of oppressed groups and how they may find their voices through counterstories. Drawing on narratives from nurses, Nelson illustrates how "a powerful group's misperception of an oppressed group results in disrespectful treatment that, as in the case of the nurses, can impede group members in carrying out their responsibilities" (50). These master narratives are *morally* oppressive to members of subordinated groups insofar as their capacity for *normative competence* is denied or diminished by the narratives. Normative competence entails not only that one is able to understand moral norms and act accordingly but also that one is capable of *normative self-disclosure*—that one may "reveal who one is, morally speaking, through what one does" (55).

Revealing oneself as a moral agent is a complex affair. One must see oneself as a moral agent, as morally trustworthy. But, if one sees oneself as a moral agent, this requires, in turn, that *others* see her as a moral agent and understand her action not only *as* a moral action but also as a moral action of a specific kind. Thus is a person's identity a function of how others understand what she does, as well as how she understands what she does, and thus is free agency a function not only of an agent's capacities and abilities but also of how others view her capacities and abilities. How others see her contributes to her understanding of herself—of what she can and should do. This gives others power to harm a person by depriving her of the identity of a morally competent agent—what Nelson calls "the harm of deprivation of opportunity"—and, in so doing, by contributing to her own sense of herself as having limited or diminished moral agency—what Nelson calls "the harm of infiltrated consciousness." In some cases, such as that involving the narratives of the nurses cited by Nelson, this harm can be repaired by means of a counterstory that aims at changing not only the perception that the powerful have of the oppressed group but also an oppressed person's perception of herself.

But such harm is a function not just of the means used but also of *the extent to which* the identities of the oppressed have been structured by these master narratives. Depending, as Nelson says, on not just *how* but also *when* a counterstory is introduced, it may or may not be possible to repair the harm of infiltrated consciousness or, at least, to right the wrong done to those whose sense of self has been undermined by oppression. Nelson cites as an example of someone with an identity beyond narrative repair a person who has never formed any notion of her free agency because of oppressive social structures combined with personal domination in an intimate relationship.

Bat-Ami Bar On takes how others view her and how she views herself as her starting point in "Violent Bodies." Bar On recounts how she developed her violent body first in response to the taunts of other children, then in accordance with the customs and expectations of a Jewish–Israeli youth in postindependence Israel, then as an adult Israeli citizen in military service, and finally as a feminist involved in a women's antirape movement in the United States. Feminist suspicions and criticisms of violent bodies are grounded in the fact that it is the male violent body that is so often the means through which women experience violence, primarily in the form of rape and battery in their everyday lives and during wartime. But what, Bar On asks, are the ethical implications of her "violent body"—a body that is ready to fight and habituated to respond to violence with violence with little or no conscious reflection about this response? To frame her analysis Bar On turns to Hannah Arendt, whose work on violence is perhaps the most sustained thinking about violence undertaken by a female philosopher—or a male philosopher, for that matter.[4] For Arendt, violent action can only be justified on ethico-political grounds, and because, as Bar On points out, we are limited in our ability to predict and control whether any action, including a violent one, will achieve the end for which it is the means, violent actions must be limited in scope and can be justified only for the short term. (Violence in self-defense is unproblematic because the danger is clear and present and the end justifying the means is immediate.) *Political* ends can thus justify instrumental violence and instruments like violent bodies, as long as violence is being used *to halt—and not to promote—the decline of political power.* Violence must always be backed by and restrained by political power, that is, the conscious and concerted action of a group of people working together not out of self-interest but out of solidarity—out of care and concern for one another and the world.

This Arendtean sense of *political* differs from standard feminist usage in which violence against women is political because it is made possible by a systemic matrix of domination and submission. For Arendt, systemic domination does not deserve the appellation *political* because people working together in concert and solidarity are central to her meaning of the term. Bar On observes that, *pace* Arendt, who objected to feminism insofar as it was motivated only by women's self-interest and not by care for the world, women's self-defense can be seen as a political project in an Arendtean understanding of the term, as can the production of violent female bodies. Because women's project of producing violent bodies serves as an "interruption of the status quo . . . what otherwise would have proceeded automatically" (71), Bar On argues that the production of women's violent bodies is transgressive. As transgressive, Bar On considers it justified ethico-politically—as long as women do not transgress boundaries "inhumanely" and "destructively" and remain aware of, and wary about, the seductive nature of violence (71).

That feminist ethics develops a theoretical framework and political strategies to contest the exercise of oppressive power is also of concern to Lisa Tessman, Margaret A. McLaren, Barbara S. Andrew, and Nancy Potter, each of whom analyzes how virtues of character and their realization in habituated actions contribute to these projects. Using a critical virtue ethics framework, Lisa Tessman argues that what is morally objectionable about oppression is that it interferes with human flourishing and that it does so for targeted social groups in a systematic way. Oppression does this by preventing or restricting access to "external goods" but also by preventing or hindering one in the development and exercise of the virtues and, in so doing, precluding one from acquiring a character that is part of a good life. Of particular concern to Tessman is that we examine how moral damage hinders members of oppressed groups from effectively resisting their oppression at the same time as we avoid dehumanizing the morally damaged group by treating that group as "a problem."

Analyzing how oppressive forces can interfere with human flourishing requires not only that we augment Aristotle's list of the factors interfering with flourishing by noting the systematic nature of this interference. We must also add goods that Aristotle did not recognize, including goods that are not captured under distributive paradigms. Of primary importance to Aristotle, of course, is the acquisition of those virtues the exercise of which results in a good life. Tessman adds the accompanying realization that if "there is injustice already at work in the formation of character, the fact that something is based on character does not imply that it is not also rooted in an oppressive social system" (82). The task—as Tessman, echoing Claudia Card, reminds us[5]—is that of distinguishing the insights of the oppressed from the moral damage that results from oppression. Such damage would include the failure to develop self-esteem, the fear of being conspicuous, and the tendencies to dissemble and to ingratiate oneself or identify with one's oppressors. Such character traits typically develop as survival mechanisms when one lives under conditions of oppression, but this does not mean that they are not morally damaging as well. Indeed, some psychological traits are doubly damaging from a moral perspective insofar as they help to convince the members of the oppressed groups that their circumstances are the result not of systemic structures and forces but of their own flawed characters and psyches.

To acknowledge that some of us have the bad "moral luck" to be members of oppressed groups does not, however, relieve us of all moral responsibility for our characters, even if their formation does not lie completely within our control. There is, of course, considerable risk of harm to members of oppressed groups in speaking of moral damage. Tessman illustrates this risk in recounting how the concept of the "damaged black psyche" became the justification for opposing changes in oppressive social structures and forces. This argument proceeds from the assumption that once the psychic damage has been done, the repair needed should come from neither economic assistance nor political empowerment but, rather, from the inculcation of "character-building" values, usually conceived of as "family values" where the heads of household are male. Indeed, an extreme version of this argument reverses the causal sequence, arguing that character deficiencies are the cause and not the consequence of such economic states as welfare dependency, despite the fact that historically economic opportunities for blacks have been so severely restricted, either in the number of opportunities or in the amount of compensation, as to be at times virtually nonexistent. Acknowledging that talk of moral damage is risky, Tessman points out that one does not have to choose between working to change structural causes of oppression and attempting to repair moral damage. Even more importantly, she suggests that changes in systemic structures and forces while necessary to undo the oppression of social groups may not be sufficient to repair the moral damage that is part of their oppression. Tessman thus proposes that radical strategies of resistance to oppression include a critical virtue ethics, for, among other things, the moral damage done to members of oppressed groups may interfere with their abilities to form such strategies of resistance. Equally important, those who have been morally damaged because of oppression have "responsibilities of their own," Card has observed, "to their peers and descendants."[6]

In "Feminist Ethics: Care as a Virtue," Margaret McLaren provides an example of how a traditionally female trait such as caring can be a resource for a feminist ethics that bases its approach in critical virtue theory. The concept of care is problematic for feminist ethics because some theorists have argued that defining care as characteristic of women and other subordinated groups is instrumental in their oppression. Such definitions can serve to "naturalize" and perpetuate oppression and can be morally damaging to the extent that women sacrifice their own interests for the interests of others, including those of their oppressors. In so doing, women fail to develop their own identity, autonomy, resources, and moral agency. However, other theorists have considered care to be a female trait that provides a foundation for a feminist ethics. McLaren argues that care ethics of the sort inspired by the work of Carol Gilligan is a *feminine* but not a *feminist* ethics because, among other things, it reinscribes the stereotypes of women that have structured and perpetuated the oppression of women. Still, McLaren insists that the concepts developed by feminist philosophers in response to care ethics provide us with the resources we need for a feminist virtue ethics.

That care has been seen as a virtue of women rather than of men is *prima facie* problematic, for seeing virtues as gender related has been one way in which ethical theory has contributed to and perpetuated oppression. Because virtue ethics is not innocent in the matter of women's oppression does not mean, however, that it has nothing to offer to feminist ethics. McLaren, like Tessman, believes that a *critical* virtue theory has much to recommend it as a normative ethical theory, for, unlike deontological theories, virtue ethics assumes that the moral agent is an embodied member of a community and, in so doing, addresses what is concrete and particular in moral situations. This becomes especially clear once we consider the attention that virtue theory pays to the contributions of character, practical judgment, emotions, and moral perception in deliberating about actions and motives.

Virtue ethics holds that human flourishing—and how one's community contributes or does not contribute to such flourishing—is both a condition for and a consequence of a moral life. Following Joan Tronto, McLaren argues that the concept of care should be *extended into the political realm* with the consequence that the boundary between morality and politics—or the public and the private—is erased.[7] When this boundary goes, so should the notion that women's virtues are those of the domestic sphere in contrast to those virtues (which, if not feminine, are presumably masculine) that allow the formulation of abstract, "universal," moral principles—principles that appear to be universal only in the public, and not the private, sphere. Finally, conceiving of care as a public or political virtue incorporates a concern for justice—the concern that care ethics allegedly slights. A *feminist* ethics that conceives of care as a political virtue will be a virtue ethics informed by feminist politics but not one in which care is the only virtue. McLaren suggests that other virtues in a feminist virtue theory would include such things as feistiness and playfulness, in addition to more readily recognized virtues of self-respect, openness, courage, and self-awareness.

The importance of contesting the image of the ethical woman as caring to the extent of being the "Angel in the House" prompts Barbara Andrew to look for another image of the ethical woman in "Angels, Rubbish Collectors, and Pursuers of Erotic Joy: The Image of the Ethical Woman."[8] Like McLaren, Andrew insists that the virtue of care should not be understood as exemplified primarily or solely by the domestic nurturer and proposes instead that we take seriously Michel Foucault's claim that ethics has its origins in "the care of the self."[9] As Foucault understands it, such care aims at a telos—"the kind of being to which we aspire when we behave in a moral way"—and thus does Andrew seek the telos of feminist ethics—the ideal image of the moral agent that inspires the ethical self to action. Andrew holds, as do Tessman and McLaren, that feminist moral action is political action and that care properly understood neglects neither the moral autonomy necessary for political action nor justice as both a means and an end of political action. Indeed, it is Andrew's claim that the ideal of ethical relationship that care ethics has helped to formulate necessarily involves autonomy and that the recognition of this ideal provides care ethics with an alternative telos to that of the Angel in the House. According to Andrew, the notion of ethical relationship fulfills the same function in care ethics that the notion of autonomy does in ethical theories centering on justice: each acts as a condition for moral actions and judgments, but each depends, in turn, on the existence of social conditions that provide the basic goods that enable its exercise. Thus, feminist ethics needs a telos that incorporates both care and autonomy.

The ideal image(s) of the ethical woman must recognize the importance of our desires both for connection with others and for autonomy; this is not accomplished by bifurcating between the (good) image of the Angel in the House and the (bad) image of the "Woman of the Streets." Following a suggestion of Drucilla Cornell's,[10] Andrew considers the *chiffionnier*—the junk or rubbish collector—as an image of the ethical woman. As a chiffionnier, the ethical woman sifts through the remnants of philosophical theories and systems for useful strategies for feminist political and ethical action. As such, she gives up the dream of the perfect philosophical system or theory, the one that will guarantee her neither loss nor oppression, and accepts that she must improvise strategies that allow her to both engage the other and care for the self. Still, even this image of the ethical woman lacks an ingredient that Andrew thinks is essential to the image of the ethical woman: the recognition of the imaginary, the domain in which, as Cornell notes, we *as embodied, sexual creatures* imagine ourselves as free and autonomous as we fulfill our desires for ourselves and for others.[11] Cornell observes that the imaginary domain as such can only be accommodated within an abstract ideal of subjectivity: "Defining the person only through a normative outline . . . [is] the only way we can preserve freedom of the personality."[12] In this way we employ the concept of the abstract person in our political analyses as one who determines for herself her values, including how best to love, even though these values have their source beyond her. In an attempt to do justice to the imaginary, Andrew turns to Simone de Beauvoir's image of woman as pursuing erotic joy as she creates "found art" and negotiates her sexual and caring relationships with others in order to experience the joys of connection and of freedom.[13] For Beauvoir, the *erotic relationship* provides the paradigm of our existence as subjects who care for ourselves and connect with others while also existing as Others for subjects who, too, desire both freedom and connection with us. Andrew concludes that whatever ethical images we propose must acknowledge that we participate with each other in relationships of power.

Nancy Potter also raises a question about our responsibilities to others in her chapter "Is Refusing to Forgive a Vice?" Potter agrees with Tessman,

McLaren, and Andrew that our moral evaluations should take the form not of testing whether our actions are instances of a universal moral principle but of asking whether an action and the disposition to which it attests are deficient or excessive—*virtuous* or *vicious*—in the context in which they occur. Potter notes that when moral theorists are asked about forgiveness they are prone to take the concept out of a religious context but are nonetheless willing to assert its central place in our moral lives. Indeed, forgiveness is commonly viewed as moral because it indicates that one who has been wronged has overcome (justifiably) negative feelings toward the person or persons responsible for the harm or injury. These negative feelings include such feelings as resentment, and the presumption is that giving in to such negative feelings indicates some moral lapse or weakness on the part of the one who has failed to overcome them. An injured party who forgives believes that the harm or injury perpetuated by the wrongdoer was morally wrong and that the wrongdoer is responsible for the action. Nonetheless, the injured party overcomes negative feelings toward the wrongdoer. In such a view, the act of forgiveness suggests that the wrongdoer in some sense transcends the harmful acts committed in the past. Accordingly, some moral theorists speak of the empathy with the wrongdoer that allows forgiveness and of the state of restoration or reconciliation that is its aim.

But Potter contends that this view of forgiveness fails to take into account that when forgiveness is viewed as a virtue there are situations in which its exercise can be seen as an excess or a deficiency. She notes that Jeffrie Murphy, for example, observes that we cannot be obligated to forgive another—or seek restoration or reconciliation at any cost—if doing so indicates that we lack self-respect, that we do not count ourselves as equal in moral importance to others.[14] In Murphy's view, forgiveness must be compatible with respect for both oneself and others as members of a moral community. Using this criterion, there will be cases in which both the action of forgiving another and the disposition to forgive will count as vices. Potter finds a case in which forgiveness would be a vice in Dorothy Allison's novel, *Bastard Out of Carolina*.[15] Bone, the protagonist in the novel, suffers repeated beatings at the hands of her stepfather—beatings about which her mother knows and which she sometimes tries to help her daughter escape. However, Bone's mother is unable to choose her daughter's well-being over what she perceives as her own—remaining with her husband. The husband's ultimatum that his wife choose him over her daughter takes the form of raping Bone, a rape that Bone's mother witnesses. Although Bone's mother and stepfather—and the larger community of which they are a part—are victims of the oppression suffered by poor whites in America's rural South, an oppression that Bone recognizes she shares with the members of her family, Bone refuses to forgive them for her injuries. As Potter notes, Bone has no reason to either forgive or seek a reconciliation with her stepfather, who scarcely acknowledges his wrongdoing or repents for it. There is no positive relationship that Bone can restore with him, no point to any reconciliation. Her resentment of her mother and her failure to forgive her, while clearly painful to Bone because she has given up the opportunity to recover her mother's love, may be necessary if Bone is to realize that she has suffered an injury that she did not deserve. Thus may Bone's refusal to forgive be seen, Potter suggests, as the mean between excess and deficiency, for it signals her respect for herself—and others—as members of a moral community, as moral agents who have a right to expect that injustice be punished. To refuse to allow a wrong to go unpunished, to refuse to forgive when to do so would be to diminish one's moral worth—and thereby commit a further injury and injustice to oneself—can hardly be counted as a vice.

In "Gender and Moral Reasoning Revisited: Reengaging Feminist Psychology," Phyllis Rooney argues, too, that feminists should redirect their attention to the *situational* character of both gender and moral psychology, specifically with the aim of enhancing our understanding of moral reasoning. Rooney shares the concern expressed by many of the contributors to this volume that, in talk of care and justice as different voices in moral deliberations, we fail to notice that some of these voices are the voices of the oppressed. Empirical studies conducted subsequent to those described in Gilligan's *In a Different Voice* contest the claim that males are more likely than females to have a disposition for moral rationalism,[16] that is, an enthusiasm for systematizing abstract rules and general principles and for seeing the primary values of moral agency as consisting in autonomy, consistency, and control. But the issue—as Rooney insists—is not merely a factual one, for traditional accounts of moral reasoning have asserted men's superiority *as a sex* over women precisely insofar as men have this proclivity toward moral rationalism and women do not. Indeed, the justification that one so often finds for denying women moral rationality is women's presumed inferiority at reasoning *in this fashion.* Thus does Rooney express the same concern as other contributors that "in the feminist literature there has been *an insufficient reading against the grain* of this traditional supposition" (156). She is especially concerned that the "care voice" attributed to women is characterized as eschewing abstract principles in favor of attending to the concrete aspects and contextual features of a moral situation. Rooney notes the imprecision with which *abstract* is used in such a characterization of the care ethic and points out that "abstracting from a (multifaceted) moral situation with respect to particular kinds of relationships and responsibilities among individuals in it, and not with respect to the specific juridical rights of those individuals as autonomous agents, is one way of abstracting from the situation; another way involves abstracting with respect to the latter and not the former (and these, clearly, need not be the only way of abstracting)" (156–57).

Rooney cites the psychological research of the past two decades that contests the view of earlier research, like Gilligan's, according to which gender consists of more or less stable intrapsychic traits and dispositions. More recent research suggests that gender is also very much a social category, one that social regulation works to produce, perpetuate, and reinforce through gender norms, practices, and expectations that can be related to power differentials. Empirical studies suggest that modifications of the experimental situation can result in the appearance—or disappearance—of gender differences and that the political dimension of different research programs may do so as well. Prompted by the possibility that Gilligan's work "exaggerates differences in disposition between women and men and overlooks differences in social structure, such as power differentials that press for different behavior in the two sexes," Nancy Clopton and Gwendolyn Sorell have studied the extent to which gender is stable versus situational in instances of moral reasoning.[17] Their conclusion is that gender differences in the orientation of moral reasoning result more from "differences in current life situation than from stable gender characteristics."[18] Rooney concludes that their study suggests that if *care* and *justice* apply to something, it is "to different kinds of moral situations in the kinds of responses they evoke" (161).

Rooney takes this shift to a more situational view of gender in moral reasoning as an impetus toward a more situational view of cognition, but she stresses that situated reasoning is not the same thing as contextual reasoning. "Care reasoning" may be contextual in a way that "justice reasoning" is supposedly not, but both kinds of moral reasoning—indeed, all kinds of moral reasoning—are situated. If one set of moral reasoners is prone to use "rights and principles" talk, we need to ask what it is about the situation of these reasoners that constrains them to reason this way. Because gender is often a salient characteristic of social location—one constructed and situated through particular norms and expectations—we may find that the gender of reasoners affects how they construct their "situatedness" and that, in specific social locations, men and women will construct their situatedness differently.

Of particular importance for ethics is that recent psychological work has given an active role to moral situations, prompting Rooney to remark that "situations, thoughtfully encountered, can bring morality to people: it is not simply that people bring morality (in the form of some 'inner' capacities and virtues, consistent sets of moral principles, and so on) to situations" (164). If ethicists have failed to recognize the extent to which this is true, it may be because the hypothetical situations often described when presenting moral problems are, as Rooney stresses, preselected for the limited forms of moral rationality they employ. Indeed, the models of cognition that they employ only scarcely apply to moral problems as distinct from mathematical or logical ones. Whether the moral situation is found in life or in literature, humans employ more cognitive and affective capacities than those exhibited in the artificial and hypothetical situations of ethical theory. Rooney asserts that these cognitive and affective capacities, "with moral practice and the development of moral integrity, enhance rather than diminish the range of human reasoning capacities" (164). Her recommendation is that feminist theorists operate with a more sophisticated picture of moral reasoning.

James Lindemann Nelson provides a complex picture of moral reasoning in his "Constructing Feelings: Jane Austen and Naomi Scheman on the Moral Role of Emotions." Nelson analyzes the views of moral reasoning presented by certain characters in Jane Austen's *Sense and Sensibility* and uses this analysis to critique Naomi Scheman's account of the role of emotions in moral cognition.[19] According to Nelson, Austen is concerned not merely with how character is developed in the Dashwood daughters but also with the "set of socially created and renewed resources" that contribute to the construction of feelings, the direction of action, and the intelligibility of the world. Indeed, that Austen captures the effects that emotions have on moral reasoning with such clarity and elegance is what prompts Nelson to see her novel as a kind of exercise in moral cognition. Nelson suggests that we might view Austen herself as refuting the view, expressed by the character of Marianne, that "feelings as such reliably indicate where propriety lies." Nelson's own view of the emotions' contributions to moral epistemology is more positive than Austen's, whose position in *Sense and Sensibility* appears also to be at odds with much recent feminist theory devoted to the positive role that emotions play in moral reasoning.

Nelson's take is also at odds with Naomi Scheman's views on the role of emotion in moral reasoning. Scheman holds that one of the primary functions of emotions is to provide for the possibility of moral objectivity; emotions are socially constructed and essential to moral judgment. Nelson reads Scheman as saying that, as a social construction, an emotion is not a state of an individual and does not have the kind of causal relations that provide for its existence as an entity independent of a social context. In Scheman's view, one could not experience an emotion outside of a social context that relates feelings, sensations, thoughts, and behavior in ways that provide for a coherent explanation; or, as Nelson observes, "Scheman's view . . . entails that emotions are not identifiable in terms of their causal effectiveness outside of particular forms of social practices and explanations" (169).

For Nelson, the ontological status of emotions—whether they exist as functions of explanatory schemes or whether they can be individuated apart from their role in social explanations—has important consequences for moral reasoning. He finds Scheman's account unclear regarding the conative or representational force of emotions—a force that he thinks is especially important when an emotion is discordant with some of our beliefs. For Nelson, emotions can and often do reveal what is morally salient in a situation; in support of this claim he cites Richmond Campbell's analysis of fear as a representation that one is in imminent danger and Alison Jaggar's account of the importance of "outlaw emotions."[20] The problem Nelson finds with Scheman's account of the moral role of emotions is that if emotions are functions of social explanations, the best that outlaw emotions can do is identify alternative strategies to the dominant strategy under which these emotions are deemed "outside of the law." Yet Scheman sees confrontations between explanatory strategies as contributing to the search for moral objectivity; to attain it requires a set of stable and sharable beliefs to emerge from challenges by the widest possible set of alternatives. Nelson does not see how emotions, *as Scheman characterizes them,* can contribute to the resolution of these contests. If emotions only exist within social explanations, can conflicting emotions indicate anything other than the existence of multiple explanatory strategies? Can they indicate that one strategy is more morally defensible than another? Nelson thinks that emotions can represent the world as being a certain way because they do have causal powers that individuate them independently of an explanatory scheme. Citing Scheman's discussion of the disagreement between the mother and son in *Torch Song Trilogy* as to whether the son's feelings of loss over his deceased homosexual lover are analogous to the mother's feelings of loss for her deceased husband, Nelson observes that there is nothing inferential or interpretative about the son's suffering. The son does not have to determine whether his emotion is located in an explanatory scheme, and it is difficult to believe that his mother would not recognize it as suffering—whether or not it qualified on her scheme as conjugal grief. Or, as Nelson observes about anger, "social practices might affect anger in many ways—trigger it, shape it, control what counts as acceptable expression of it, associate it and the forms of its expression in different ways according to gender or class—but not by providing it with the conditions that are essential to its having its identity at all" (179). He notes, in a similar vein, that although in *Sense and Sensibility* Marianne and her sister, Elinor, have different views of the explanatory scheme that holds that "feelings as such reliably indicate where propriety lies," Elinor does not deny that Marianne feels what she feels. Marianne's defense of her emotions and of their role in her view of propriety suggests that Marianne's emotions, *pace* Austen, may not have been so unreliable after all. Indeed, one might argue that these "outlaw emotions" represented the moral indefensibility of an explanatory scheme that causes women to feel so much shame over having done so little harm.

In the concluding section of this volume contributors discuss how the insights of feminist ethics can be applied in specific social contexts. Joan C. Tronto, whose *Moral Boundaries: A Political Argument for an Ethic of Care* has influenced many contemporary theorists—including contributors to this volume—urges those working in professional ethics to follow feminists in their examination of the meanings assigned to moral principles in reflexive moral practices. In "Does Managing Professionals Affect Professional Ethics? Competence, Autonomy, and Care," she examines the claim—frequently criticized by those whose job it is to manage professionals—that formulating and monitoring ethical standards for the professions is properly left to their practitioners. Professionals defend their right to devise their own standards by appealing to notions of professional autonomy and professional competence. More than one feminist theorist has pointed out the ways in which professionals tend to cast themselves as autonomous (masculine) figures who are nearly heroic, who have to struggle to maintain their autonomy against controlling (feminine) managers who resort to manipulation and indirection. Tronto believes that the notion of managing professionals is ethically dubious, and she thinks that the best way for professionals to make this case is to extend their idea of competence beyond knowing and applying technical expertise to include "caring well." "Caring well" should not be equated with providing a "reasonable standard of care," which is usually understood to be a matter of conforming to a set of technical requirements, for caring well involves focusing not merely on the requirements of the moment but on the entire caring process. Accordingly, the competent professional— the caregiver—must be not only technically competent but also attentive, responsible, and responsive. This will entail, among other things, using "multiple perspectives to make certain that care is not being distorted by relations of power and imposed or ignored needs" (192).

But professional autonomy, and not just professional competence, needs to be reconceptualized if one is to find a solution to the problem of regulating professionals other than introducing nonprofessional managers. Tronto suggests that traditional views of professional autonomy tend to see professional practice as consisting of a relationship of only two parties: professional and client (patient). But this picture neglects the extent to which professional activities as they are currently carried out involve contributions from a number of other professionals. Tronto notes empirical studies suggesting that the greater the extent that professionals see themselves as a team and to the extent that they are willing to see each others as equals and to acknowledge their vulnerabilities to other members of the team, the less likely they will be to find their work stressful and the more likely the team will be effective. Professionals who see themselves as separated from others with whom they work—and from their clients—because of differentials of power, distance, and professional hierarchies are less likely to communicate and acknowledge the possibility of error. Tronto suggests that professional competence should be understood as a quality exhibited not so much by individuals as by teams or groups of professionals. Professional autonomy may then be seen as requiring professionals to take responsibility for the organizations of their professions, including their relationships with other professionals. In so doing, all professionals need to see themselves as similar to those of us in society who also give care and *not* as markedly different from others because of their professional competence. They need to see professional ethics as not so different from the ethical responsibilities of people in society generally.

The self-definition of many professionals emphasizes having expert knowledge—and a "calling"—that differentiates them from others. Thus do they claim to be self-regulating, wrapping themselves, as Tronto says, in their "cloak of competence" and denying that nonprofessional managers are qualified to challenge their professional judgment. Tronto suggests that professionals are, perhaps, even more concerned than others to assert their autonomy and demand the kind of self-control denied others for fear that their professions will be seen as like the more "feminine" caring professions. Given the extent to which contemporary society seems committed to "flat hierarchies," professionals may worry that their work is being devalued, and they may feel the need to reassert its value. But defending the value of one's own profession by devaluing the work of others seems unlikely to be a successful strategy in the long run. As a result, Tronto proposes that the professions give up their claim to a special status based on their possession of expert knowledge that differentiates them from others. She urges, instead, that they acknowledge that they are able to care for others as a consequence of their competence and that caring well requires working with other professionals. Finally, she urges them to view caring well as central to the practice of all professions. They will then hold themselves and others with whom they work to the same standard as we would hold anyone else in society—to a standard that includes the responsibility to care for others.

Natalie Brender is also concerned with care as an ethical concept in the public sphere. Brender begins by recounting historical antecedents in which ethical theorists, usually men, have expressed anxiety about the shortcomings of those, usually women, who allow emotions or emotional dispositions such as care to dictate actions and policies in the public realm. Still, care can be a problematic concept in the political sphere, as Brender notes in her discussion of humanitarian relief. Suffering is prolonged rather than reduced if and when humanitarian relief permits political power to remain with those who are responsible for initiating and perpetuating the conditions causing the suffering. Brender argues that we must cultivate a degree of analytical detachment when responding to graphic representations of the suffering of those sufficiently distant from us that we are uncertain of the suffering's causes and the consequences of our financial help. Brender cites Margaret Walker's work on representational practices and moral recognition to argue that the "moral graphics" of many calls for humanitarian relief seem designed to block recognition by the audience that the suffering being represented is occurring in a specific sociopolitical and economic context.[21] Brender takes Walker's implications to be that "such a failure of recognition is not *consequentially* but *intrinsically ethically* deficient" (209) and that "notwithstanding the images' success in producing a salutary emotional and practical response, it is grounds for ethical criticism of the images that they foster a cognitive failure of recognition" (209). Brender wants to insist, however, that analytical detachment of the kind required to respond ethically to these images is not incompatible with care. Drawing on the work of Joan Tronto, Brender suggests problematic aspects of Western audience members responding to images of, say, starving children—and "showing that they care"—by writing checks to relief agencies. Care, as Tronto has pointed out, differs in terms of its object(s): one can care *about* someone in the sense of being generally concerned for her well-being and can care *for* someone, which requires attention to another's needs—physical, emotional, spiritual, intellectual, and psychic.[22] Both of these can be done well or poorly, and to care well one must have knowledge about the needs, priorities, and demands of the specific situation and choose the appropriate course of action using the correct means. Writing a check to a relief agency is not an instance of *caring for* those who are suffering. Rather, it indicates that one *cares about* their suffering, although not enough to investigate the cause(s) of their suffering. It is true that the humanitarian response may be inhibited if emotional appeals are accompanied by political analysis, but Brender notes that there is also a danger that those confronted with repeated images will cease to respond altogether. What makes both compassion and analytic detachment possible—and not inherently incompatible—is the cognitive content as well as the corrigibility of emotions. Representations that fail to acknowledge these aspects of our emotional lives will, in the final analysis, be short-lived and limited in their effectiveness to provoke responses—humanitarian or otherwise.

Alison Bailey is also concerned with how feminism can inform analyses of political and social problems—but in a different context. She is concerned with how we conceive of our responsibility for hate crimes in the communities of which we are members. She cites the crimes committed against Bridget Ward, an African American single head of household, after moving to Bridesburg, a suburban area sometimes characterized as one of "Philadelphia's best kept secrets." Ward and her family moved out of their house in Bridesburg in less than two months because of repeated threats and acts of violence against them. Some residents of Bridesburg decried the hate campaign against the Ward family and insisted that they were not racists, that this campaign was the work of a "few bad apples," and that the community as a whole did not want to be blamed for the acts of violence. In a traditional view of collective responsibility—what Bailey refers to as the liberal response—a group is assigned responsibility for harms perpetrated by some of its members and it is the group's responsibility to hold the individual perpetrators accountable for their (past) actions. The focus, as Bailey notes, is "on the relationships between individuals in groups and the causal contribution each makes to a particular state of affairs," (221) and the perspective taken on this state of affairs is primarily down and backward, that is, those who neither contributed to nor were the victims of the harmful act assign responsibility to other members of their group for what these members have already done. In this view, the residents of Bridesburg are discharging whatever responsibility they have in condemning the members of their community who performed the acts. Bailey, echoing concerns of other feminists, argues that the liberal account of collective responsibility is inadequate in the case of hate crimes. It fails to acknowledge that the identity of the victim is not incidental to the crime; rather, this individual was chosen to be the victim of the crime because he or she was a member of a targeted group. As a result, this conception of collective responsibility fails to recognize the social and systemic dimensions of the particular act of violence and thus conceives of responsibility too narrowly. "To fully address the harms resulting from practices such as rape, gay bashing, and racially motivated violence," Bailey says, "our notion of responsibility must look beyond the moral moment of the crime itself" (222). Such crimes are a consequence not only of isolated intentions and actions of individuals but also of a social system of oppression, and thus we must consider the roles that communities play in keeping in place systems that increase the likelihood of such intentions and actions.

As part of her analysis, Bailey cites Larry May's work on collective responsibility. May recognizes that the attitudes of a community toward minority groups may increase the odds that hate crimes will occur in a community.[23] In May's account of shared responsibility, then, members of a community are held responsible for their attitudes and should look not only "down and backward" but also forward to changing the shared attitudes that foster a tolerance of hate crimes in the community. Still, Bailey worries that this attempt to share responsibility focuses only on the attitudes, feelings, and behavior of the majority members of the community and not on the minority members who have been the victims of the hate crimes. Bailey wonders how successful this endeavor to change the majority's attitude toward the population's minority members can be if the latter's views and experiences are not taken into consideration. Indeed, she speculates that the motivation for preventing any further hate crimes from occurring in this community may well be the result of shame rather than genuine concern for the well-being of others. The problem, as Claudia Card has observed, is that what we see when we look up and forward will vary with our social location.[24] If one is "at home" in one's community, one may have a great deal of difficulty not only in understanding *why* others feel ill at ease but also in knowing *what* causes them to have such feelings. Invoking Maria Lugones's notion of "world traveling,"[25] Bailey suggests that we view oppressed members of a society as those who have to world travel out of necessity in the hope of escaping their oppression. In so doing, they are forced to travel to places where they are not "at home" and where even well-meaning others may see them as outsiders. Those who inhabit positions of privilege travel to other worlds when, if, and how they choose and are at least predisposed to feel at ease wherever they are. As long as the "outsiders" remain the subject of conversation rather than a party to it, those who are privileged are unlikely to have any idea of whether and how their actions—even well-intentioned ones—contribute to the "outsider" being ill at ease. In place of May's notion of shared responsibility, Bailey thus proposes a more open-ended account of responsibility in which we see ourselves as "acting with" rather than "acting for" the victims of hate crimes. In this account of responsibility, we need to ask how a *community* should respond to prevent future harmful acts as well as past ones. In so doing, we need to include in our discussions of responsibility those who have been—and may be—harmed by hate crimes. Bailey closes by citing the example of Billings, Montana, a community that mobilized itself in the face of a series of hate crimes against African Americans, Jews, and Native Americans. In this case, various organizations and community members, prompted by the suggestions and support of community leaders, demonstrated their opposition to those who had committed these hate crimes, their support of the victims of the crimes, and their intention of preventing any such crimes in the future. They engaged in such activities as attending services with the victims at their (defaced) church, displaying menorahs in their windows, and repairing the damaged homes of the victims. Such acts of solidarity exhibit the kind of collective responsibility that empowers moral communities and their members.

Empowering moral communities and their members must be a goal of ethical theory as long as moral authority and moral responsibility are necessary for us to survive and flourish. Achieving this end requires an analysis of how power is implicated in the moral structure of our social practices. In other words, we must do what feminists who do ethics—especially those in this volume—have done: see power in morality and morality in power. This is, we think, no small achievement.

NOTES

1. The Feminist Ethics Revisited Conference was sponsored by the Department of Philosophy and the Ethics Center of the University of South Florida and took place in October 1999 in Clearwater, Florida. The palpable excitement of the participants at this conference was the impetus for us—along with Hilde Lindemann Nelson and Sara Ruddick, the editors of the Feminist Constructions Series at Rowman and Littlefield—to pursue the publication of this volume. It includes expanded versions of a number of the papers presented at the conference and some essays not presented there. We would like to thank all who contributed to the conference and to the volume.

2. Sustained discussions of the historical realities cited by Walker include Carole Pateman, *The Sexual Contract* (Stanford: Stanford University Press, 1988); Linda Nicholson, *Gender and History: The Limits of Social Theory in the Age of the Family* (New York: Columbia University Press, 1986); Patricia Mann, *Micro-Politics: Agency in a Postfeminist Era* (Minneapolis: University of Minnesota Press, 1994); Wendy Brown, *States of Injury: Power and Freedom in Late Modernity* (Princeton: Princeton University Press, 1995); and Charles W. Mills, *The Racial Contract* (Ithaca: Cornell University Press, 1997).

3. Marilyn Frye, "The Possibility of Feminist Theory," in *Theoretical Perspectives on Sexual Difference,* ed. Deborah L. Rhode (New Haven, Conn.: Yale University Press, 1990).

4. An earlier but classic work on the subject is, of course, Georges Sorel's 1906 volume, *Reflections on Violence,* trans. T. E. Hulme (New York: Peter Smith, 1941). Since the last decade of the twentieth century has seen the publication of many new studies on violence, there may soon be works added to those of Sorel and Arendt.

5. Claudia Card, *The Unnatural Lottery: Character and Moral Luck* (Philadelphia: Temple University Press, 1996), 41.

6. Card, *The Unnatural Lottery,* 41.

7. Joan C. Tronto, *Moral Boundaries: A Political Argument for an Ethic of Care* (New York: Routledge, 1993).

8. "Angel in the House" is what Virginia Woolf dubs the ideal woman in *The Death of the Moth and Other Essays* (New York: Harcourt Brace Jovanovich, 1970), 236–38.

9. See Michel Foucault, *Ethics,* in *Essential Works of Foucault 1954–1984,* vol. 1, ed. Paul Rabinow, trans. Robert Hurley (New York: The New Press, 1997); and Foucault, *The Uses of Pleasure,* in *The History of Sexuality,* vol. 2, trans. Robert Hurley (New York: Random House, 1985).

10. Drucilla Cornell, *The Philosophy of the Limit* (New York: Routledge, 1992).

11. Drucilla Cornell, *At the Heart of Freedom: Feminism, Sex and Equality* (Princeton: Princeton University Press, 1998).

12. Cornell, *At the Heart of Freedom,* 38–39.

13. Simone de Beauvoir, *The Second Sex,* trans. H. M. Parshley (New York: Random House, 1974).

14. Jeffrie Murphy, "Forgiveness and Resentment," *Midwest Studies in Philosophy* 8 (1982): 503–36.

15. Dorothy Allison, *Bastard Out of Carolina* (New York: Plume, 1993).

16. Carol Gilligan, *In a Different Voice: Psychological Theory and Women's Development* (Cambridge: Harvard University Press, 1982).

17. Nancy Clopton and Gwendolyn Sorell, "Gender Differences in Moral Reasoning: Stable or Situational?" *Psychology of Women Quarterly* 17 (1993): 85–101.

18. Clopton and Sorell, "Gender Differences in Moral Reasoning," 85.

19. Naomi Scheman, "Feeling Our Way toward Moral Objectivity," in *Mind and Morals: Essays on Cognitive Science and Ethics,* ed. Larry May, Marilyn Friedman, and Andy Clark (Cambridge: MIT Press, 1996).

20. Richmond Campbell, *Illusions of Paradox: A Feminist Epistemology Naturalized* (Lanham, Md.: Rowman & Littlefield, 1998); Alison Jaggar, "Love and Knowledge: Emotion and Feminist Epistemology," in *Women, Knowledge, and Reality,* ed. Ann Garry and Marilyn Pearsall (Boston: Hyman, Unwin, 1989), 145. Nelson also cites

Cheshire Calhoun's "Cognitive Emotions?" in *What Is an Emotion?* ed. Cheshire Calhoun and Robert Solomon (Oxford: Oxford University Press, 1984).

21. Margaret Urban Walker, *Moral Understandings: A Feminist Study in Ethics* (New York: Routledge, 1998).

22. Tronto, *Moral Boundaries.*

23. Larry May, *Sharing Responsibility* (Chicago: University of Chicago Press, 1992).

24. Card, *The Unnatural Lottery.*

25. Maria Lugones, "On the Logic of Pluralist Feminism," in *Feminist Ethics,* ed. Claudia Card (Lawrence: University of Kansas Press, 1991).

I

THEORY MATTERS

1

Seeing Power in Morality: A Proposal for Feminist Naturalism in Ethics

Margaret Urban Walker

It is often said that the opposition of morality to power is virtually coextensive with canonical Western moral thought. It is supposedly installed as a founding distinction in the dialogues of Plato, where Socrates more than once defeats the view that justice is the advantage of the stronger. But this is not quite right. Socrates opposes not "power" but brute force and the unbridled exercise of rapacious desire on or in spite of others. Indeed, in Plato's *Republic* the ideal state Socrates envisions can only achieve a true moral order in this world through detailed and extensive coordination of coercive, controlling, and productive powers of several types.

The Platonic root of canonical Western moral theory is really something else: the conviction that morality "itself" is something ideal. Plato's Socrates sees any imperfect, power-dependent worldly realization of moral order as an unstable and shadowy semblance of something itself fully real, true, perfect, and unchanging, not within the plane of ordinary human existence or within the range of those cognitive powers through which we know things of the ordinary world. This Platonic legacy of the *ideality* or *transcendent nature* of morality still reigns. Through most of the canonized Western tradition moral theory has consistently been done as if morality were ideal, and most philosophers today continue to make theory about morality as if it were effectively ideal, even if they do not literally believe that—that is, they treat it is a subject matter largely independent of empirical information about the real histories and contingencies of human relations in society. This legacy underlies many philosophers' boredom with or contempt for too much interest in how human beings actually live and what it has been or is like for them—each of them—to live that way. They think that there is little to be learned from what is about what ought to be.

3

The ideality of morality has enjoyed many formulations: a vision of The Good, a divine command, an unchanging natural moral law; an intuition of nonnatural properties, the transcendental logic of pure practical reason, the logic of moral language, the necessary conditions of agency as such, the pragmatic transcendental presuppositions of the ideal speech situation, or what certain imagined beings would have to endorse in certain imagined situations in which they mostly cannot know things about actual human beings in actual situations. I do not see strong prospects for any longer defending the view of morality as truly ideal or transcendent. Yet many feminist philosophers, too, share in the tradition that sees the ideality of morality as both inspiring and protective.

A continuing fear is that if morality is too much a matter of what is, and of who has the power to make it so, then those without or with less power are left without moral appeal. This fear has real basis: Power unconstrained by moral compunction and unanswerable in fact to standards with moral authority is always something to be feared—and not only by the weakest. But it is a mistake to think that a naturalistic and power-sensitive view of morality itself must "reduce" morality to power or make morality disappear in favor of power. Instead, it should be an instrument for testing the legitimacy of powers that claim moral justification. Still, there is the philosopher's wish, in feminist philosophy serving a political vision, to stand on moral ground that cannot shift. I do not believe that the desire for apodictically secured foundations for morality can be satisfied. That is not, however, some problem about the infirmity of morality. In a postfoundationalist era, it is only to say that our moral grounds cannot be better, epistemically, than the others that anchor our understanding of the world.

There is an alternative to the idealism of a transcendent view, on the one hand, and, on the other, the normative emptiness of a view that rejects morality wholesale in favor of "amoral contests about the just and the good in which truth is always grasped as coterminous with power, always already power, as the voice of power."[1] I cannot defend an entire view of morality here, but I make a proposal for an empirically obligated and politically emancipatory naturalism in ethics that sees the ineliminable roles of power in morality "itself."[2]

MORALITY OF POWER, MORALITY IN POWER

Feminist ethics is inevitably, and fundamentally, a discourse about morality and power. The most obvious way feminist ethics and politics connect morality and power is in examining the morality of specific distributions and exercises of power. Feminism's traditional critique challenges morally the coercive, arbitrary, cruel, and oppressive powers of men over women in many systems of gender. Feminism claims for women on moral grounds economic, political, social, sexual, epistemic, discursive, and symbolic powers denied them by individual, institutional, and cultural male dominance. Feminism must also oppose domination structured by hierarchies or exclusions of class, race, sexuality, age, and ability, for these always partly organize gender even as they are themselves realized in part through specific organizations of gender. To acknowledge this obligation is not, however, to have in hand either the theoretical or the political strategies necessary to fulfill it.

Feminist moral theory also continues to produce unprecedented theoretical understandings of the moral meaning of relations of unequal power, especially asymmetric relations of dependency as well as interdependencies that do not even approximate reciprocal exchanges. This theorization of the morality of unequal power, of "power-over," "responsibility-for," "depending-on," and "trusting-to," reaches to the roots of our conceptualization of human beings as moral beings and requires us to see our moral being in terms of varied relations, both symmetrical and asymmetrical, immediate and highly mediated, to others. The full impact of this reconception on ethical theory and practice is still at the edge of imagination; it remains unclear whether or in what versions some familiar moral and political conceptions can meet the realities of human society as a scene of inescapable connection, dependence, vulnerability, and entrustment.

Feminism's insistent reexaminations of morality and power on these fronts are connected by the need to explore likenesses and differences among legitimate and illegitimate powers, their conditions, and their effects in relations of many kinds. Socially enforced dominance must do quite a lot of things to and with people to make coerced vulnerabilities appear as inevitable ones. Feminist, race, culture, and postcolonial theory continue to reveal this. We cannot distinguish inevitable vulnerabilities and dependencies from manipulated ones until we understand both the manipulated ones in all their subtle and overt varieties and the inevitable ones from the viewpoints of both those who are vulnerable *and* those who respond to them, as care, ageism, and disability theories show. Works of lesbians, gay men, transsexuals, and sex workers on constructions of sexuality and their implications for identity, citizenship, and family dissect the powers of modern institutions and expert discourses to naturalize norms and to moralize what is natural only for some.

To understand the moral necessity, arbitrariness, or catastrophe of giving some people powers over others or of reserving certain powers for some people rather than others, it seems we need the whole manifold of objects of comparison: people in relations of reciprocal risk and trust; people positioned higher or lower by socially enforced hierarchies of power and privilege, whether legitimately or not; those variously less physically able than most others; the immature and the less mature; the cognitively or socially limited or incompetent; those inescapably or radically dependent. Ours then becomes a question of moral terms for the equivalent political and social membership, the essential material and personal support, and the dignifying care, participation, governance, and representation *of all of us*. It is not clear to me that this question has ever really been set before in the 2,500-year history of the canonical, and usually ostensibly "universalist," Western tradition. Feminist thought has played a crucial role in formulating and pressing this question, showing how tirelessly one must think through ethical problems posed by many relationships and exercises of power.

I suggest now that these mutually deepening insights about the morality of power be joined to another kind of view about the powers of and for morality. This is a naturalist view in which morality "itself" is *a disposition of powers through an arrangement of responsibilities*. In this view the very existence of morality requires many social powers. Powers to control, educate, and influence are required to cultivate and foster senses of responsibility. Powers to govern, persuade, inspire, reward, recruit, and punish are necessary to impose and enforce distributions of responsibility, norms for who may do what to whom, who must do what for whom, and whose business anyone's welfare or behavior is. Powers to give or pay, to speak, silence, or credit speaking, to rule and punish, to represent, ritualize, and memorialize are needed to nourish relations of responsibility materially, discursively, legally, and symbolically.

But social orders require as well the sustenance of distinctively moral powers: the powers of morality when embodied in the self-understandings of agents and in the structure of discourses and institutions. Even as moral understandings are carried by social arrangements, they imbue these arrangements with (ideally) mutually understood importance and depth. Moral understandings thus create meaning for us in reproducing our social arrangements and sustain pride, gratitude, and trust among us in doing so. They mobilize resentment toward, and shame in, those who deny or undermine them. Where moral understandings command our confidence, they move us in trust and hope to continue or adopt a certain way of living, and we invoke them to move others to do so with us. Social arrangements, limited and enabled by many powers, give body to morality in the world. Morality in turn disciplines many natural human powers of self-direction, expression, attention, reason, feeling, imagination, and mutual responsiveness—in service of a shared way of life whose authority inheres in being understood always as more than *simply* that.

The central point of this view is that morality is *not socially modular*. Morality is neither a dimension of reality beyond or separate from shared life nor a distinct and detachable set of understandings within it. Our moral practices are not extricable from other social ones. Moral practices in particular lifeways are entirely enmeshed with other social practices; and moral identities, with social roles and positions. Moral understandings are effected through social arrangements, while all important social arrangements include moral practices as working parts. Moral concepts and judgments are an integral part, but only one part, of practices that attempt to organize feelings, behavior, and judgment in ways that keep people's expectations in rough equilibrium.

This has implications for moral philosophy. In moral theory we abstract moral ideas from social practice, imaginatively varying, simplifying, or idealizing them. This is unavoidable but leaves questions about how the social provenance of ideas shapes what they can mean, whether novel applications we imagine for them can be achieved, and at what costs. None of us can access by pure reflection necessary moral precepts or pure moral concepts that are not in fact derived from our socially situated experiences of actual forms of social life or our socially constrained imagination of others. If there were a fund of purely moral knowledge accessible to some kind of purely reflective inquiry, then we could do this. But there could be such a fund of purely moral knowledge only if morality completely transcended history and culture, if it were, once again, something *ideal or transcendent*. To speak of morality as a disposition of powers through an arrangement of responsibilities is to say that morality is not like this. Morality is not a norm that either exists independently of human activity and judgment or remains invariant because it is in no way a function of changes in the course of the histories of human beings in societies. This means that philosophers must ask themselves on what socially cultured experience of morality they draw in making claims about "morality itself"; about the presuppositions of being a "person" or an "agent"; or about the intuitions, sense of justice, or concept of responsibility they claim is "ours." It also means that philosophers need to investigate whether and how moral views can be seated in and sustained by actual social arrangements. What disposition of powers do moral views assume and effect, at whose service or expense, with what methods of recruitment and enforcement, and through what ecologies of feeling and attitude? Finally, philosophers will have to acknowledge that many types of empirical information are necessary in investigating the possibility and justifiability of forms of moral life.

No other kind of moral philosophy has explored these issues as persistently and with as profound results as has feminist ethics. A lot of moral philosophy does not explore them at all. My proposal is that feminist and other politically emancipatory ethics adopt the methodological framework that makes sense of this theoretical practice, what I am calling a "naturalistic" one.

WHAT KIND OF NATURALISM?

Naturalism is a protean and loaded term that sparks suspicions and resistance of several kinds. *Naturalism* may suggest a commitment to natural kinds or natural essences, a presumption in favor of scientific knowledge or a scientific basis for morality, or an essentially descriptive and explanatory enterprise that will miss the "normative" character of morality and the critical character of moral philosophy. None of this is what I mean by "naturalism."

I mean by it that morality is a naturally occurring structure of all human social groups. It recruits and produces many powers to shape interpersonal response and self-direction around shared understandings that guide judgment, action, and expectation. Moral theory needs to study this structure in its various forms but also to grasp the characteristic way that this kind of structure presents itself to its participants. To investigate how the patterning that constitutes moral relations has the kinds of force and meaning that it does is to ask, What are some distinctive aspects of people's grasp of their social relations that make those relations *moral* ones, that give them the kinds of *authority* that we associate with morality? Moral theory has to use this descriptive and explanatory understanding of the specifically *moral authority of morality* in turn to take up its normative critical task: to investigate whether specific moral arrangements are what they must present themselves to be to have this force and meaning. The descriptive and analytical work constructs a working model of what moral relations are like that can guide the normative inquiry. The normative inquiry, testing how supposedly moral arrangements may or may not turn out to be what their authority requires, in turn refines the model: It reveals more about the ways the various working parts of social arrangements and self-understandings must either pull together or be kept safely apart for a social-moral order to roll (or lurch) on.

My own analytical model of morality is that moral structure shows itself in practices of responsibility. The practices implement and enforce understandings of who may do what to whom, who must do what for whom, and to whom various ones of us have to account. This model directs us to look very closely at how these practices construct and circulate understandings of people's identities, their relations to others (or lack thereof), and commonly intelligible values that sustain a given distribution of responsibilities. Actual attention to our own and others' moral cultures reveals that typically there are different responsibilities assigned to or withheld from different groups of people within the same society. In fact, the differences between groups are defined in important part by the forms and limits of agency these distributions of responsibility impute to them. Practices of responsibility show what is valued (at least by those with most power to define the practices) as well as who is valued by whom for what.

But moral practices are ways of going on together that claim something more for themselves than the inertia of habit and tradition, which are already crumbling as soon as their adherents see them as exactly and *only* that. And moral practices claim something quite other for their specific kind of power over us than main force, coercive threat, or manipulation. At the core of any moral-social order there must be trust that certain basic understandings are common, that the common understandings are the operative ones shaping shared life, and that these operative understandings constitute a way of life that is not only "how we live" but also "how to live," a way worthy of people's allegiance, effort, restraint, or sacrifice. Without this, there really are just ways some people can make others behave.

The "normativity" of morality—the specifically moral authority of morality, whatever powers hold its practices in place—does not descend from someplace outside all human judgment; it inheres in the durability of our understandings and the trust they support under the right kind of tests. The relevant tests are those that reassure us that we do understand how we live and that how we live is indeed worthy, considered in its own conditions and effects or considered in comparison to some other way. So, the tests must tap the experiences and understandings of those who live the lifeway under test. If our way of life in reality betrays our shared understandings, or if these understandings turn out to be driven by deception, manipulation, coercion, or violence directed at some of us by others, where all are nonetheless supposed to "share" in this purported vision of the good, then our trust is not sustained and our practices lose their *moral* authority, whatever other powers continue to hold them in place. They become then nothing more than habits or customs, ways we live that are no longer credible or trustworthy as "how to live." Substantial parts of moral-social orders commonly fail to be credible to, or trustworthy for, many participants who are less valued, protected, or rewarded than others in their orders' differential distributions of responsibility.

This "transparency testing" is both a tool of normative philosophical critique and an actual social process that may be relatively inchoate and undirected or politically accentuated and mobilized.[3] Yet moral understandings in life or philosophy are only ever tested for their worthiness in light of some moral standards or other. We always stand on some moral values as we consider the authority of others; sometimes we stand on certain applications of a moral standard to contest other applications of the same one. This only means that, with respect to moral beliefs, we are not in a different situation than is now widely acknowledged for other empirical beliefs: We are always in the position of using some of what we know to discover whether, and how, we know anything else. So it is for moral knowledge: We never get completely behind or beneath all moral beliefs. And any moral standards we apply in testing others are realized in or abstracted from human practices, discourses, and institutions that are themselves configured and reproduced by power. We cannot get behind or under the powers for and of morality, either.

In this view there is no standpoint completely transcendent to and neutral among all forms of social practice and the conceptions of value and responsibilities they implement. But this does not mean that we "lose" the essential dimension of normativity. It means that we never get outside of it, but are never done with reconfirming it, by testing the actual social conditions and effects of the moral practices that claim our trust. Testing the moral authority of our practices means discovering how they actually go, what they actually mean, and what it is actually like to live them from particular places within them. It means examining the power-bound social arrangements that necessarily embody morality. The moral authority of these arrangements, however, is in no way reducible to the fact of their existence.

Scientific knowledge enjoys no hegemony or even privilege in this critical project. It is one source of our understanding of some features of how we live, but it does not trump historical, ethnographic, hermeneutic, cultural, political, and critical studies of lived experience and its meanings; nor can it replace the mutually situating testimonies of all those whose experience of a way of life bears on its claims to authority. Attention to variety in moral practices and appreciation of how they work for people placed variously within them tend to undermine rather than support essentialist generalizations about *how* beings must live to *be* human ones. These studies lead us to explore instead the intricate social architectures that produce specific understandings of ourselves as human beings. This naturalism installs precisely an open-ended and open-minded need to *look and see* how moral ideas materialize in social practices that then constrain at a given time what these moral ideas mean.

A feminist naturalism finds it both too soon and too late for ideal theory. It is too late to turn back from some things we know. We know that past and existing practices of responsibility have encoded oppressive and demeaning social hierarchies covered by deceptively inclusive-sounding ideas like "the good life for man," or "the kingdom of ends," or "our sense of justice." Yet it is too soon to rest confident in what little we know. We may not fully grasp the material conditions and practical constraints under which moral theories and ideals can achieve the emancipatory applications *for all of us* that many of us desire.

RECONSIDERING MODERN UNIVERSALISM

I want to use an example, very briefly, of one such uncertain place to which we are delivered by the parallel efforts of feminist theory and critical race theory. Insistently tracking the real intrication of morality and power, feminist and race theory have established a deeply unsettling assessment of one of the most powerful paradigms of modern liberal moral and political theory: the social contract. This conceptual model is still central to moral philosophy today and remains for many feminists a best hope as a model for moral egalitarianism.

Feminist deconstructions of the social contract have uncovered the inescapably gendered conceptual and practical foundations of early modern and contemporary contractarian thinking.[4] The mutually accepted equality of certain Anglo-European men made them free by their own agreement to view *each other* that way. They agreed among themselves to positions for certain women that were defined by their relations to those women—specifically, relations of power over, or access to, them. That is, mutual recognition of these men's rights over certain women is one of the significant respects in which the men define themselves as equal. Furthermore, the hierarchical sexual division of labor is a material condition for men to be free to engage in the economic competition, social participation, and political contests that both express and measure their equality in society's public sphere. This pattern continued well into the twentieth century with assumptions that the discourse of justice and equality defines statuses within the "public" lives of household "heads."

Race theorists have excavated the historical foundations of modern Europe's self-definition as the universe of civilized men. Enlightenment ideals of reason and personhood played central roles in constituting—again deliberately, consciously, and violently—a raced equality that defined white men as moral subjects and political peers in important part by entitling them to power over or access to nonwhite people and what nonwhite people have. As Charles Mills puts it, a "racial contract" has always underwritten the still-invoked social one.[5] Mills, along with other race theorists, makes a compelling case from textual and historical evidence that the equality of Anglo-European men was imagined from the outset in terms of who these men were not, and were not like. More tellingly, separate moral and juridical statuses were explicitly elaborated for nonwhite others in the course of, and for the purpose of, explicitly elaborating and justifying white men's entitlements to work, rule, displace, civilize, own, or kill them.[6] Now the pattern continues in the form of widespread denial by whites of pervasive racism and persisting disadvantage, strategic exclusion, and raced violence in a society organized, politically and epistemically, to sustain this deniability.

Neither of these compelling bodies of critique has yet been joined to the other in a unifying, or at least mutually clarifying, analysis of the contractarian constructions of equality as both Whiteness and Maleness (and perhaps of each in terms of the other). Each of these inquiries, however, powerfully confronts the unsavory historical amnesia and institutional legitimation that allow us to keep thinking about, and circulating, and teaching these views "as if" they "really" proclaimed the universally inclusive freedom and equality, or equal moral worth, of all human beings. In demonstrable and demonstrated fact, they did not. Nor did they intend to. They intended and did the reverse, intentionally erecting the ideal of *equality for equals* to assure mutually the rights of certain people in part by defining them as rights over other people. In all versions of this contract equality was seen as conferred by a restricted class of men on its members, and among the things conferred was the right of those equal to each other to distinguish themselves from the rest, particularly by specific powers *over* those not equal to them.

These historically informed analyses exhibit a central feature of the modern liberal idea of equality *in the context of the actual social arrangements that made sense of it.* This construction of equality requires there to be something *other* than equality. What is other is not merely different but must define and support the equality of equals. Despite claims for its revolutionary nature, the ostensible universalism of modern equality repeats the subsumptive universalism of classical thought. In this conceptual structure, some nature or possible perfection of humanity (usually "Man") was to be realized in the persons of a few human beings suited to it. But the many others are not left out; they occupy *indispensable* roles in relation to the few. Legitimized asymmetrical exercises of power over the many lesser others distinguish the few who enjoy these powers over the many, and not over each other, *as equals.* Concretely, those who are able but not equal supply the wherewithal of common life that is necessary to sustain the "achievement" of equality by some.[7]

This persistent logic of equality (as we have always known it and as it has in fact evolved in tandem with the practices that make sense of it) is that it qualifies some by subsuming or subjecting others. The fundamental problem with the status of women and nonwhite men in the social contract (and the actual society it images) is *not* capricious and arbitrary exclusion from a status they might just as well have occupied alongside white men if the qualifications were fair, although efforts to "correct" contractarian thought tend to "add in" or "add on" some of those historically excluded. The problem is instead a kind of pointed and invidious *inclusion* in subordinate or diminished statuses that serve to define entitlements of the equals and the nature of equality itself. Equals do not just have different and greater powers and entitlements *relative* to those below; they are defined *as equal* to one another by their shared entitlements *to* and powers *over* those below. The former aspect of unequal status, "distributive" inequality, can be remedied by equalizing "shares" in available goods or access to them. But there is a real puzzle in fixing the latter key feature of equality: If powers *over* others are what defines the equals, then when equality is extended to those below, over whom are they entitled to rule? In other words, the part of the equality status that is defined structurally by "power over Xs" cannot be reduced to any version of "difference from Xs." Yet what we have learned from studies of race and gender oppression shows that it is "power over" that is fundamental; distributive inequality and the social marking of "differences" are *effects* of systemic powers of some over others.

For me, this persistently subsuming and subjecting logic of consensual equality poses the question of whether an "association of equals" can in fact be rendered universal. One profound contribution of feminist ethics has been its insistence that moral theory address immaturity, vulnerability, disability, dependency, and incapacity as inevitable, central, and normal in human life. The model of an association of equals does not seem capable of including all of us and will not give the needed guidance, as Eva Kittay puts it, "on our unequal vulnerability in dependency, on our moral power to respond to others in need, and on the primacy of human relations to happiness and well-being."[8] In pursuing an encompassing moral universalism—this time, *for the first time*—we cannot ignore theoretically what we cannot dispense with humanly: many "powers over" are indispensable "powers for," that is, on behalf of, the infant, the immature, the frail, the ill; the occasionally, developmentally, or permanently dependent; the mildly or severely incapacitated. These are not different (kinds of) people. *They are all of us at some times—and necessarily.* It remains unclear to me whether there really can be a single universal and substantive moral status; if there is, I doubt that it can be the status of equality. I do not yet see the deeper logic of moral equality, or a fully inclusive logic beyond equality, that is universal in its moral embrace while it differentiates not only among persons but fluidly within the lives of persons, over times and contexts, in its assignments of responsibility.

MORALITY, NOT IDEOLOGY

A moral inquiry that reflects on practices of responsibility for an actual social life will not talk about morality instead of power but, rather, will explore the moral authority of some powers and the arbitrariness, cruelty, or wastefulness of others. It is a heavy irony that interrogating the ways that power (inevitably) constructs morality so often prompts the charge that one is "reducing morality to ideology." In fact, exactly the reverse is true. In one useful characterization of ideology, it is a practice of presenting claims as existing "above the fray of power and politics," for instance, as being "theoretical, rational, or spiritual and, on that basis, justified in acting as the final arbiter over others,"[9] thus "hiding the social histories and circumstances from which ideas . . . derive their logics."[10] Claims about or within morality are used ideologically when they pretend to operate beyond or above all social powers, rather than as a means of distributing and authorizing social powers and so needing justification as such. The alternative, I have argued, is always to see the power in morality—and to "see through" it to its conditions and costs. This is what I am calling naturalism in moral philosophy. It is something feminist moral philosophers are usually already very good at doing.

NOTES

1. Wendy Brown, *States of Injury: Power and Freedom in Late Modernity* (Princeton, N.J.: Princeton University Press, 1995), 45. Brown argues that "surrendering epistemological foundations means giving up the ground of specifically *moral* claims against domination" (45), but this is true only if moral claims cannot receive an alternative epistemological account, just as other knowledge claims now usually do. Brown repeats the view that the discursive roots of a morality-power antagonism go back to Plato.
2. This is the view I defend at length in *Moral Understandings: A Feminist Study in Ethics* (New York: Routledge, 1998).

3. See *Moral Understandings,* chapters 3 and 9, for fuller discussion of transparency as a moral and epistemic ideal and of transparency testing as an aspect of actual social processes in real times and spaces.

4. Many people have contributed to this analysis. Some examples of sustained discussions of the historical realities include Carol Pateman, *The Sexual Contract* (Stanford: Stanford University Press, 1988); Linda Nicholson, *Gender and History: The Limits of Social Theory in the Age of the Family* (New York: Columbia University Press, 1986); Patricia S. Mann, *Micro-Politics: Agency in a Postfeminist Era* (Minneapolis: University of Minnesota Press, 1994); and Brown, *States of Injury.* Exposures of the continuing occlusion and exclusion of women in Rawls's thought include Susan Moller Okin, *Justice, Gender, and the Family* (New York: Basic Books, 1989), and Eva Feder Kittay, *Love's Labor: Essays on Women, Equality, and Dependency* (New York: Routledge, 1999).

5. Charles W. Mills, *Racial Contract* (Ithaca, N.Y.: Cornell University Press, 1997), 93.

6. Two incisive accounts are those of Mills, *The Racial Contract,* especially chapters 1 and 2, and Lucius T. Outlaw Jr., *On Race and Philosophy* (New York: Routledge, 1996), especially chapter 3. A provocative collection of classical modern philosophical texts that construct race distinctions is Emmanual Chukwudi Eze, *Race and the Enlightenment: A Reader* (Cambridge, Mass.: Blackwell Publishers, 1997). On the specifically American construction of black/white distinction in the context of Anglo-European philosophy and culture, see Winthrop D. Jordan's massive study, *White over Black: American Attitudes toward the Negro, 1550–1812* (Chapel Hill: University of North Carolina Press, 1968). Richard H. Popkin provides an interesting account of the intertwining histories of biblical and philosophical thinking about race in "The Philosophical Bases of Modern Racism," in *Philosophy and the Civilizing Arts,* ed. Craig Walton and John P. Austen (Athens: Ohio University Press, 1974), 126–53.

7. In *Doctrine of Right* Kant distinguishes "passive citizens" who do not have the same schedule of rights as "active" ones. As Tamar Shapiro explains, passive citizens include not only the "natural" ones, women and children, but also those economically dependent, including apprentices, domestic servants, domestic laborers, private tutors, and tenant farmers. Shapiro explains that Kant distinguishes this restricted citizenship from the "freedom and equality *as human beings*" shared by all and disallows the treatment of passive citizens as things or as members of a permanent underclass, although the possibilities for women to work their way up remains doubtful. See Tamar Shapiro, "What Is a Child?" *Ethics* 109 (1999): 715–38. Shapiro's discussion illustrates how the category of those subsumed as "dependent" has encompassed all those whose labor materially supported the "independence" that qualifies relatively few as equals. This "independence" is an amalgam of entitlement to, power over, and exemption from the labors of others. It also dramatizes the question of what moral conceptions like "freedom and equality" mean divorced from actual social implementation of these statuses. In one straightforward sense, they *do not* mean "freedom and equality." Tellingly, Shapiro reconstructs childhood as a "moral predicament," an unfortunate situation to be overcome.

8. Kittay, *Love's Labor,* 113.

9. E. Doyle McCarthy, *Knowledge as Culture: The New Sociology of Knowledge* (New York: Routledge, 1996), 31.

10. McCarthy, *Knowledge as Culture,* 7.

2

The Scope of Our Concerns: Reflections on "Woman" as the Subject of Feminist Politics

Uma Narayan

In the light of some recent discussions and readings,[1] I have the impression that a number of feminists feel that feminism, both as a political movement and as a framework for analysis, needs to retain the category "Woman" as the central constitutive element of its self-definition. This has been a view that I myself accepted for many years, but it is a position I am no longer convinced about. However, I have had a difficult time articulating the considerations that were causing me to question this view. This chapter is my attempt to give an account of some of the reasons for my changed position on this matter.

I would like to start by posing three questions pertaining to the overall scope of feminist politics and political concerns and explore the answers to them. The three questions I will discuss are

1. Can the scope of feminist politics amount to "fighting for all the significant interests of all women"?
2. Is shared oppression a necessary basis for political solidarity, and, if so, should membership in feminist groups or political activism be restricted to women?
3. Can the scope of feminist analyses, and the agenda of feminist moral and political engagement, be justifiably restricted to "issues pertaining to the interests of women"?

I am inclined to answer no to all three questions. I believe that the inclination to answer yes to these three questions is rooted in a vision of feminist politics indebted to some forms of 1970s radical feminism. I will begin by briefly sketching the radical feminist vision that suggests that the answer to these questions is yes. Next, I will briefly outline the critique of "mainstream feminism," made primarily, but not exclusively, by feminists of color and les-bian feminists, which strongly stresses the need for feminist analyses to "take differences among women" into account. I shall call this the "Differences Critique" for short. While the Differences Critique has been very influential, many who endorse it, myself included, do not always register how different the vision of the scope of feminist concerns that it entails is from that endorsed by radical feminism. Most of my chapter will be spent examining the Differences Critique's implications for my three initial questions, and I will argue that taking the Differences Critique seriously implies that the answer to these questions is no. However, some who endorse the Differences Critique are nevertheless inclined to answer yes to these questions. I will try to explain why some feminists who endorse the Differences Critique might answer these questions in the affirmative. I will argue for the negative answer in all three cases by pointing to problems with the affirmative answer to these questions.

RADICAL FEMINISM AND ITS VISION OF FEMINIST POLITICS

In significant forms of radical feminism such as those found in the work of Mary Daly, Shulamith Firestone, and Catharine MacKinnon,[2] the Marxist notion of the proletariat as the oppressed class is replaced by "Women"—conceived of as a classlike group that is oppressed and controlled by the ruling class "Men" and is subject to a systematic form of oppression, namely, "patriarchy." Just as the Marxist position suggests that the proletariat must come together to develop "class consciousness," radical feminism suggests that women need to come together to develop a feminist consciousness that will challenge patriarchy. Thus, for the radical feminist vision of feminist politics, women are the revolutionary class, the agents of political struggle against patriarchy.

For radical feminism, the feminist political agenda is to fight to dismantle patriarchal structures of oppression—understood as those that affect *all women as women*. Consciousness raising was considered a central method whereby women could come together and recognize their oppression as "common and shared." This recognition of shared oppression was seen as providing the basis for solidarity or sisterhood with other women, needed to sustain collective struggles for changing patriarchal norms and structures. Because shared oppression was deemed to create shared interests, and because consciousness of shared oppression was considered to engender political solidarity, membership in feminist groups and participation in feminist struggles were restricted to those who *experienced* patriarchal oppression, namely, women.[3]

These elements of radical feminism's political vision collaborate, I believe, in suggesting that the answer to all my three initial questions is yes. Feminist political struggles fight for the important shared interests of all women; genuinely feminist agendas are restricted to issues pertaining to women's interests; and membership in feminist struggle is restricted to those who suffer patriarchal oppression, namely, women.

THE DIFFERENCES AMONG WOMEN CRITIQUE

I will now proceed to briefly sketch the Differences Critique. What I refer to as the Differences Critique covers various critiques of mainstream feminism articulated by feminists such as bell hooks, Maria Lugones, and Elizabeth Spelman.[4] These critiques collectively point out that many mainstream feminist analyses have ignored the ways in which factors such as race, class, and sexual orientation affect women's interests and oppression, hegemonically privileging the interests of mainstream women in their articulation of "feminist issues." These critiques argue that it is imperative for feminists to attend to these differences among women in order to generate feminist analyses that are adequately responsive to the interests of various marginalized groups of women.

The Differences Critique questions whether patriarchal structures uniformly afflict "all women" in identical ways, pointing to the ways in which other aspects of women's social identities inflect and structure the patriarchal oppressions they suffer. It points out that the forms taken by "patriarchal oppression" are not concretely describable apart from factors such as class, race, and sexual orientation that variously mark different groups of women. Furthermore, it underscores the fact that many women suffer not only "specific sorts of patriarchal oppression" but also forms of *class-based, race-based, and heterosexist oppression* that are, in turn, *inflected and affected by their gender.* The Differences Critique constitutes a "critique of mainstream feminist hegemony" in which the interests of one subset of women masquerade as the "interests of All Women" and in which the interests of privileged women are often put at the center of feminist concerns.

IMPLICATIONS OF THE "DIFFERENCES CRITIQUE" FOR THE FIRST QUESTION

Let me now turn to the implications of the Differences Critique for the first of my three questions and ask, Can paying adequate attention to various differences among women result in feminist analyses or political positions that fully represent "all the significant interests of all women"? The position that endorses the Differences Critique but nevertheless answers yes to this question I shall call the "affirmative answer," and the one that answers no, the "negative answer." I will clarify my sense of what leads to the disagreement between these two answers and explain why I favor the negative answer.

I believe that the answer one gives to the first question depends on the picture one has of "women's interests," a picture that affects the way in which one sees these interests represented by feminist analyses. I myself have in the past subscribed to the affirmative answer while endorsing the Differences Critique, and it is helpful to clarify the picture of "women's interests" I held at that time. I understood the Differences Critique as pointing out that when "differences among women" are not taken into account, mainstream women's interests are misrepresented as "the interests of all women." I also understood the Differences Critique as saying that when various differences among women are adequately taken into account, feminist analyses *can* adequately represent "the interests of all women." At that time, I understood the Differences Critique in terms of what I now think of as a "Jigsaw Puzzle Picture Model of Women's Interests." When subscribing to the Jigsaw Puzzle Picture Model of Women's Interests, I understood the Differences Critique as saying that mainstream feminist accounts put together a *part* of this picture and took it for the *whole* or put the "pieces" that represent the interests of nonmainstream women at the *margins* of the puzzle when they properly belonged in the *center*. In addition, I understood the Differences Critique as holding that, when feminists adequately take all relevant differences among women into account, we can in fact represent and fight for the *full* Jigsaw Puzzle Picture of "All Women's Interests" with all the pieces in their right place. In short, I assumed that the interests of different groups of women, *if adequately attended to,* would always coherently fit alongside each other like pieces of a jigsaw puzzle, enabling feminists to struggle for all the significant interests of all women. It was my unreflective subscription to the Jigsaw Puzzle Picture Model of Women's Interests that led me to initially favor the affirmative answer to the first question, even as I endorsed the Differences Critique.

I now endorse the negative answer to this first question because I see this Jigsaw Puzzle Model as seriously flawed. I have come to believe, upon reflection, that taking "differences among women" into account *often* entails recognizing that some interests of some women (say minority or working-class women) might well be *opposed to* (and not fit neatly alongside) the interests of other, privileged, women. It is not simply that *some* of the interests of privileged groups of women belong at the *margins* of the jigsaw puzzle; they may not belong *at all* in the picture of the interests that feminists should fight for. I have come to endorse the negative answer because I have come to believe that it is not just that some women's *class-* or *race-based* interests are opposed to those of other women but that, as a result, their *interests as differently situated women* are likely to be in conflict as well. Thus, I have come to endorse the negative answer and to reject the idea that the scope of feminist political agendas could *very often* neatly coincide with fighting for the significant interests of *all* women.

As examples of situations in which the interests of some groups of women are arguably opposed to those of other women, I offer the following. The interests of nineteenth-century British feminists who fought for their own suffrage and empowerment by invoking the role they could play in the colonial enterprise with respect to the uplift of colonized women is a situation in which women from colonizing countries clearly had gender interests different from those of many colonized women.[5] The interests of women workers in a manufacturing plant in the United States that moves to a Third World country may be opposed to the interests of the women elsewhere who will now have access to more employment. Improving the wages and working conditions of women who work as child care providers may adversely affect the interests of some women who can now currently afford their services only because they are badly paid.[6] I believe the negative answer is correct in insisting that there are significant feminist issues that do involve such conflicts among the interests of different groups of women and thus require moral and political decisions to be made about *which interests of which group of women* deserve feminist political support. I would contend that the affirmative answer to the first question is an unthought-through residual effect of a radical feminist vision that thinks feminism should be able to "struggle for the interests of all women." If the negative answer is correct, and I think it is, the scope of feminist politics is often *narrower* than "fighting for all the significant interests of all women."

IMPLICATIONS OF THE "DIFFERENCES CRITIQUE" FOR THE SECOND QUESTION

Let me turn to the second of my three initial questions and ask, Is endorsing the Differences Critique compatible with support for the position that shared oppression is a *necessary basis* for political solidarity and for the related position that membership in feminist groups or political activism should be *restricted to women*? Once again, the position that endorses the Differences Critique but nevertheless answers yes to this second question I call the affirmative answer, and the one that answers no, I call the negative answer. Once again, I favor the negative answer to this question and will attempt to clarify my reasons. I shall begin by describing one train of thought that might lead someone who endorses the Differences Critique to subscribe to the affirmative answer to this second question.

The Differences Critique implies that sustained political solidarity among different groups of women requires that feminists who are privileged with respect to factors such as class, race, or sexual orientation be prepared to recognize, and work against, the adverse effects these privileges might have—both with respect to their theoretical understandings of issues and with respect to the ways in which they personally interact with less privileged women. The Differences Critique implies that it is *necessary* that feminists work against their privileges and that it is *possible* (although difficult) to do so.

The affirmative answer to the second question arises, I believe, from the sense that, although "working against one's privileges" is essential for feminist solidarity, underneath our differences, all women do in fact also share the *common experience* of oppression by patriarchy. What "patriarchal oppression" amounts to in each case is certainly affected by a woman's class, race, or sexual identity, but even if different groups of women are patriarchally oppressed in different ways, it is undeniable that they *are* in fact patriarchally oppressed. The affirmative answer often stems from the conviction that this shared status of being subject to patriarchal oppression provides women with an underlying basis for solidarity with each other and with the motivation and commitment to work across their other differences. Because men are not subject to patriarchal oppression, they lack this underlying basis for solidarity with women and for the motivation and commitment to work against their privileges. These views collaborate in making the affirmative answer appear correct, for they suggest that shared patriarchal oppression constitutes a necessary basis for feminist solidarity and that men, who do not suffer patriarchal oppression, should not be granted membership in feminist political groups.

I will begin defending the negative answer to the second question by arguing against the claim that it is the shared status of being subject to patriarchal oppression that necessarily provides women with an underlying basis for a sense of solidarity with each other despite their differences. My inclination to favor the negative answer stems from the conviction that if one takes the implications of the Differences Critique seriously, there may be few *concrete* "common elements of patriarchal oppression" that all women experience that they recognize as the basis for their solidarity across all their other differences. If, in fact, it is likely that a privileged woman's location and interests may constitute a direct part of the structure of race-, class-, and gender-based oppression suffered by a less privileged woman, this fact would weaken rather than strengthen the prospects of solidarity between them.

I favor the negative answer because I believe that shared oppression is not a *necessary* (let alone a *sufficient*) condition for political solidarity. Rather, I would suggest that political solidarity between any two persons often depends *less* on "shared oppression" and *more* on shared political categories and analyses, on shared willingness to work against one's privileges and differences, and on shared political organizations and institutional spaces that enable coming together to articulate and struggle for shared agendas.[7] My endorsement of the negative answer to the second question rests on my conviction that the basis for political solidarity is fundamentally *political*. I would argue that this understanding of political solidarity enables us to explain why many women are far from endorsing any version of feminist politics, even though they suffer from patriarchal oppression, and to explain why there are some men who are clearly feminist in their understandings and commitments.

My position does not reject the view that even if "shared oppression" is not a *necessary condition* for political solidarity, it often *facilitates* political solidarity. However, it would also insist that the Differences Critique shows us that some men *do* experience "shared oppression" with some women. For instance, we should not ignore the fact that for some men the basis for their feminist political sensibilities and commitments is in fact *personal experience of patriarchal oppression*. I have had male students whose interest in feminism was spurred by the violence that they, and their mothers, experienced at the hands of abusive fathers. Furthermore, changes in social contexts often transform certain patriarchal norms and practices that were once relatively undiluted patriarchal privileges into structures that are burdensome for both men and women. For instance, norms of purdah in areas of India or Bangladesh that require the seclusion of women from public arenas of paid work have weakened in part because of the fact that the patriarchal role of being the breadwinner is an impossible burden for many men to sustain under changing economic conditions of hardship. I am inclined to believe that we conceive of patriarchal oppression *too narrowly* when we think of it, as we often do, as always *only* adversely affecting women.

To the degree that "shared oppression" might facilitate political solidarity, the negative answer would argue that attending to the interests and experiences of less privileged groups of women, as the Differences Critique endorses, would bring home the ways in which some men do "share specific forms of oppression" with some women—for instance, African American men "share racial oppression" with African American women, poor or working-class men "share class oppression" with poor or working-class women, and men who belong to sexual minorities "share heterosexist oppression" with women who belong to sexual minorities—even though gender continuously inflects the ways in which these factors differently affect men and women. Some men do acquire feminist commitments as a result of working alongside women in organizations centrally concerned to challenge racist, heterosexist, or class-based forms of oppression. Politically working with feminist women makes these men conscious of the ways in which gender inflects the organization, dynamics, or policies of those groups and makes them aware of the need to support feminist perspectives within those groups. Their feminist commitments are partly rooted in the political solidarity they develop working with feminist women with whom they share other forms of oppression.

If different men can have different ways in which they come to develop a sense of solidarity with feminist concerns, I believe there is no cogent reason for excluding men as a class from membership in groups devoted to struggling for feminist agendas. I believe that taking the Differences Critique seriously entails this position. Feminists who endorse the Differences Critique agree that privileged women in feminist groups can and must work against their *class, race, or heterosexist privileges*. It does not seem consistent or reasonable to deny that it is similarly possible for men to work against their *gender privileges*. Additionally, in democratic contexts where numbers count, the support of men willing to work against their gender privileges would be beneficial to feminist agendas. Thus, I would argue that there are good reasons for allowing the participation in feminist groups of men prepared to work against their gender privileges. On the basis of such considerations, the negative answer to the second question offers a different vision of political solidarity, with wider implications for feminist membership, than the affirmative answer, which appears to remain more closely aligned with the perspectives of radical feminism.[8]

IMPLICATIONS OF THE "DIFFERENCES CRITIQUE" FOR THE THIRD QUESTION

I will now turn to my third and final question—whether the *agenda* of feminist analyses and politics should be restricted in *scope* to "issues pertaining to the interests of women." Once again, what I call the affirmative answer replies yes while the negative answer replies no. The underlying factor leading to these two different answers is, I think, connected to the way in which the *reasons* given by the Differences Critique, for feminists needing to take factors such as class, race, or sexual orientation into account, are cashed out. The affirmative answer understands the reason for "taking differences into account" as centrally grounded in the fact that these factors of "difference" adversely affect *women* and need to be taken into account to adequately represent the problems of different groups of *women*.

The negative answer, which I favor, would go further and insist that the widest or most basic reason for attending to factors such as class, race, or sexual orientation is because they too, like gender, *constitute systematic forms of oppression and injustice* that restrict and diminish the lives of many. While feminists always have good reason to consider how class-, race-, or sexual orientation–based oppression cash out in gender-inflected ways, often having worse effects on the lives of women in contrast to those of men, I think it would be morally arbitrary and politically unwise for feminists to care about these injustices and oppressions only insofar as they affect women. If, as feminists, we care about the ways in which systemic oppression based on class, race, or sexual orientation affects and circumscribes the lives of women, we have analogous reasons to care about how systemic oppression based on class, race, or sexual orientation affects and circumscribes *the lives of men* (i.e., these factors impoverish their opportunities, expose them to violence or discrimination, and so forth). In addition, I endorse the negative answer because it strikes me that if we really wish to fully understand, analyze, and oppose systemic forms of oppression and injustice based on class, race, or sexual orientation, we cannot do so if we ignore how these oppressions adversely affect men. If we ignore their effects on men, we have only a partial understanding of, and partial political responses to, the ways in which these systemic forms of oppression work.

I believe that many feminists, perhaps especially feminists of color, have felt the force of these considerations advanced by the negative answer to the third question but have often not confronted them head-on. This has sometimes resulted in a tendency to shift between definitions of the scope of feminist concerns that endorse the affirmative answer to this third question and those that endorse the negative answer. For example, the first chapter of bell hooks's *Feminist Theory: From Margin to Center* shifts between defining feminism as "the movement to end *sexist oppression*" (which is in fact the title of her chapter) and defining feminism as "the movement to end *all interconnected forms of oppression*." These are clearly not coextensive terms. The affirmative answer to the third question suggests a seeming middle ground—that feminism is *more* than a movement to only end "sexist oppression" because it is committed to engaging with issues of class, race, and so on *when they pertain to women*. However, feminism is *less* than a movement to "end *all* interconnected forms of oppression" because it does not concern itself, *qua feminism,* with these interconnected forms of oppression when they adversely affect men. However, this middle ground is clearly unstable and raises the question of *why* the scope of feminist concerns should be limited in this way. Someone who favors the affirmative answer to the third question might answer thus:

> When I work or think as a *feminist,* "Woman" does function as a "limit" or a "cut-off category" for my concerns. As a feminist, I am concerned with factors such as class, race, sexual orientation, and so forth only insofar as they affect women. I agree that I have moral and political reasons to also care about how these factors affect men. However, when I analyze or struggle about how these factors adversely affect men, I do not do so as a *feminist*. Rather, I do so as an anti-racism activist, or as a left-wing activist, or as a gay rights activist.

Here are some considerations that I would offer to show that the above move is not very successful. Take a hypothetical African American feminist who works both with a feminist group, where "Woman" functions as a "cut-off category" for defining the agenda, and in a progressive group committed to working on issues pertaining to the African American community, where "African American" functions as such a "cutoff category" for defining the agenda. This hypothetical feminist may well have reason to feel resistant to the claim that when she works within and for the issues of the feminist group she functions "as a feminist" but that when she works within and for the issues of the progressive African American group she does not "function as a feminist" but, rather, as something else, say, an "antiracism activist." She may justifiably argue that she does function "as a feminist" within the African American group, for she and other feminists are often instrumental in shaping the formulation of issues in ways sensitive to *feminist concerns*—so that the group does not, as it might otherwise, focus only on issues that predominantly affect African American men or characterize issues in ways that inadequately attend to interests of women in the community.

Those who favor the affirmative answer to the third question may respond to this hypothetical figure by saying,

> Yes, you do function "as a feminist" within the African American group when you do engage in these sorts of activities. However, there are other moments in the African American group at which you do not function "as a feminist" in the work you do—for instance, you do not function "as a feminist" when you take up within the group issues that *do* predominantly or exclusively focus on African American men, such as issues pertaining to African American men's racist treatment by the criminal justice system.

This hypothetical African American feminist may not be satisfied by this answer because this description does not feel correct to her on the *phenomenological* level—she does not feel as if she is a feminist at some moments and not at others, depending on the issue being addressed. At a more conceptual level, she might say,

> I am a feminist even when I work with the group on African American men's racist treatment by the criminal justice system—for instance, I help to raise questions about how the criminalization of African American men contributes to problematic stereotypes of African American *masculinity* both outside and within the community. Surely my interest in and sensitivity to such gender constructions is both a legacy and a sign of my commitments to feminist politics?

In order to defend its endorsement of "Woman" as a cutoff category for feminist political agendas and concerns, an endorser of the affirmative answer to the third question might then say, "Well, analyses of masculinity *count as feminist* when they reveal how these scripts of masculinity *adversely affect women* but not when they focus on how these scripts *adversely affect men*." Many feminists of color, including our hypothetical African American feminist, would more than likely find this unappealing, for they have often been at the forefront in examining how certain problematic racialized scripts of masculinity have adverse effects on both men *and* women within communities of color. Or take, for example, an analysis such as that in Mrinalini Sinha's *Colonial Masculinity: The "Manly Englishman" and the "Effeminate Bengali,"*[9] which shows how British colonial scripts of "effeminate Indian masculinity" had adverse effects on many Indian men *and* women and had problematically power-conferring effects on *both* British men and British women. It would be more than a little odd to read this text as "being feminist" when it considers the adverse effects of this colonial script on Indian women but not when it attends to its adverse effects on Indian men.

Some endorsers of the affirmative answer to the third question might say at this point, "All right, maybe it is not *adverse effects on women* but *attention to problematic scripts of gender* that is the crucial and definitive characteristic of feminist work." However, if they make such a concession, they have in effect come around to endorsing the negative answer to my third question. The negative answer, as I would construe it, can endorse the view that feminist work on issues pertaining to class, race, colonialism, and so on should be attentive to the ways in which these issues are "gender inflected." However, this position makes the scope of feminist concerns *far wider* than that described in the third question—where it is restricted to "issues pertaining to the interests of women."

MOVING BEYOND THE "CUTOFF CATEGORY" MODEL OF POLITICS

The versions of radical feminism I have described most clearly endorse what I call an "Oppressed Identity–Based Cutoff Model" of political membership whereby *membership* in feminist groups is restricted to those who suffer from patriarchal oppression. Such an "Oppressed Identity–Based Cutoff Model" is also operative in *some* existing political groups organized to struggle around other axes of systemic oppression such as race or sexual orientation—serving to normalize and make normative a vision of political membership restricted to those who suffer from a particular form of oppression. It strikes me that this Oppressed Identity–Based Cutoff Model of membership is perhaps least prevalent in traditional left-wing groups engaged with issues of class struggle and class oppression. While the interests of the poor or of the working class were the center of the political *agenda* in these groups, *membership* was not restricted to those who themselves suffered from class oppression. This was certainly the case in India, where the sons and daughters of the bourgeoisie were a significant presence both in formal Left political parties and in more informal Left groups, something perhaps true in the United States as well. With groups organized around fighting racial injustices, there appears to be more of a real *mixture*—some groups do operate with an Oppressed Identity–Based Cutoff Model of political group membership (where membership may be restricted, say, to African Americans, Asian Americans, or more broadly to "persons of color"), but others do not, working in multiracial coalitions even as the *agendas* they fight for pertain to the welfare of those who suffer from racial injustice and oppression. There seems something of the same kind of mixture when it comes to issues affecting sexual minorities—gays, lesbians, bisexuals, and transgendered people. It seems to me that, in terms of the political landscape in the United States as a whole, the Oppressed Identity–Based Cutoff Model of political membership is fairly widely accepted by feminist groups—often operating at a de facto level even in those feminist groups that do not explicitly see themselves as committed to radical feminism.

Even in political groups in which a particular form of oppressed identity has not functioned as a cutoff for *membership,* it has very often functioned as a cutoff for defining the *political agenda* of the group. There are clear historical reasons for this phenomenon. Historically, a number of specific and different axes of oppression were not adequately attended to in mainstream moral and political theories or in mainstream social and political agendas. It is not historically surprising that each axis of oppression initially became a *specific site* of political analysis and activism—allowing *specific structures* of oppression based on class, race, gender, and so forth to be named and theorized and to become the specific agenda-setting bases of discrete political movements.

Over time, each of these initially discrete analyses and political movements has been challenged and enriched by the others—drawing our attention to the ways in which each of these seemingly discrete categories of oppression was deeply inflected by and affected by the others. The credit for this enrichment belongs to different versions of the Differences Critique, and the political terrain in which many of us work is considerably shaped by these lessons we have learned from the Differences Critique. At the present time, many of us mostly work in groups whose agendas, if not membership, are defined by one or another cutoff category but in which we register and insist on the need to take "differences into account" *within these groups.* For instance, one might work in a feminist group in which "Woman" functions as the cutoff category for its agendas and membership but within which members struggle to deal with differences based on factors such as class, race, or sexual orientation insofar as they affect different groups of women. Or one might work in a group fighting for racial justice in which, say, "African Americans" functions as the cutoff category for its agendas but within which members struggle to deal with factors such as class, gender, or sexual orientation insofar as they affect different groups of African Americans. This process is admittedly something that continues to be difficult, even in groups that have come to recognize the need to be attentive to such differences.

The fact that many groups we currently work with have one or another cutoff category for their agendas often leads to effects I find perturbing. People who suffer from multiple forms of oppression or who work for several such groups with agendas shaped by different cutoff categories often end up having an overall *wider scope of political concerns* than those who suffer from fewer forms of oppression or work in fewer such groups with agendas shaped by different cutoff categories. Thus, the African American feminist who works both within a feminist group and in a progressive African American political group often ends up with more demands on her time, attention, and energy than, say, a white feminist who works only in the feminist group or an African American man who works only in the African American political group. And while the African American feminist may be instrumental in facilitating certain kinds of political cooperation among some members of each group, the cutoff categories that define these political organizations often function to limit the kinds of political cooperation she can expect from many of her fellow members. Thus, many white feminists from her feminist group might attend and support a demonstration against the antiwoman agenda of the Million Man March organized by the African American group but may often feel neither a need to attend and support nor political propriety in attending and supporting a demonstration organized by the African American group against a local instance of police brutality against African American men. Similarly, many of her African American male comrades may attend and support a meeting organized by the feminist group to discuss the raced and gendered discourses around the Anita Hill/Clarence Thomas hearings but may feel neither a need to attend and support nor political propriety in attending and supporting a campus demonstration organized by the feminist group against an incident of sexual violence against a white woman. In each case, the cutoff category defining the group's political agenda functions to legitimate the idea that the white women and African American men need to actively care about or engage with *a narrower set of issues* than the African American feminist. In many such instances, the result is not only that the African American feminist is left burdened by the feeling that she is expected to have the time and energy for a wider set of political concerns than her male African American comrades or her white women comrades. She is often also left frustrated that she can feel only a *partial political solidarity* with these comrades in both groups, for they only actively care about a part of what she cares about.

I think that it is time for us to recognize the need to *weaken* the limits set by various cutoff categories on the scope of our concerns. I believe that we need political discourses that forcefully endorse the need for all of us who are politically concerned and involved to widen the scopes of our concerns so that they are not wholly circumscribed by the bounds of any of these particular cutoff categories. And I believe that we need political organizations and routines that help all of us to more consistently work together on a wider range of political issues than is possible when most of the organizations currently available to us function on the basis of cutoff categories.[10] I am not denying that there may be functional reasons to maintain forms of political organization that still operate with cutoff categories for their agendas.[11] I am simply arguing that we need other, wider forms of political organization in addition that will *complement* the cutoff category–based organizations, which are often all that many of us have now, and wider forms of political vision that encourage all of us to widen the scope of our concerns beyond the limits set by any particular cutoff category.

I believe that we have urgent political reasons to do so. Many of the issues and problems that currently confront concerned and progressive citizens in this country and in others—ranging from the social instability, human misery, and environmental degradation caused by current forms of global economic development, to cuts in welfare and other forms of state-funded support for different groups of vulnerable citizens, to anti-immigrant policies, to various forms of fundamentalism and fundamentalist nationalism, to genocidal ethnic violence and military violence, and to the backlash against affirmative action and gay rights—affect a great many people in a great many ways and cut across the constituencies of the various cutoff categories that structure many of our political organizations today. All too often, these cutoff categories function to hinder and limit vital forms of political cooperation among organizations.[12] I believe that we all urgently need to build on the lessons we have learned in our attempts at "attending to differences" *within* one or more cutoff categories and to learn to extend our political concerns beyond these cutoff categories while remaining attentive to the different ways in which these various systemic forms of injustice affect different groups of people.

Cutoff categories have operated as "boundaries" for political agendas and organizations, and boundaries always have a dual aspect. They help us to focus on and attend to what is *inside* the boundary, but they often also help to seal off attention from what lies *outside*. We have all learned a great deal politically from the focus provided by these boundaries as they have helped shape the contours of the political organizations in which we work. I think it is time that we become more willing to also care about and attend to important and connected matters that may lie outside the boundaries that define the current scope of our political concerns.

I will conclude by saying that many of these changes seem to be already under way. There is in fact a considerable body of feminist work that is not restricted to "issues affecting women," and there is increasing political willingness to work across cutoff categories. One purpose of my chapter is to make this process explicit and to clarify the reasons that might support this development.

NOTES

1. See Iris Young, "Gender as Seriality," in her *Intersecting Voices: Dilemmas of Gender, Political Philosophy and Policy* (Princeton, N.J.: Princeton University Press, 1997).

2. See Mary Daly, *Gyn/Ecology: The Metaethics of Radical Feminism* (Boston: Beacon Press, 1978); Shulamith Firestone, *The Dialectic of Sex* (New York: William Morrow, 1970); and Catharine MacKinnon, *Towards a Feminist Theory of the State* (Cambridge, Mass.: Harvard University Press, 1989). In Firestone's and MacKinnon's work, Marxist categories such as "capitalism" and "the proletariat" seem self-consciously and explicitly replaced by "patriarchy" and "women," respectively. Daly does not make this move explicitly, but her theoretical position is substantially similar to that of MacKinnon or Firestone with respect to the positions I am ascribing here to radical feminism.

3. Different reasons have been given for the exclusion of men from feminist organizations. At one extreme, some radical feminists have seen all men as "The Enemy," as so deeply invested in their patriarchal privileges that removing one's life as far as possible from the presence and influence of men was imperative. I think there is much in Daly's work that reflects this sense of things. At a less extreme level, men have been constituted as "Untrustworthy Outsiders," who would not be reliable allies in struggles against patriarchy because they were likely to lack sustained commitment to critiquing and surrendering their patriarchal privileges and because their lack of experience of patriarchal oppression would not generate reliable understandings of oppression. At the "weakest" level, men have been excluded because they were regarded as "Impediments to Feminist Activism." Given the patriarchal context, men would tend, despite their best intentions, to dominate the conversation in these groups, to distract women's attention either by guilty self-flagellation or by expecting praise from women for their presence, or to prevent women from feeling comfortable discussing issues such as rape or domestic violence.

4. See bell hooks, *Ain't I a Woman* (Boston: South End Press, 1981) and *Feminist Theory: From Margin to Center* (Boston: South End Press, 1984); Maria Lugones and Elizabeth V. Spelman, "Have We Got a Theory for You!: Feminist Theory, Cultural Imperialism and the Demand for 'the Woman's Voice,'" in *Women and Values: Readings in Recent Feminist Philosophy,* ed. Marilyn Pearsall (Belmont, Calif.: Wadsworth Publishing Co., 1999); and Elizabeth V. Spelman, *Inessential Woman: Problems of Exclusion in Feminist Thought* (Boston: Beacon Press, 1988).

5. For a historical account of this process, see Antoinette Burton, *Burdens of History: British Feminists, Indian Women and Imperial Culture, 1865–1915* (Chapel Hill: University of North Carolina Press, 1994).

6. I have been asked by more than one person whether I think that such "apparent conflicts of interests among women" would disappear if I considered feminism to be a movement that fights only for the "morally justifiable interests of all women." I feel resistant to this move and can only briefly clarify my reasons for resistance. First, I am afraid that this is one of those all-too-comfortable stipulative moves so loved by philosophers—whereby something that is in effect a "stipulation" is taken to be a "solution." Second, I am wary of engaging in discussions in which every example of a "conflict of interest" is deemed resolved by the idea that "if we had the right moral

analysis, the apparent conflict would vanish." The idea that "the apparent conflict between one woman's interests and those of another group of women would disappear
if we only had the right moral analysis" appears comforting, but it does not strike me
as plausible. Further, even if in cases like that of the conflicting interests of Western
and Third World women factory workers, or between child care providers and those
who can afford them only because they are badly paid right now, it is possible to conceive of a *long-term solution* that might bring both sets of interests back into align-
ment, there are clear *short-term conflicts* that cannot be wished away. And it arguably
seems that both sets of interests in both examples are "morally legitimate interests" in
one sense. Both groups of workers need employment. The woman who can afford
child care now only because the worker is badly paid cannot wait for a far-off Utopia
where, say, there would be state-funded child care that would both be affordable for
her and pay the workers well. Right now in both cases there is a genuine conflict—
and political agendas ignore these sorts of tensions at their peril.

7. Experiencing oppression or sharing oppression clearly do not constitute *necessary conditions* for political solidarity because we can find several examples, both historical and contemporary, of people who have fought against forms of oppression they
were not subject to and of people who have fought against forms of oppression even
when they were privileged in every important respect. John Stuart Mill is an example.

8. I am not opposed "in principle" to certain feminist forums excluding men. I
would like to make an analogy here to the ways in which some feminist forums may
exclude white women or straight women. Working across "differences among
women" has been, and continues to be, a serious challenge for many feminist groups.
Sometimes, there has been a felt need for some of the women in the organization
who belong to marginalized groups to create supplementary forums within the organization, open only to women from a particular marginalized group, which meet
to think about issues specific to them. I am thinking about forums such as a "Women
of Color Caucus" or a "Lesbian Feminist Caucus" that operate "under the umbrella" of
the central feminist organization. I am not at all opposed to this sort of move *in principle*—there may often be times when this is politically crucial and useful to do. What
I do want to insist on, however, is that this formation suggests an answer to how to
handle the inclusion of men into feminist groups while maintaining the possibility of
excluding them from certain meetings or discussions. While meetings and discussions of the "central organization" would be open to men, there may be a need to
sometimes have "women-only" meetings. One could do this on the same lines as the
Women of Color Caucus—there would be some meetings of the organization open
only to women of color and some open only to women.

9. Mrinalini Sinha, *Colonial Masculinity: The "Manly Englishman" and the "Effeminate Bengali" in the Late Nineteenth Century* (Manchester: Manchester University Press, 1995).

10. I am arguing that many of us need to take a deserved measure of self-
responsibility for our own adherence to "cutoff category politics." Feminist groups
open only to women create a general atmosphere in which many feminist men feel
really guilty about even thinking of using the term *feminist* to describe themselves.
Many think, in a hazy way, that their role is to work on transforming *themselves* in
an antipatriarchal direction—but not to work with women on political agendas. Not
only does such a "focus on the self" run the danger of becoming tedious and nar-

cissistic, I think that these men would have a better sense of what they need to change if they worked alongside feminist women. Many of us feminist women have learned a great deal of our feminist understanding and sensibilities by working in feminist groups. By keeping men out, we are denying them precisely the kinds of political opportunities that consolidated our own understandings of, and commitments to, feminist politics.

11. I think that there has often been a confusion in feminist thought and in feminist political groups between "the practical level" and "the principled or conceptual level." There may sometimes be good *practical* reasons for talking *as if* feminism represented "Women's Interests as a Whole," for excluding men from membership, and for having agendas restricted to "Women's Interests." In other instances such practical reasons may be absent or may pull in the opposite direction. Radical feminism offers "principled or conceptual reasons" (albeit mistaken ones, I believe) for all these things. Many of us remain partially in the "grip" of radical feminist conceptual frameworks and are confused about whether the reasons why we may endorse these things are practical or principled. We may think we have principled reasons for these positions when all we have are practical considerations that apply only in some instances. We end up building into the very framework of our organizations and political agendas decisions about the scope of our membership and agendas that should be made only in a pragmatic and piecemeal way—for example, instead of excluding men from some forums or meetings when there are specific concrete reasons for so doing or focusing on "women's interests" when there are specific concrete reasons for so doing. We take these to be permanent and principled commitments and build them into the institutional frameworks of our political organizations and into the conceptual vision of our political agendas.

12. I will offer a concrete example of the ways in which such cutoff categories function as impediments to political cooperation. A few years ago, in the midst of the backlash against affirmative action, my colleague, Luke Harris, and I were invited to talk to the NAACP Legal Defense Fund in New York on the subject of affirmative action. Among other things, we questioned their construction of affirmative action as a purely race-based issue and one that only affected African Americans. In the ensuing conversation, it emerged that the Puerto Rican Legal Defense Fund and the NOW Legal Defense Fund had their headquarters in the very same building but that there had been no attempt to coordinate their various legal struggles on this issue. This particular situation subsequently changed, but I believe that this phenomenon remains common, hindering the sustained forms of progressive coalition politics that we need to adequately address many urgent issues that confront us today. I am calling for a political perspective that is deeply sensitive to the lesson of the Differences Critique—one that stresses the need to morally and politically attend to a variety of intersecting and interlinking forms of oppression that unjustly impoverish and distort the lives of a great many different groups of inhabitants of our nations. I believe that this sort of "serious attention to differences," which operates without any cutoff category setting political limits to what we care about, is imperative for the kinds of democratic coalitions we need to successfully fight for many of the concrete issues that confront all of us in a variety of national and international contexts.

II

FORMING SELVES, BEING AGENTS

3

Social Groups and Individual Identities—Individuality, Agency, and Theory

Diana Tietjens Meyers

I must assume, not just as history but as an ongoing psychological force, that, in the eyes of white culture, irrationality, lack of control, and ugliness signify not just the whole slave personality, but me.

—Patricia Williams, *The Alchemy of Race and Rights* (Cambridge: Harvard University Press, 1991), 11

I don't recall ever choosing to identify as a male; but being male has shaped many of my plans and actions.

—K. Anthony Appiah, *Color Consciousness: The Political Morality of Race* (Princeton, N.J.: Princeton University Press, 1996), 80

Race and gender are thrust on us, and it is not within our power as individuals to expel race or gender from our lives. That our society and the people we associate with classify us according to race and gender is not controversial. The U.S. census expects individuals to classify themselves by race and gender. Although public toilets are no longer segregated by race, they are still reserved for "men" or "women." Most expectant mothers eagerly await news of whether their fetuses are boys or girls, and few adoptive parents are willing to accept a child from a racial background different from their own. Likewise, it is not controversial that access to social, economic, and political opportunities as well as to other goods differs depending on race and gender. Although nothing legally bars women or African American men from running for the U.S. presidency, they have not had much electoral success so far. Moreover, major gaps persist between women's earnings and men's and between the earnings of Euro-Americans and those of people of color.

35

Yet, in recent feminist theory, a controversy has emerged about whether women have gender identities—that is, whether social institutions and cultural traditions instill gender in our cognitive, emotional, and motivational infrastructures. Some feminist scholars deny that women have gender identities. Specifically, they deny that gender structures people's attitudes, values, desires, and expectations, and they deny that women as a group have anything in common. I agree that women do not share the same identity—there is no set of personality traits or values that every woman has. Nevertheless, in this chapter I take issue with the claim that women do not have gender identities, and I urge that both gender and race are internalized and become integral to individualized identities.[1] Moreover, I explicate the epistemological contribution of individualized, subordinated identities to social critique, and I defend the epistemological feasibility of developing theories about the personal and social meanings of subordinated group identities.

GROUP MEMBERSHIP, IDENTITY, AND INDIVIDUALITY

According to Iris Young, a leading exponent of the anti-identity view, women are members of a group precursor, but they do not necessarily have a gender identity.[2] To explain gender, Young invokes Jean-Paul Sartre's idea of seriality. A social series is "a social collective whose members are unified passively by the objects around which their actions are oriented or by the objectified results of the material effects of the actions of others."[3] In other words, a series is constituted by a behavior-directing, meaning-defining environment. The lives of series members are affected by being assigned to particular social series, for serial existence is experienced as a "felt necessity" that leaves individuals feeling powerless.[4] People feel impelled to act in ways that conform to their series memberships. Yet series membership "*does not define the person's identity* in the sense of forming his/her individual purposes, projects, and sense of self in relation to others."[5] Indeed, individuals can *choose* to make none of their serial memberships important for their individual identity.[6]

Young's view is premised on a false dichotomy: Either social positioning is constitutive of individual identity, and all similarly positioned individuals share a common identity, or else social positioning is external to individual identity unless a person decides to let it in. Because it is indisputable that women do not share a common identity—the same can be said of members of racial, sexuality, class, and ethnic groups—Young opts for the voluntarist position. One is a member of this or that social series whether one likes it or not. One becomes a member of a social group only when one elects to join one. Group membership shapes one's identity only if one allows it to do so.

The alternative to this individualist voluntarism is not gender (race, sexuality, class, or ethnic) essentialism and a common feminine (racial, sexual, class, or ethnic) identity. The alternative is gendered *and* individualized identities. At one point, Young seems to concede this very point. No woman's identity "will escape the *markings of gender*," she observes, "but how gender marks her life is her own."[7] I agree—identities are individualized. But I hasten to add that how gender marks a woman's (or a man's) identity will not be entirely her (or his) own choice. Gender worms its way into identity in ways that we may not be conscious of and in ways that we may not be able to change no matter how much we try.[8] Gender is constitutive of who we are—our personalities, our capabilities and liabilities, our aspirations, and how we feel about all of these dimensions of identity. Yet there is no feature of identity that all women or that all men share. The same is true of other subordinated and privileged identity categories. How is this possible?

Nancy Chodorow uses psychoanalytic theory to make sense of individualized, gendered identities. Psychoanalysis explains how individuals "personally animate and tint . . . the anatomic, cultural, interpersonal, and cognitive world we experience."[9] One's affective dispositions, unconscious fantasies, and interpersonal relationships filter the culturally entrenched conception of gender one encounters. Through various psychic processes—projection and introjection together with defense mechanisms—gender acquires a "personal meaning" that is inspired by, but does not wholly replicate, culturally transmitted strictures and iconography.[10] As Chodorow somewhat paradoxically puts it, each woman creates "her own personal-cultural gender."[11]

It is a mistake to picture attributes like gender as toxic capsules full of norms and interpretive schemas that individuals swallow whole and that lodge intact in their psychic structure. The diversity of individuals' experience of gender belies this view. But as the epigrams taken from Williams and Appiah attest, it is also a mistake to picture attributes like gender as systems of social and economic opportunities, constraints, rewards, and penalties that never impinge on individual identity.[12] The seeming naturalness of enacting gendered characteristics, the passion with which people cling to their sense of their gender, and the intractability of many gendered attributes when people seek to change them testify to the embeddedness of gender in identity.

Cultural gender, race, sexuality, class, and ethnicity conceptions are internalized, to be sure, but they are also processed psychologically. This lifelong processing individualizes these socially mandated dimensions of identity. However, this processing neither dissolves the individual's ties to her cultural milieu and its regnant conceptions of these identities nor endows the individual with complete control over her identity insofar as it bears imprints of gender, race, class, and ethnicity.

I wish to stress, however, that individuals can exert a good deal of control over their group-based identities.[13] They can become conscious of how gender, for instance, is limiting and frustrating them; they can become estranged from these features of their identity; and they can seek out transformative practices—

for example, consciousness raising or psychotherapy—and undertake to overcome them. Likewise, they can participate in movements that aim to redefine
gender along emancipatory lines and thus seek to spare future generations of
women the need to struggle against some of the pernicious strictures and
meanings that they internalized as girls and had to fight as women.

SUBORDINATED IDENTITIES, SOCIAL CRITIQUE, AND POLITICAL AGENCY

I shall now turn to the question of why it is important to see womanhood and
other subordinated social identities as dimensions of individual identity. Let us
listen to Patricia Williams again: "I think: my raciality is socially constructed, and
I experience it as such. I feel my blackself as an eddy of conflicted meanings—
and meaninglessness—in which my self can get lost, in which agency and con-
sent are tumbled in constant motion. This sense of motion, the constant windy
sound of manipulation whistling in my ears, is a reminder of society's constant
construction of my blackness."[14] Because Williams distinguishes between her
"blackself" and her self and comments that her blackself threatens to eclipse her
self, it might seem that she is reifying and compartmentalizing her socially imposed blackself and her imperiled own self. Thus, it is tempting to suppose that
she is reviving some sort of notion of an innate, core, authentic self surrounded
by layers of socially constructed, inauthentic, overpowering self-toids. I doubt,
though, that she is endorsing such a simplistic and discredited view.[15] Rather, I
would urge that she is succinctly and poignantly accomplishing several goals:
(1) she acknowledges the power of social structures and discourses to invade
and inhabit individual psyches by asserting that she has a blackself; (2) she insists on the disparity between the cultural stereotype (her blackself) and the inner reality (her own self); (3) she highlights the agentic resources of individuality by affirming that her own self resists the destructive forces of social
construction; (4) she communicates the excruciating bewilderment and conflict
that such racialized, subordinated subjectivity inflicts. The rest of Williams's essay is a probing examination and trenchant critique of the construction of
African American womanhood and manhood in the United States today.

  I shall take my cue from Williams's text—that is, I shall focus on the inter-
play among group-based identities, alienation, and moral reflection. In my
view, the kind of alienation Williams describes is, alas, desirable as long as
we live in societies that subordinate some social groups while privileging
others, for this unsettled, disquieting sense of self can spark insightful moral
reflection and emancipatory social critique.

  What is so awful about having a subordinated, perhaps multiply subordinated, identity is that one seldom feels at ease in one's own skin. One may
be plagued by layers of consciousness—one's objectives and intentions;

how others, especially members of other social groups, are likely to perceive one's conduct; how others' various possible misperceptions may spoil one's undertakings; and so forth. Of course, people are never transparent to one another, and misunderstandings abound in all interpersonal relations. However, it is quite another matter when stereotyping unconsciously, but systematically, blocks mutual understanding.

Maria Lugones describes herself as an intense person, yet she knows that Anglos routinely stereotype her as an "Intense Latin."[16] Thus, when she is speaking or gesturing intensely, her consciousness is often split—split between her desire to demonstrate the gravity of her point and to give expression to her distinctive personality traits, on the one hand, and her knowledge that her behavior will be dismissed as merely typical and that her ideas will not be accorded the weight they deserve, on the other. From one point of view, such communication blocks are tragic—they isolate us from others and impoverish our lives. But Lugones does not dwell exclusively on the misery and injustice that stem from these barriers. She also invites subordinated individuals to take delight in the absurdity of their predicament and to deliberately toy with others' bigoted preconceptions—sometimes masquerading in the stereotype, and sometimes feeling intense and acting that way, but always knowing that the Other cannot tell which is which.[17]

What needs to be underscored here is that Lugones's strategy presupposes a complex understanding of who she is, an understanding that is not limited to but does incorporate her membership in social groups. She can only make a mockery of bigotry and manipulate it for her own ends if she recognizes both the potency of the social construction of her identity and the laughable megalomania of its pretensions to total control over who she is and who she can be. In a similar vein, Williams's essay documents the insidious ways in which African American women and men are recruited into subordinated gender identities that they then inflict on one another and which whites use as excuses for despising them. But through her own simultaneous avowal and refusal of her "blackself," Williams marshals critical acuity that enables her to depict the pathos of this complicity and to decry the oppression that secures it.

Who one is affects the way one thinks about society—what issues will be salient, how one conceptualizes and interrelates them, what policies and practices seem benign, and what sorts of change seem urgent. Few young dotcom turks are concerned about the same issues that galvanize single mothers who never completed high school. One's moral outlook is not independent of one's identity, and one's identity is not independent of one's position in the world. Yet, as we have seen, one's identity is individualized. Coupled with crosscutting group allegiances, individuality often splinters subordinated groups and (lamentably) hinders mass political mobilization. Nevertheless, I would urge that the individualization of subordinated identities is indispensable to social dissidence. Each individual has peculiar talents and deficiencies, satisfactions and frustrations, fancies and antipathies, yearnings and dreads, ambitions and resignations, and the like. Not only do these attributes make people unique, they also leverage critique. Lugones, noting that she is playful in some contexts but not in others, argues that the contexts that make her unplayful are oppressive.[18] Conflicts between one's individualized subordinated identity and dominant cultural norms or authoritative institutions provide a vital impetus to social analysis and oppositional activism, for people care deeply about living a life that expresses their sense of self.

Iris Young is right, then, to stress that the specific circumstances of women's lives give rise to specific affinities around which they may choose to organize and act.[19] However, these affinities should not be severed from subordinated identities. It is the clash within the individualized subordinated identity and between the individualized subordinated identity and the subordinating social context that fuels these affinities.

THE EPISTEMIC STATUS OF "ESSENTIALIST" THEORY

Now, it might seem that my view of subordinated identity, moral reflection, and political engagement throws the whole project of theorizing subordinated groups into disrepute. If gender identity is individualized, it seems doubtful that there could be any general explanations of gender. And if the line of thought I have developed does not altogether dispose of gender theory, it might seem that it collapses gender theory into the project of explicating the psychological mechanisms of identity consolidation. In my view, however, drawing this inference rests on a misunderstanding of the epistemic status of accounts of subordinated groups.

My argument takes off from my conviction that many of the gender theories that have been most convincingly condemned as "essentialist"—such as Chodorow's account of the perpetuation of exclusively female mothering and Catharine MacKinnon's account of women's objectified sexuality—are nevertheless insightful and illuminating. Chodorow argues that because the vast majority of girls receive primary care from women, and because they identify with these female caregivers, girls develop relational personalities.[20] Empathic and at ease with intimacy, women are good at caregiving and gain satisfaction from caring for others. Thus, they are disposed to have children and assume primary responsibility for caring for their own children. In contrast, MacKinnon focuses on heterosexuality and argues that women's sexuality is a sexuality for men.[21] Feminine softness, pliancy, vulnerability, and so forth are qualities that mark women as available to men on men's terms. Women's desire to be alluring is nothing more than a desire to please and appease those in power, namely, men, by complying with the sexual norms codified in the pornography that turns men on. These are very different but equally sweeping claims about the nature of feminine identity.

How can it be true that charges of essentialism against these theories are telling and also that these theories are insightful and illuminating? If, contrary to Chodorow, some women are not relational and nurturant, and if, contrary to MacKinnon, some women's sexuality defies pornographic imagery and male violation, it seems to follow that these theories are false and therefore worthless.

If one regards these theories as inductive generalizations about women, they certainly are false as they stand. They couch their claims in universalist terms, and the empirical data furnish ample disconfirming evidence. However, I believe that this social scientific epistemic model is not the best one to adopt. Instead, I propose that we think of gender theories like Chodorow's and MacKinnon's on the model of interpretation of literary texts. Literary interpretations cannot ignore the texts they purport to analyze and explain. They must cite supporting passages in the texts and explain away apparent inconsistencies between the text and the interpretation being proffered. However, because the text itself may not be perfectly coherent, there may be no single interpretation that leaves nothing in it unexplained. Thus, there is general consensus that a single text can reasonably be interpreted in more than one way and that many of these interpretations are insightful and illuminating. In other words, literary texts are rich enough to sustain a number of divergent interpretations. No text conveys just one meaning to every reader, and readers can deepen their appreciation of works of literature by familiarizing themselves with other readers' interpretations.

Similarly, social phenomena, such as gender, race, sexuality, class, and ethnicity, and psychological phenomena, such as gendered, raced, sexualized, classed, and ethnically imprinted identities, are extremely complex and variable, and they look different from different angles. Consequently, it would be foolish to expect to capture these phenomena in one comprehensive account. Nevertheless, as Marilyn Frye maintains, it is imperative that we study them and try to identify patterns in the phenomena—social forces that maintain these hierarchical social systems and motifs running through different individuals' subjective senses of their gender, race, sexuality, class, and ethnicity.[22] Frye suggests that we regard gender theory as akin to metaphors.[23] Good metaphors are apt and revealing. However, a metaphor asserts an equivalence that will prove misleading if it is taken literally and pursued too far, and no one metaphor ever expresses the complete and definitive truth about a phenomenon.

If theories of subordinated groups resemble tropes more than they resemble statistical tabulations, it is worth recalling that hyperbole numbers among the canonical figures of speech. Thus, the universalist language in which many gender theories are articulated can be understood as an instance of the rhetorical device of exaggeration. But here it might be objected that the trouble with hyperbole is that it is all too similar to yelling. The practical effect of relatively privileged feminists' hyperbolic theorizing may be to drown out the voices of other women and to enshrine their interpretations of gender as authoritative. Worse, perhaps, when relatively privileged feminists base their political activism on a gender theory that makes sense of their experience while neglecting the experience of many other women, these gender tropes may get translated into exclusionary institutions and policies. Thus, it is necessary to consider whether these unacceptable consequences can be averted without repudiating such theories.

I would like to propose several ways of mitigating the adverse impact of theories of gender. First, theorists can tone down the rhetoric in which they couch accounts of gender without shutting down the project of theorizing gender—the restraint of classical style is no less stirring than the flamboyance of the baroque. By adopting less flashy, more tentative and reflexive rhetoric, theorists can acknowledge their own social locations and the need for multiple interpretations. Second, many relatively privileged feminists are educators, and as teachers we function as sales agents for publishers. Through our reading assignments, we can and should expand the market for diverse feminist theorizing, pressure book publishers and journals to meet this demand, and ensure that these "other" voices reach as wide an audience as possible. Finally, I would emphasize that activists would be far less likely to advocate privilege-perpetuating initiatives were they to recognize that the theories guiding their politics are analogous to literary interpretations and are, therefore, partial in both senses of the term—that is, incomplete and perspectival.

Although African American feminists sometimes focus on experience quite unlike my own, my thinking about gender has been immeasurably enriched by studying their theorizing. For example, I find their analysis of intersectionality—that is, the consequences of converging vectors of social stratification—widely applicable.[24] It is as important, in my judgment, that middle-class, heterosexual, Euro-American women grasp how class, sexuality, and race privilege ameliorate the effects of gender subordination as it is that multiply subordinated women grasp how their injuries are compounded. Instead of complacently generating counterexamples to gender theories, then, I would urge readers to scrutinize the rhetoric of each theory to see what literary effects it is designed to achieve and to assess whether this language successfully achieves these aims. If gender theories are epistemic relatives of literary interpretations, ostensibly essentialist gender theories are not defeated by the discovery of disconfirming data. Moreover, such theories can be suggestive and helpful even though none conveys the Truth about gender. I would urge, then, that my view of individualized, subordinated identities not only advances our understanding of the epistemology of social critique; it also epistemically vindicates the project of theorizing internally diverse, subordinated social groups.

NOTES

1. Subordination of social groups is not a uniform phenomenon. Different subordinated groups are assigned to different social positions, and the prejudices against different subordinated groups vary in form and content. Women, for example, are not an isolated minority. Yet manhood is the cultural norm of humanity, whereas womanhood is culturally coded as a defective form of manhood. Moreover, gender segmentation persists in labor markets worldwide, and women wield little political power compared with men of similar backgrounds. Likewise, minority groups may be more or less isolated—for example, in the United States, Jews are more socially and economically integrated than African Americans. Prejudices against different groups are not uniform—homophobia is significantly different from racial bigotry. These variations notwithstanding, we may ask whether there are continuities with respect to the relationship between membership in a subordinated social group and the constitution of individual identities, and that question is the focus of this chapter.

2. Iris Marion Young, "Gender as Seriality: Thinking about Women as a Social Collective," *Signs* 19 (1994): 713–38. Young suggests that sexual orientation, class, race, and nationality are amenable to analysis as seriality, too (731–32). For related discussion, see Linda Alcoff, "Cultural Feminism versus Post-Structuralism: The Identity Crisis in Feminist Theory," in *Culture/Power/History,* ed. Nicholas Dirks, Geoffrey Eley, and Sherry Ortner (Princeton, N.J.: Princeton University Press, 1994).

3. Young, "Gender as Seriality," 724.

4. Young, "Gender as Seriality," 726.

5. Young, "Gender as Seriality," 727, emphasis added.

6. Young, "Gender as Seriality," 733.

7. Young, "Gender as Seriality," 734.

8. Sandra Lee Bartky's discussion, in *Femininity and Domination* (New York: Routledge, 1990), chapter 4, of women's masochistic sexual fantasies provides a poignant and convincing demonstration of this point.

9. Nancy J. Chodorow, "Gender as Personal and Cultural Construction," *Signs* 20 (1995): 520.

10. Chodorow, "Gender as Personal and Cultural Construction," 517.

11. Chodorow, "Gender as Personal and Cultural Construction," 518. Elizabeth Abel develops a parallel line of thought with respect to race and class in "Race, Class, and Psychoanalysis? Opening Questions," in *Conflicts in Feminism,* ed. Marianne Hirsch and Evelyn Fox Keller (New York: Routledge, 1990).

12. For related discussion, see Bartky, *Femininity and Domination,* chapter 5.

13. For discussion of some of the ways in which people individually and collectively exert control over their group-based identities, see Diana Tietjens Meyers, "Intersectional Identity and the Authentic Self? Opposites Attract!" in *Relational Autonomy,* ed. Catriona Mackenzie and Natalie Stoljar (New York: Oxford University Press, 1999).

14. Williams, *The Alchemy of Race and Rights* (Cambridge: Harvard University Press, 1991), 168.

15. For a critique of this view, see Jean Grimshaw, "Autonomy and Identity in Feminist Thinking," in *Feminist Perspectives in Philosophy,* ed. Morwenna Griffiths and Margaret Whitford (Bloomington: Indiana University Press, 1988), 95–96; and

Diana Tietjens Meyers, *Self, Society, and Personal Choice* (New York: Columbia University Press, 1989), 19–21.

16. Maria C. Lugones, "Playfulness, World-Travelling, and Loving Perception," in *Feminist Social Thought: A Reader,* ed. Diana Tietjens Meyers (New York: Routledge, 1997), 156.

17. Lugones, "Playfulness," 156. Also see Patricia Mann's remarks about women's identification with eroticized beauty ideals in "Glancing at Pornography: Recognizing Men," in *Feminist Social Thought: A Reader,* ed. Diana Tietjens Meyers (New York: Routledge, 1997), 434.

18. Lugones, "Playfulness," 152, 155–56.

19. Young, "Gender as Seriality," 737.

20. Nancy J. Chodorow, *The Reproduction of Mothering* (Berkeley: University of California Press, 1978).

21. Catharine MacKinnon, "Feminism, Marxism, Method, and the State: An Agenda for Theory," in *Feminist Social Thought: A Reader,* ed. Diana Tietjens Meyers (New York: Routledge, 1997).

22. Marilyn Frye, "The Possibility of Feminist Theory," in *Theoretical Perspectives on Sexual Difference,* ed. Deborah L. Rhode (New Haven, Conn.: Yale University Press, 1990), 180.

23. Frye, "The Possibility of Feminist Theory," 181–83. For readings of Chodorow's and MacKinnon's theories as extended tropes, see Diana Tietjens Meyers, *Subjection and Subjectivity: Psychoanalytic Feminism and Moral Philosophy* (New York: Routledge, 1994), 78–83, 106–07.

24. Meyers, "Intersectional Identity and the Authentic Self? Opposites Attract!"

4

Identity and Free Agency

Hilde Lindemann Nelson

A consideration of how power operates in oppressive group relations shows us something interesting about the connection between identity and agency. The coercive forces within an abusive power system—patriarchy, for example—create the identities that are required by the system. These oppressive identities then determine the degree to which those who bear them may exercise their moral agency.

Because identities are narratively constructed, however, their faults can be narratively repaired. I call the tool for such repair a "counterstory." The concept of the counterstory furnishes a valuable clue to the relationship between identity and agency, for it is premised on the idea that damage to a person's identity constricts her agency, while repairing the damaged identity frees her agency. And so I shall argue. But let me begin with a narrative of how a counterstory is developed.

VIRGINIA MARTIN'S COUNTERSTORY

In the small city of Cranford somewhere in the Midwest there was a 225-bed hospital. Virginia Martin did her floor training there when she was a nursing student at Eton College, and when she graduated in 1989 she found full-time work on the orthopedic service almost immediately. She was thirty then, kindly and plump, married since she was nineteen. She would have liked to go to medical school and was certainly bright enough to get the degree, but because her husband's law school loans still had to be repaid and their two children needed her, nursing seemed the next best thing. She was good at it. She liked it.

Virginia Martin's hospital had four different kinds of nurses. Many of them were young or middle-aged baccalaureate nurses like her, trained to the work of a particular unit and qualified to rise to the rank of head nurse. The older nurses tended to be diploma nurses with years of practical experience. Then there were RNs with associate degrees, many of whom were part-timers. And finally there were RNs with master's degrees who served as the hospital's nurse educators and directed the chemotherapy and nuclear medicine units. As only 6 percent of nurses in the United States are men, perhaps it is not surprising that, at the time when these events unfolded, all the nurses at Cranford Community Hospital were women.

Like all hospitals, Cranford Community had its frictions. The diploma nurses were galled when they trained a baccalaureate nurse to do the work of the unit only to see her promoted to be their head nurse. As a cost-cutting move, the hospital administrators had hired more unlicensed personnel to do bedside tasks that none of the nurses considered them qualified to do. And physicians at Cranford continued to see their job as "managing the numbers"—getting white cell counts down to normal levels, measuring blood gases, monitoring electrolyte imbalances—while leaving the nurses to do what the chief of medicine was once overheard to call the "touchy-feely stuff" of providing patients and their families with human sympathy.

Every year in the first week of May the nurses at Cranford Community Hospital and Eton College sponsored a Nurse Recognition Day, involving speakers, student events, media attention, and a sit-down dinner for 400 of the city's RNs to honor the recipient of that year's Distinguished Service Award. Virginia Martin volunteered to serve on the steering committee, which meets twice a month throughout the year. She was not sure why she offered. If you needed a Recognition Day, it must be because you knew you weren't recognized, and why would you want to draw attention to your lack of prestige? Doctors don't bother with days like that, she thought. She found, however, that she really enjoyed getting to know the fourteen other members of the committee. They quickly coalesced into their own little community.

And a diverse community it was. Nursing was about the only thing the committee members had in common. One was a fundamentalist Christian, some were atheists, two were observant Jews. Political stances ranged from Left leaning (like herself), to apathetic, to those who favored big business. Three sexual orientations were represented: lesbian, bi, and straight. Most committee members had full-time careers; three were "refrigerator nurses" who saw their jobs mainly in terms of supplemental income. Some, like herself, were comfortably maternal; some, feisty and funny; still others, quietly elegant, or timid, or driven.

As the committee sifted through the nominations and planned the events, the conversation moved naturally to the qualities that make someone an admirable nurse and to the future of the profession. But the talk also drifted to the ethical problems that nurses encounter in the course of their work. Linda Adams, a public health nurse, had visited a new mother and baby in a tumbledown farmhouse and suspected that the baby's failure to thrive was caused by the mother's inability to cope—it was just a feeling she'd had when she was there. Sally Martinson, the emergency room nurse, had started an intravenous drip on a patient without orders because the physician seemed slow and unsure of herself. Chris Johnson, the director of the chemotherapy unit, remarked that she never knew how much she should tell her patients about side effects, for she believed in honesty but not in "truth-dumping." And so on.

At the fourth meeting of the Nurse Recognition Day Committee, Pilar Sanchez arrived with a tale of a sixteen-year-old patient who had been in and out of the hospital many times over the last few years with a form of leukemia that is usually curable in kids of his age. Jake was unlucky, though. His oncologist thought he had defeated the cancer, but it came back, and now even a last-ditch bone marrow transplant had failed. Jake's mother insisted that he not be told that he was dying, and the physicians, saying they had to respect her wishes, forbade the staff to discuss Jake's prognosis with him. Pilar Sanchez, who had been taking care of Jake every time he was hospitalized, was very troubled by this. She was convinced that he could handle the truth, and she felt as if she had lied to him every time she smiled encouragingly when he told her about his plans for the future. She tactfully tried to broach the subject with Jake's oncologist, but he was abrupt, telling her that she was emotionally overinvolved and professionally out of line.

Everybody on the committee was interested and indignant, and everybody had something to say. In Sally Martinson's opinion, this was yet another case of physicians' treating nurses as not-very-bright children. Chris Johnson declared that the reason doctors didn't listen to you was that they didn't take you seriously, and the reason they didn't take you seriously was that you were only doing women's work. Linda Adams bitterly agreed. They do the science. We just do the touchy-feely stuff. Pilar Sanchez added that the oncologist might just as well have said right out that she was an excitable Hispanic. Virginia Martin didn't think they needed to drag gender or ethnicity into this—it was just a doctor–nurse thing. It happened all the time. Only last week, one of the orthopedic surgeons on her unit had put her off when she asked him for a medical consult for a patient with high blood pressure. She hated that. She was the one who would have to cope if the patient stroked out.

And so the committee settled down to a full-bodied grouse. Then, the eldest member, Patricia Kent, a crisply tailored professor of nursing at Eton College, suggested that instead of merely complaining about the friction at the hospital, the committee take some time at each meeting to figure out how to challenge the "technical" versus "touchy-feely" division of labor between doctors and nurses. A picture of nursing seemed to be holding the physicians captive—the Earth Mother with the Bedpan, one might call it. The Earth Mother, of course, was a character in an old story that badly needed to be updated. What better story could be told about the nurses' professional identity that would allow the physicians to see them more clearly? If the nurses could challenge the story about Earth Mothers that the physicians seemed to be telling themselves and substitute one that invited more respectful treatment, maybe it would be easier for them to do their jobs properly.

Nancy Schmidt, one of the older diploma nurses, thought that all this business of nursing as a profession has been taken too far and that if nurses want to be professionals, they should become doctors. Virginia Martin secretly agreed with her, but aloud she merely pointed out that there didn't seem to be any one story they could all tell about their professional identity. There were too many differences among them.

Perhaps, Patricia Kent suggested, they could at least agree that the "touchy-feely" story was a damaging one because it got in the way of their work. And she traced the history of that story, reminding the others of its connections to nineteenth-century military models of nursing, whereby male officers gave the orders and female nurses served and obeyed them. If the committee members were to resist the "touchy-feely" identity, she argued, they would have to challenge the stories that fed it, including those that identify women as subservient to men, as emotional rather than rational, as mothers rather than scientists. Those were the stories the physicians seemed to endorse. To get them to stop, the nurses would have to counter the destructive stories with better ones of their own.

Virginia Martin drove home feeling a little flat, like a tire without quite enough air. She had managed to stay clear of the frictions at the hospital by being nice to everybody and keeping her mouth shut, but she had hoped that this strategy would not be necessary in her newly acquired circle of friends. While she was all for equality with men, she was no feminist. The thought of quoting Gloria Steinem to the orthopedic doctors on her unit made her blink. *There* was an image for you. Why were the committee members making so much of a fuss over what was, after all, just a case of docs being docs? A savvy nurse soon learned how to work around these petty obstructions.

Still, as the weeks went by and many committee members continued to want to think about who they were and how willing the physicians were to let them be it, Virginia Martin and Nancy Schmidt reluctantly went along. The anecdotes about encounters with physicians displayed a disturbing pattern. For example, there was the story of a dehydrated and disoriented elderly patient with no previous history of dementia who, after being restrained in the emergency room, managed to free her right arm, pull out her IV tubes and Foley catheter, and tangle herself in the bedding, all the while wailing loudly. Sally Martinson helped her to sit in a chair while she remade the bed; gave her juice and water to drink; calmed her by stroking her forehead; roused her hourly all night for fluids, toileting, and neurological checks; and by morning found her oriented and talking of going home. The patient was discharged that afternoon. A week later, the night-shift supervisor formally reprimanded Sally for not following the physician's orders concerning restraints, IVs, and Haldol. Apparently the physician had gone straight to the supervisor to complain. Virginia Martin could identify with this story. She too had been the target of complaints from physicians who didn't bother to talk to her first. And somehow that brought to mind her husband's law firm, where the senior partner had recently made it clear—to her husband, not to her—that he expected her to give a dinner party for an important client.

Over time, Virginia Martin's perception of the hospital underwent a significant shift. In the beginning this was largely due to her respect for Patricia Kent. She had a great deal of affection for her witty and magisterial former professor and an equally high opinion of her intelligence. And Sally Martinson, who was no fool either, took almost as radical a view as Patricia Kent. Virginia Martin's trust in these women allowed her to try on their perspective.

The stories ultimately contributed just as much to her change of heart as the people who told them, however. They spoke to her own experiences, but because they were actually about other people she was fond of, they aroused feelings of indignation that her own experiences had never seemed to merit. And because they were her stories as well, the patterns they displayed of contempt for women had to be acknowledged as a pattern in her own life. That acknowledgment made it possible for her to agree that the doctors' story about nurses, as the others were piecing it together, needed to be resisted. She saw that, despite their differences, she and the others could construct a better story—one that identified nurses more accurately and respectfully as skilled professionals with serious responsibilities.

Bit by bit, the nurses connected one fragment of their own story to another, offering ethical interpretations of the various anecdotes and telling fresh ones that, in the light of these interpretations, now seemed relevant. Some were stories of admirable nursing practice. Patricia Kent, for instance, told the others of the time when Virginia Martin, while a nursing student, had arranged for a dying patient to take a little walk outside the hospital in the spring rain and had gotten thoroughly soaked while keeping him company. Others were stories of why the nurses had been attracted to nursing in the first place. As the narrative work went on, the committee members came to a clearer, shared understanding of who they were on the job.

They realized that this shared understanding was only a first step. They knew they would have to start telling their improved story *within* the hospital if their work conditions were ever to change. Moreover, the physicians would not only have to hear that story but accept it and alter their behavior accordingly. And that would take a lot of doing. The day they succeeded would indeed be a Nurse Recognition Day.[1]

COUNTERSTORIES

The cluster of histories, anecdotes, and other narrative fragments the nurses began weaving together is a counterstory—a story that resists an oppressive identity and attempts to replace it with one that commands respect.[2] By piecing together the fragments of various narratives that have gone into the construction of the oppressive identity and challenging the unjust assumptions that lie hidden in those narrative fragments, the nurses began to develop a counterstory that identifies them more accurately and fairly.

Many counterstories are told in two steps. The first is to identify the fragments of master narratives that have gone into the construction of an oppressive identity, noting how these fragments misrepresent persons—here, nurses—and situations. The second is to retell the story about the person or the group to which the person belongs in such a way as to make visible the morally relevant details that the master narratives suppress. If the retelling is successful, the group members will stand revealed as moral agents worthy of respect. Because a powerful group's misperception of an oppressed group results in disrespectful treatment that, as in the case of the nurses, can impede group members in carrying out their responsibilities, the counterstory's repair of the injured group identity opens up the possibility that group members could enjoy greater freedom to do what they ought—Virginia Martin and her colleagues might now be able to care for their patients properly.

Counterstories can provide a significant form of resistance to the evil of diminished moral agency. First, by interacting in a number of different ways with master narratives that identify the members of a particular social group as candidates for oppression, counterstories aim to alter the *oppressors'* perception of the group. If the counterstory moves the dominant group to see the subgroup members as developed moral agents, the more powerful group may be less willing to deprive those belonging to the subgroup of the opportunity to enjoy valuable roles, relationships, and access to the goods on offer in their society. This could permit members of the oppressed group to exercise their agency more freely.

Second, counterstories aim to alter, when necessary, an oppressed person's perception of *herself.* Oppression often infiltrates a person's consciousness, so that she comes to operate, from her own point of view, as her oppressors want her to, rating herself as they rate her. By helping a person with an infiltrated consciousness change her self-understanding, counterstories permit the agent to put greater trust in her own moral worth. If the counterstory moves her to see herself as a competent moral agent, she may be less willing to accept others' oppressive valuations of her, and this too could permit her to exercise her agency more freely.

Note that both injuries to the identity—call them deprivation of opportunity and infiltrated consciousness—constrict a person's freedom of agency.

A strong case can be made, I think, for the view that free agency is a function not only of the agent's capacities and abilities but also of uptake on the part of others. How others see us, and how their perception contributes to our own self-understanding, plays a crucial role in determining how freely we can exercise our moral agency. Identity, understood as a complex interaction between a person's self-conception and others' understanding of who the person is, can thus be conceptualized as something like a lever that constricts or frees agency. A damaged identity constricts agency, but if the damage can be repaired, the person who bears the identity can exercise her agency more freely.

With the help of two important articles by Paul Benson,[3] I will argue that the connection between identity and agency is an internal one, for my actions disclose not only who I am but who I am taken—or take myself—to be, which directly affects how freely I may act. Identity is a question of how others understand what I am doing, as well as how I understand what I am doing. If others' conception of who I am keeps them from seeing my actions as those of a morally responsible person, they will treat me as a moral incompetent. This is the harm of deprivation of opportunity. If my own conception of who I am keeps me from trusting my own moral judgments, I will treat myself as a moral incompetent. This is the harm of infiltrated consciousness. Both others' recognition that I am a morally responsible person and my own sense of myself as a morally responsible person, then, are necessary for the free exercise of moral agency.

I will make my argument in two steps. First, I will make the case that how others identify me has a direct bearing on how freely I can exercise my agency. Second, I will demonstrate that how I see myself also determines how freely I can act.

HOW OTHERS IDENTIFY ME: DEPRIVATION OF OPPORTUNITY

Modern and contemporary philosophers often talk of moral agency as if it were merely a capacity one has, involving competencies that we possess in our own right. Many prominent contemporary theories, including Gerald Dworkin's, Harry Frankfurt's, Wright Neely's, Gary Watson's, and Daniel Dennett's,[4] have characterized free agency as consisting in the competency to govern one's conduct willfully and the capacity to regulate one's will reflectively—neither of which is represented as having anything at all to do with one's relationships to other people.

Freedom of agency, however, requires not only certain capacities, competencies, and intentions that lie within the individual but also recognition on the part of others of who one is, morally speaking. To see how this works, let us return to the story of the young leukemia patient who was not told that he was dying. Because the physician identified Pilar Sanchez as a fond (in the sense of foolish) caregiver, her considered moral judgment that Jake be told of his prognosis was not registered as a *moral* judgment at all. It was registered as emotional overinvolvement—assisted, perhaps, by ethnic stereotypes about excitable Hispanics. The physician's inability to identify Pilar Sanchez as a morally developed agent forecloses the possibility of any discussion with him, let alone a case consult, and this deprives her of the opportunity to care for Jake as well as she thinks she should.

In "Feminist Second Thoughts about Free Agency," Benson contends that most theories of free agency have misdescribed cases of diminished freedom in which the agent is, say, a young child or someone who has been diagnosed with a serious mental illness. In cases of this kind, the theories hold, the agents have no "power to control their conduct through deliberate choices which express what they 'really' want to do."[5] So, for example, Frankfurt classifies young children as "wantons," incapable of adopting second-order desires that control which first-order desires they are willing to act on. The insistence on a control condition as sufficient for free agency, Benson suggests, is a mistake that could only be made by a philosopher who has never been the primary caregiver of a young child. Who else would think that a five-year-old boy who has been warned not to tease his baby sister but does it anyway must be out of control, incapable of stopping what he is doing? That the control condition is inadequate is, to hark back to the title of the essay, Benson's "first feminist thought" about free agency.

The five-year-old may be perfectly capable of leaving his sister alone, says Benson. What he has not yet developed, however, is the capacity for "normative self-disclosure"—the ability to reveal through his actions who he is, morally speaking.[6] The little boy's teasing does not license the inference that he is a cruel or obnoxious person because he probably cannot fully appreciate the evaluations that others place on this kind of behavior and so should not be held morally responsible for it. Because the capacity for normative self-disclosure is, for Benson, a crucial component of normative competence, and the boy has not yet attained normative competence, his agency is not free even though he *can* control his behavior.

In Benson's view, then, agency is free to the extent that two conditions are present. One is the control condition, and the other is normative competence, which involves the ability to express one's identity through one's deeds. As Benson puts it,

> Powers of control are only one part of a much broader, and hopefully more adequate, conception of free agency. On this new conception, free agency requires *normative competence,* an array of abilities to be aware of applicable normative standards, to appreciate those standards, and to bring them competently to bear in one's evaluations of open courses of action. . . . At the heart of

free agency is the power of our actions to reveal who we are, both to ourselves and to others, in the context of potential normative assessments of what we do. Our level of awareness and understanding of the standards expressed in those assessments is as crucial to our freedom as our ability to control what we do.[7]

In keying free agency to the expression of one's identity, Benson points to something that P. F. Strawson has famously described in "Freedom and Resentment."[8] In that essay, Strawson contrasts our ordinary attitudes of interpersonal engagement, such as "gratitude, resentment, forgiveness, love, and hurt feelings,"[9] which we display toward people whose actions reveal them to be participants in the moral community, with attitudes that preclude such engagement because the persons' deeds show them to be morally sub- or abnormal. "Participant reactive attitudes," says Strawson, "are essentially natural human reactions to the good or ill will or indifference of others towards us, as displayed in *their* attitudes and actions"; they are attitudes we take toward people who by their attitudes and actions have shown themselves to be among "the normal and the mature."[10]

Objective attitudes, by contrast, are those we exhibit toward people whose actions disclose them to be psychologically abnormal or morally undeveloped (note that these are Benson's two cases of unfree agency). "To adopt the objective attitude to another human being," as Strawson memorably puts it, "is to see him, perhaps, as an object of social policy; as a subject for what, in a wide range of sense, might be called treatment; as something certainly to be taken account, perhaps precautionary account, of; to be managed or handled or cured or trained."[11] Which attitude we take toward someone depends on whether we think they are morally responsible or morally defective, and we decide this by interpreting, in accordance with some set of evaluative standards, what their actions say about who they are. How we register what someone is doing thus determines whether we will allow them to exercise their agency freely, on the one hand, or constrain them by disciplining them, refusing them a driver's license, denying them custody of their children, or confining them to a locked psychiatric ward, on the other.

But, as Benson goes on to point out (this is his "second thought"), whether we will be seen as the sorts of people who can be held morally responsible for what we are doing has as much to do with the norms of those who assess us as with our ability to understand those norms.[12] Not all of us who fail to qualify as fully free agents do so because we do not appreciate the evaluative standards that others use to take our measure. We may know those standards very well but reject them—and so court persistent misreading. Here Benson is thinking, for instance, of a woman in a sexist society. She may be perfectly aware of how others will perceive her "unladylike" behavior but not accept mainstream standards of how a lady should behave. It is possible that those in the mainstream will then judge from her actions that she is not morally trustworthy—she obviously does not know the rules. As Benson points out, agents who are at the margins of society are particularly open to having their actions evaluated as evidence of sub- or abnormality precisely because they do not conform to the standards adopted by those in the mainstream.

If Benson is right—and I think he is—then normative competence is not just a matter of capacities and capabilities that reside within the agent. Capacities and capabilities are always relative to an environment. Because other people are a part of that environment, the successful exercise of our capacities and capabilities depends in part on others. Normative competence is therefore genuinely interpersonal, for one of its components, the capacity for normative self-disclosure, embraces not only the agent's ability to appreciate the moral construction that others will place on one's actions but also recognition, on the part of those others, that the actions are those of a morally developed person. The role that other people's recognition of one's identity plays in Benson's account of free agency explains, in a way that most contemporary theories cannot, what went wrong between Pilar Sanchez and the dismissive oncologist. According to the standard theories, Pilar Sanchez is a free agent. She is able to govern her behavior by means of her will and is also capable of regulating the content of her will. So the control condition is met. Yet there are good reasons to think that her moral agency is less than fully free, and that is because one component of the normative competence condition is not met. She is aware of and appreciates applicable normative standards and can bring them to bear in her assessments of her options, but she cannot make her actions reveal who she is because others have imposed an oppressive identity on her.

The oncologist has perceived Pilar Sanchez's involvement with her young, dying patient as saying something morally discreditable about her. He sees her as a defective agent and therefore as in no position to hold him accountable. By his standards, which are the mainstream standards in the hospital, she is someone to be managed or handled (if not cured or trained). The problem is not, however, that Pilar Sanchez is morally underdeveloped. Rather, it is that there is something wrong with the norms in the mainstream. These norms produce the oncologist's objective attitude toward her, and it is that which keeps her from being fully free.

If the constrictions on Pilar Sanchez's agency are to be loosened, the oncologist must be persuaded to identify her differently. If he comes to perceive her as a colleague rather than an emotional Latina, he is more likely to include her in the moral deliberations regarding Jake's care. His change in perception would remove obstacles to her free exercise of agency. The injury the oncologist has inflicted on her identity is that of deprivation of opportunity. The counterstory that is required to reidentify her, then, is a story about her moral trustworthiness that *he* is willing to endorse.

So far, it looks as if the degree to which agency is free depends on how well two conditions are met. One is the control condition, which ranges over both one's ability to act willfully and the ability to regulate one's will reflectively, and the other is normative competence, conceived as (1) the ability to understand moral norms, act in accordance with them, and reveal who one is, morally speaking, through what one does; and (2) the ability of others to recognize by one's actions that one is a morally responsible person. Alternatively, the normative competence condition may be thought of as a refinement of the control condition: control over one's actions requires that others not put obstacles in one's path. Seeing that self-disclosure is a matter of what others perceive, as well as what a person expresses, helps us to explain why repairing the damage to a person's identity might permit her to exercise her agency more freely, at least when the injury in question is that of deprivation of opportunity.

HOW I IDENTIFY ME: INFILTRATED CONSCIOUSNESS

When we consider the other sort of damage that oppression inflicts on people's identities, however, it quickly becomes apparent that our understanding of the normative competence condition needs to be expanded. In another article, "Free Agency and Self-Worth," Benson considers the problem of what I have been calling infiltrated consciousness, arguing that in addition to whatever other capacities are necessary, "free agents must have a certain sense of their own worthiness to act."[13] In other words, not only do *others* have to identify the agent as morally trustworthy—she has to identify *herself* as trustworthy as well.

Benson begins by looking at an instance, not of oppression, but of personal domination.[14] In the 1944 film *Gaslight* the character played by Ingrid Bergman is the wife of an evil man, played by Charles Boyer. The Boyer character, who has murdered the Bergman character's aunt, marries the Bergman character so that he can steal the valuable jewels the aunt hid before she died. Bergman, of course, is unaware of his nefarious intent and believes he truly loves her. To keep her from finding out what he is doing, Boyer tries to confuse and disorient her, making her believe that she cannot remember things she has recently done, that she loses things, and that she has hallucinations. Through plausible suggestions he isolates her from people, reducing her to bewildered helplessness. By these means he dramatically diminishes her freedom as an agent.

She can act intentionally even though she believes she is going mad, and her will does not seem to be plagued by unregulated motives. As most free agency theorists understand it, then, the control condition is met. Likewise, her normative competence, as we understand it so far, seems to have survived intact. She can wield moral norms and reveal herself through her actions, and others identify her as the sort of person toward whom one appropriately takes the reactive attitude. But she is still not free. Why? Benson's answer is that "she has lost her former sense of her own status as a worthy agent. She has ceased to trust herself to govern her conduct competently."[15] If he is right, then we have to refine the normative competence condition. We must now conceive of normative competence as (1) the ability to understand moral norms, act in accordance with them, and reveal who one is, morally speaking, through what one does; (2) the ability of others to recognize by one's actions that one is a morally responsible person; and (3) the ability of the agent to see herself as a morally responsible person.

Benson thinks that a historical theory of free agency, such as John Christman's,[16] could explain Bergman's lack of freedom by showing that the process by which she came to her present beliefs could not bear her scrutiny. If she knew what Boyer had done to manipulate her, "she would surely resist the beliefs and desires that resulted from it."[17] So Benson moves to a case of oppression, which he views as blocking this response. He imagines a feminist remake of *Gaslight,* also set in the 1880s, in which the husband is a kindly soul who takes his wife's interests to heart, but, because he is a physician and the medical science of his day pathologizes women, he regards the wife's active imagination and strong passions as symptomatic of a serious psychological illness. The wife trusts her husband's diagnosis and comes to believe that she is mentally ill. In this case, Benson argues, "the woman would not be likely to resist the process by which her beliefs and desires were altered in the wake of her diagnosis, if she were to attend reflectively to that process. For she arrives at her sense of incompetence and estrangement from her conduct on the basis of reasons that are accepted by a scientific establishment which is socially validated and which she trusts."[18]

Here the loss of free agency extends beyond the institutional impediments that others place in the agent's way. Whereas the social mechanisms that sustain oppression thwarted Pilar Sanchez's ability to register a moral judgment regarding her young patient, the mechanisms reach even further in Benson's case of medical "gaslighting," infiltrating the agent's consciousness and destroying her *sense of who she is.* Oppression takes the place of Boyer's machinations to make the medically gaslighted wife lose, to a significant degree, confidence in her worthiness to be the author of her own conduct. Like Bergman in the original film, her view of herself has been altered so that she no longer regards herself as competent to answer for her actions in light of normative demands that she herself thinks other people might reasonably apply to her.[19]

While Benson's explanation of why someone with an infiltrated consciousness is not a free agent strikes me as largely correct, I believe that he has misdescribed what happens when one is gaslighted by deceit, as opposed to being gaslighted by oppression. Benson accepts Christman's view that the agent's regulative power over her will is free just in case "the agent's will was acquired through a process that could be sustained under reflection."[20] Under reflection, the agent concludes that her beliefs about her will have been formed in the right way: they have been properly connected to reality and are therefore warranted. Because Bergman's belief that she ought not to trust her judgment was formed by Boyer's systematic deception, rather than by any actual psychological impairment, it is not warranted and so, Christman would say, she is not free.

Benson endorses this account of how deception takes away an agent's freedom and follows it up by a psychological claim: when an agent whose beliefs about her unworthiness to act are not warranted, she can repair the damage and free her will simply by reflecting on the process by which her beliefs were formed. That is why Benson thinks that if Bergman was aware of Boyer's manipulation, she would "surely resist the beliefs and desires that resulted from it." This is an argument about transparency. Benson claims that if Boyer's chicanery could be made transparent, Bergman would drop her beliefs that her judgments are worthless: what was done by deceit can be undone by unmasking the deceiver. The unstated inference is that because the medically gaslighted wife has no way to see through the medical ideology of her day, she cannot, like Bergman, free herself.

But Benson ought not to suppose that the Bergman character would "surely" resist the belief in her own unworthiness if only she knew the belief was not warranted. He attaches too much importance to the consequence of being shown the hidden mechanism. Knowing that there is no rational warrant for the belief that she is morally untrustworthy does not guarantee that the agent can rid herself of the belief. Her ability to resist depends on *her ability to trust her own judgments,* and in both of the gaslighting cases, that is precisely what has been so badly broken down.

In the original case, Bergman might discard the belief in her own untrustworthiness if she knew of Boyer's deception and if he had only been playing with her mind for a few days or weeks, for that is too short a time to do a thoroughgoing job of corrupting someone's sense of self-worth. Self-worth is resilient and survives repeated blows. As long as Bergman retains enough of it to believe that her mental processes are reliable, she may be able to assess the evidence pointing to her husband's machinations and draw her own conclusions, and that will be enough to restore her to her premarital level of confidence in her agency.

If, however, Boyer is given sufficient time to destroy Bergman's sense of self-worth altogether, and if her loving trust in him causes her to accept his verdict regarding her mental state as definitive, then Bergman will not be able to rely on her judgments, no matter how much evidence presents itself regarding his deception. Her beliefs will be evidence resistant precisely because she no longer trusts herself to exercise her moral agency competently.

She is then in no better an epistemic position than the medically gaslighted wife who, having lived all her life in a society that discounts women's judgments, and having now been authoritatively diagnosed as seriously ill, no longer regards herself as mentally competent. For the doctor's wife too, the ability to resist the belief that she is insane depends less on *whether* she is shown the hidden mechanism that drives the diagnosis than on *when*. If the evidence that the science is wrong comes too late and she no longer has any faith in her ability to judge it for herself, the evidence will not free her.

The relevant difference between the two gaslighting cases, then, is not (as Benson supposes) that there is something the wife could find out about that would free her agency in the first case, but nothing she could know that would do so in the second. Rather, the difference is that, in the first case, the wife's sense of self-worth has not yet been completely corrupted. If it were, what she knew or did not know about the warrant for her beliefs could make no positive difference to her because her ability to know anything would be precisely what she no longer trusted. Indeed, the knowledge that her beliefs are without rational warrant could well serve to make her feel even more crazy.

There are other relevant differences, too, and these have to do with both the *extent* to which the women's beliefs have been manipulated and the *means* used to manipulate them. The woman who has been medically gaslighted has been extensively manipulated. Because hers is a case of oppression, she has perhaps never seen herself as a fully competent moral agent. Those in authority are likely always to have treated her as if she were morally deficient, and this means the normative competence condition was never fully met. The social constriction on her agency would then have been compounded by the medical judgment that she is hysterical, which corrupts what little sense of self-worth she might once have had. She, having internalized both the prevailing judgment about women and the judgment of medical science, is thereby thrice bound: once by patriarchy, again by doctors, and finally by herself. As she has never exercised her agency very freely, talk of narrative *repair* seems inappropriate. What the medically gaslighted woman needs are stories that let her *acquire* ordinary levels of free agency for the first time. She needs counterstories that her husband and his colleagues will endorse and counterstories that she can endorse. Only when her identity is more fully formed—in terms of how others see her and how she sees herself—can the normative competence condition be satisfied.

The Bergman character's problem lies more in the *means* by which her beliefs are manipulated. She once, it appears, enjoyed normal levels of free agency: before she was married, both conditions for freedom were met reasonably well. That being the case, we can say that her beliefs have not been extensively manipulated. Nevertheless, if Boyer had been given a long enough time, he might have been able to corrupt her will even more thoroughly than did the husband of the medically gaslighted woman, for the means Boyer employed were Bergman's own love and trust in him. He used the special vulnerability that is attendant on intimacy to bend her to his will, taking advantage of the confidence she reposed in him not only to implant the suggestion that she was going mad but also to isolate her from anyone who might reassure her as to her sanity.

Had he been completely successful in this program of personal deception, he might well have stripped her of all the resources that would allow her to take back her normal epistemic position. Bereft of everything except her intimacy with him and no longer able to trust herself, she would have had to rely entirely on his judgments rather than her own. There would be no communities to which she could turn for help, for her world would now contain only herself and her husband. In that world there would be no one to free her, for she could no longer convincingly tell a counterstory on her own behalf and her husband would be the last person to tell it for her.[21]

Sustained and systematic deception by an intimate, then, is potentially even more destructive to a person's sense of her own worthiness to act than is oppression. In either case, however, the difficulty for someone who identifies *herself* as unworthy of answering for her own conduct is that she cannot reidentify herself as morally accountable simply by coming to the rational conclusion that her feelings of worthlessness are not warranted or by having others point this out to her. Because she does not trust her own judgment, it will be hard for her to hear, much less create, a counterstory that reidentifies her as a worthy person. She can always come up with another story that explains why she *ought* to be treated badly. She can always remind herself, as Virginia Martin did, that docs will be docs.

How, then, can a counterstory serve to repair an infiltrated consciousness? The short answer is that sometimes it cannot. As in the case of deprivation of opportunity, where there can be a great deal of difficulty in getting the persons who are misperceiving someone to endorse a counterstory that identifies the person as morally competent, so, in the case of infiltrated consciousness, the necessary story may be impossible for the oppressed person to develop. Because, however, consciousnesses can be infiltrated to greater or lesser degrees, the agent whose trust in herself is not yet completely corrupted might be able, under the right conditions, to construct the story she needs in order to free herself.

Virginia Martin, for example, has a comparatively mild case of infiltrated consciousness. When the Nurse Recognition Day Committee meetings first began, she shared the mainstream view in the hospital that a nurse is a kind of second-rate doctor who does not deserve a great deal of professional courtesy. When she encountered evidence that this view was unwarranted, she was generally able to resolve the cognitive dissonance this set up in her by dismissing the evidence as unimportant or telling a story about it that made it fit better with her other beliefs. She resisted the idea that she and her

Nelson

colleagues needed to reidentify themselves and was equally suspicious of the move to link this reidentification to any kind of feminist framework.

Because a moral space was available to her in which to reflect on who she was with other nurses whose opinions she respected, however, and because these others had a very different view of nurses than the one that infiltrated her consciousness, a cognitive dissonance arose that she could not simply dismiss. She tried to laugh it off, caricaturing the project of strong moral self-definition as a Gloria Steinem–meets–orthopedic surgeon absurdity. Ultimately, however, her affection for, and trust in, her former professor and the new friends of her chosen community made it possible for her to take for her own the counterstory the others were telling about themselves.

As these arguments suggest, the connection between identity and agency is an intimate one. Not only do we *express* who we are by how we act, but our *ability to act* depends heavily on who we and others think we are. If this is so, then whether any of us gets to be a free moral agent is partly a matter of moral luck. Our ability to enjoy the good of participating in the daily practices of responsibility that characterize the moral community depends at least in part on something that is not in our control—namely, other people. They must recognize us as moral agents if they are to treat us accordingly, and how they treat us can have a significant impact on how we see ourselves. In this respect, then, as in so many others, it would seem that we are all at the mercy of others.

NOTES

Margaret Urban Walker and James Lindemann Nelson improved this essay considerably by their close reading and thoughtful comments. Thanks are also due to John Greco, Christopher Gowans, Marilyn Frye, Howard Brody, Peggy DesAutels, and Joanne Waugh for pushing me to clarify various points.

1. Jeannine Ross Boyer, RN, supplied the texture for this story. The anecdote told by Pilar Sanchez is adapted from a case study presented by Wayne Vaught at the Annual Meeting of the Society for Health and Human Values, 10 November 1997, Baltimore, Md. Sally Martinson's story is taken from the *American Journal of Nursing* 89, no. 11 (1989): 1466–67.

2. Hilde Lindemann Nelson, "Resistance and Insubordination," *Hypatia* 10, no. 2 (1995): 23–40.

3. Paul Benson, "Feminist Second Thoughts about Free Agency," *Hypatia* 5, no. 3 (1990): 47–64; and Benson, "Free Agency and Self-Worth," *Journal of Philosophy* 91, no. 12 (1994): 650–68.

4. Gerald Dworkin, "Acting Freely," *Noûs* 4, no. 4 (1970): 367–83; Dworkin, *The Theory and Practice of Autonomy* (New York: Cambridge, 1988); Harry G. Frankfurt, "Freedom of the Will and the Concept of a Person," *Journal of Philosophy* 68 (1971): 5–20; Wright Neely, "Freedom and Desire," *Philosophical Review* 83, no. 1 (1974): 32–54; Gary Watson, "Free Agency," *Journal of Philosophy* 72 (1975): 205–20; and Daniel Dennett, *Elbow Room* (Cambridge: MIT Press, 1984).

5. Benson, "Feminist Second Thoughts about Free Agency," 52.

6. Benson, "Feminist Second Thoughts about Free Agency," 53.

7. Benson, "Feminist Second Thoughts about Free Agency," 54–55.

8. Peter Strawson, "Freedom and Resentment," *Proceedings of the British Academy* 48 (1962): 1–25, reprinted in *Free Will*, ed. Gary Watson (New York: Oxford University Press, 1982).

9. Strawson, "Freedom and Resentment," 62.

10. Strawson, "Freedom and Resentment," 67.

11. Strawson, "Freedom and Resentment," 66.

12. Benson, "Feminist Second Thoughts about Free Agency," 58.

13. Benson, "Free Agency and Self-Worth," 650.

14. Oppression consists in systematic institutional processes that prevent certain groups of people from developing and exercising their capacities or gaining access to material goods (Iris Marion Young, *Justice and the Politics of Difference* [Princeton: Princeton University Press, 1990], 38, 40). Personal domination consists in one person preventing another from determining her actions.

15. Benson, "Free Agency and Self-Worth," 657.

16. John Christman, "Autonomy and Personal History," *Canadian Journal of Philosophy* 21, no. 1 (1991): 1–24.

17. Benson, "Free Agency and Self-Worth," 656.

18. Benson, "Free Agency and Self-Worth," 657.

19. Benson, "Free Agency and Self-Worth," 660.

20. Benson, "Free Agency and Self-Worth," 654.

21. In the film, Boyer makes the mistake of permitting his wife to go out with him on a sight-seeing expedition. Her beauty and mystery attract the attention of a handsome police investigator, played by Joseph Cotten, who ultimately comes to Bergman's rescue. So her world never does consist of just herself and her husband.

5

Violent Bodies

Bat-Ami Bar On

IN THE BACKGROUND

When I was about four years old, I came home one day crying because some children in the neighborhood with whom I was playing had hit me. My mother responded to my crying rather harshly, saying that since my father left her and I had no brothers, I had no one to defend me but myself. She proceeded to send me back to the streets to learn to fight. Though far from an obedient daughter even then, sensing her desperation at what she took as the fact that I had no protection other than what I could devise, I did as I was told. This began the construction of my body as a ready-to-fight body and, as such, a violent body, a body habituated to use violence or, more precisely, a body habituated to act violently.[1]

The construction of my body as a violent body was not merely my project. It was, in addition, a national project carried out in multiple formal and informal ways alike.[2] Living as Jewish–Israeli children in just postindependence Israel, I and my peers, most of them boys but also a few girls, played a variety of games in which, by imitating fighting, we learned how to fight. We made wooden swords and lances, bows and arrows, and slingshots. We used our arsenal in elaborate battles and brief skirmishes that we designed, having in mind this or that violent encounter of Jews with what we took as "our enemies." These included the Romans against whose tyranny "we" rebelled, who eventually destroyed Jerusalem and in their efforts to erase Jewish resistance exiled everyone they could and changed the name of the Judean–Israeli territory to Palestine. "Our enemies" also comprised the Nazis, whom "we" had to fight uncompromisingly because "we" had to differentiate ourselves from diaspora Jews who, "we" were told, acquiesced in "their" own murder but for a few special cases like that of the resistance to death of the Warsaw ghetto warriors. "We" had other "enemies" as well, such as the military and police forces of the colonial British Mandate and the Palestinian and "foreign" Arab forces that they supported who might still attack "us."

Not only did I and my peers play war games in our neighborhoods after school, at school during breaks, and while on vacations, we also played them in our various youth movements, be these left-wing or right-wing oriented, where the games were used as part of the teaching of specific skills like day and night orientation and navigation, the making of topographic maps, silent movement, and different kinds of crawling. These skills were also taught in premilitary training, a regular part of the four-year Jewish–Israeli secular high school curriculum of the time. Premilitary training covered, in addition, hand-to-hand combat techniques; moving through an obstacle course under barbed wire, through window-like structures, and over walls; climbing ropes and jumping back down from a tower; and the use of rifles.

Some of the skills I learned in the youth movement and in premilitary training were taught to me again during military basic training and its repetitive and constant drilling.[3] Following that, and contrary to the case for Jewish–Israeli men, especially those trained as combatants, the maintenance and reproduction of my body as a violent body was up to me. Having joined the women's movement in the United States and having become an activist in a local feminist antirape group, I maintained and reproduced my body as a violent body through self-defense training and the study of the martial arts. I did discontinue my studies of the martial arts for about ten years, yet I have returned to them again, this time very aware that what I am doing as I train in the martial arts, because it is the maintenance and reproduction of a ready-to-fight body, is the maintenance and reproduction of my body as a violent body.

This is a disquieting awareness. I could probably comfort myself by trying to draw a sharp distinction between the ready-to-fight body as just potentially violent and the violent body as the one that actually acts violently. Still, the ready-to-fight body is a practice-habituated body, a body for which the line between "imitation" and "reality" is schooled to be thin so that it could actually act violently quickly,[4] and I am not sure that the distinction between the potential and the actual violent body could be interestingly sharp. Moreover, I suspect that what motivates an attempt at a clear-cut distinction is anxiety about and a need for innocence, a need to be as clean handed as the pacifist that I feel that I cannot be, burdened as I am by the materiality of my violent body. Because I have post-traumatic stress disorder, I am not certain whether my feelings are justified because the appropriation and internalization of the source of a trauma as a form of its mastery, conjoined as they are with doubts about what I am doing, could be symptomatic in my case. At the same time, though, how can I not be seriously troubled by my continued engagement in the maintenance and reproduction of my body as a violent body when many feminists are very critical and suspicious of violent bodies, seeing, just as I do, the violent man's body as the primary implement of violence in the everyday kinds of violence that women experience, such as rape and battering, as well as in war?[5] Is my violent body so very different from a man's violent body? Could his and my body be two significantly divergent kinds of implements of violence? Might it be the case that my violent body is ethico-politically acceptable while a man's violent body is not?

THE PROBLEM OF VIOLENCE

Few women theoreticians have engaged issues of violence in their work, and among them Hannah Arendt is of particular importance.[6] In her 1969 *On Violence*,[7] written in critical and qualified support of the 1960s student movements in the United States and Europe, Arendt calls attention to the implements of violence and violence's own instrumentality. For her, though, while violence is usually instrumental, it is also, first and foremost, a kind of action.[8] As such, and very generally speaking, because of its capacity for harm, violence requires ethico-political justification.[9] According to Arendt, violence can be ethico-politically justified because, even if potentially harmful, it is not intrinsically evil. So, like all action, if violence is rationalizable at all, it must be purposive, and, consequently, its ethico-political justification is of the means–ends variety. But for Arendt, again as in the case of all action, the means–ends ethico-political justification in question must be limited temporally and in scope. Thus, she says, "Violence[,] being instrumental by nature, is rational to the extent that it is effective in reaching the end that must justify it. And since when we act we never know with any certainty the eventual consequences of what we are doing, violence can remain rational only if it pursues short-term goals."[10] And she adds, "The danger of violence, even if it moves consciously within the nonextremist framework of short-term goals, will always be that the means overwhelm the end. If goals are not achieved rapidly, the result will be not merely defeat but the introduction of the practice of violence into the body politic."[11]

From what Arendt claims when she discusses how violence is to be ethico-politically justified, it is clear that, for her, violence is ethico-politically problematic in two senses. In the first sense, violence is ethico-politically problematic in a simple, straightforward way just because it is potentially harmful. This ethico-political problem, Arendt seems to believe, may be taken care of in particular cases only, rather then universally, and with a good enough means–ends type of ethico-political justification. In the second and more complicated sense, which is the one that articulates most profoundly the ethico-political problem that is violence for Arendt, violence is ethico-politically problematic because it is a kind of action. As it is a kind of action, there is always something

uncontrollable and unpredictable about it, and, as a result, it does not necessarily stay within the dictated boundaries of its means–ends ethico-political justifications but may, in fact, exceed them.

This, then, is the problem of violence that bothers Arendt as she thinks and
tries to make sense of violence—violence cut loose and running amok. Arendt
refers to this problem in a few very revealing lines in *On Violence* that gesture
toward and situate her thinking in that book in relation to her thinking in *On
the Origins of Totalitarianism* and *On Revolution*. In these lines she writes,

> Where violence is no longer backed and restrained by power, the well known re-
> versal in reckoning with means and ends has taken place. The means, the means
> of destruction, now determine the end—with the consequence that the end will be
> the destruction of all power. Nowhere is the self-defeating factor in the victory of
> violence over power more evident than in the use of terror to maintain domina-
> tion, about whose weird successes and eventual failures we know perhaps more
> than any generation before us. Terror is not the same as violence; it is rather the
> form of government that comes into being when violence, having destroyed all
> power, does not abdicate but, on the contrary, remains in full control.[12]

Arendt not only formulates the problem that is violence as she sees it but also
explores the conditions that make it possible for violence to be cut loose and
run amok. For her, they are all intertwined with one phenomenon—the decline
of political power, the power that is generated by people getting together to act
in concert politically.[13] Thus, she states almost definitionally that "power and violence are opposites; where the one rules absolutely, the other is absent,"
pointing out that "violence appears where power is in jeopardy" and that when
"left to its course it ends in power's disappearance," suggesting in conclusion
that while "violence can destroy power[,] it is utterly incapable of creating it."[14]

There are, according to Arendt, a variety of conditions that contribute to
the decline of political power. Of these she discusses two. The first is centralization, specifically in its bureaucratic form. Though quite efficient and
according to some a means to augment power, centralization, according to
Arendt, augments the ability to control and coerce but diminishes political
power,[15] standing as it does in contradiction to radical democratic ideals and
possibilities "drying up and oozing away . . . all authentic power sources" in
a society by limiting the paths for people's political action.[16] The second condition that Arendt discusses is the mixture of technoscience with government. This mix contributes to the decline of political power because it increases the reliance on experts even in the case of decisions that should be
made through radical democratic processes.[17] The mixture of technoscience
with government is, according to Arendt, particularly dangerous in the case
of decisions about violence that are among the decisions governments must
concern themselves with. Having in mind the development of nuclear strategy in the United States, Arendt claims,

There are few things that are more frightening than the steadily increasing prestige of scientific minded brain trusters in the councils of government during the
last decades. The trouble is not that they are cold-blooded enough to "think the
unthinkable," but that they do not think. Instead of indulging in such an old
fashion, uncomputerized activity, they reckon with the consequences of certain
hypothetically assumed constellations without, however, being able to test their
hypotheses against actual occurrences.[18]

JUSTIFYING VIOLENCE, NONETHELESS

Arendt's identification of bureaucratic centralization and technoscientific influences on government as two of the conditions that are essential to an understanding of the decline of political power leads her to repeat, in an insistent voice, the danger of a violence cut loose and run amok that
accompanies the decline of political power. The obvious, though far from
easy to bring about, solution to the problem of violence that follows from
Arendt's understanding of how the danger of violence comes about is halt-
ing the decline of political power. Arendt believed that at least some of the
social movements of the 1960s were attempting, and in a promising way, to
counter the decline of political power because they were creating it through
their formation and political action. Although she was concerned about an
excitement for and a nostalgic romanticization of violence that she thought
some of the social movements of the 1960s had,[19] her concern was not motivated by a rejection of violence as such.

Arendt did not reject violence as such not only because, as already mentioned, she did not take it to be intrinsically evil but also because she took it as
one of those instruments that sometimes simply must be deployed. According
to Arendt, risky as a deployment of violence is, there are contexts in which
people acting in concert politically must do so, most importantly because political power alone is never stronger than violence. As Arendt states, "Violence
can always destroy power: out of the barrel of a gun grows the most effective
command, resulting in the most instant and perfect obedience. . . . In a head-
on clash between violence and power the outcome is hardly in doubt."[20]

Given the sharp distinction that Arendt draws between political power and
violence, Arendt's openness to the mixture of political power and violence,
or, stated a bit differently and more strongly, to violent political action, is surprising. But, for Arendt herself, there is something rather factual about the
mixture of political power and violence—that is, for her, violent political action is a fact; "power and violence," she asserts, "though they are distinct
phenomena, usually appear together."[21]

Arendt's belief that there is something one could think of as violent political action leads to a need to distinguish between two senses that the instrumentality of violence can have. According to one, violence is instrumental in

the sense that it is used just like a tool. According to the other, violence is instrumental in the sense that it cannot take place without the use of instruments. Violence is inherently instrumental in both senses, and as a result it seems that Arendt's willingness to find an ethico-political place for violence must lead to some kind of ethico-political permissiveness toward the production of the instruments, or what Arendt calls the "implements" of violence.[22] Though she does not say much about this, from what she does say about violence one could expect Arendt to have suggested a means–ends ethico-political justification for the production of the implements of violence that is limited temporally and in its scope. And, while she expected the actual developments of the implements of violence to be such that they replace people, hence, actual fighting bodies, if bodies are among the possible implements of violence, then Arendt would have had to consider the ethico-political justifiability of their production as such. So, might it be right, in an Arendtean sort of way, to produce violent bodies? Very specifically, could one, in an Arendtean sort of way, ethico-politically justify the production of violent women bodies rather then any violent body, which is too general a task for an ethico-political justification that Arendt could have accepted given her limits for the ethico-political justification of action and, in particular, violent action?

BODIES AND IMPLEMENTS

Because Arendt thought of self-defense as ethico-politically unproblematic, believing that "no one questions the use of violence in self-defense, because the danger is not only clear but also present, and the end justifying the means is immediate,"[23] it seems that, in an Arendtean sort of way, one could justify the production of violent women bodies ethico-politically if one were able to show that such bodies are needed for women's own protection. There are self-defense-based ethico-political justifications of the production of violent women bodies. These began to be developed in the United States in the early 1970s by feminists in the antirape movement,[24] and they are so taken for granted now that, for example, in her recent discussion of lesbian self-fashioning, Diane Griffin Crowder explains her observation that lesbians want to develop bodily strength and express it physically, saying,

> I believe there are two important aspects of lesbians' interest in strength. The most obvious, shared by many heterosexual feminists who practice martial arts and weight lifting, is the need for self-defense in a world where women are physically threatened with rape and other forms of violence. "Out" lesbians are a special target for "gay bashing," and the incidents of violence against gays and lesbians is rising. Hence, increasing physical strength is a survival mechanism.[25]

Still, things are not this simple, for the production of violent women bodies is only in one respect a production of women bodies that are able to defend themselves. In another sense, it is a production of bodies that are particularly transgressive because as implements of violence they are skilled and competent in ways that are usually reserved for men.[26] The following story, reported in *Yediot Achronot*, the largest selling Israeli newspaper, illustrates this sense.[27] According to the story, a twenty-five-year-old woman, while serving as an officer in the Border Police, participated in many of her unit's military activities in the West Bank. She even led some of these and caught dozens of men sought by the Border Police, many of whom were armed. While the story does not tell this, after 1948 women were excluded from the Israeli Defense Forces combat units, though they may serve in them in support roles, and so the woman officer in the story is quite unique. The tellers of her story, recognizing this, hint that her uniqueness was a form of transgression. This is done not only by pointing out that some men were upset about her participation but also by trying to recuperate through her normalization via her symbolic refeminization. Thus, she is shown in several photographs in a sexually suggestive manner wearing a sundress. Moreover, she is described as blond and as having a well-sculptured figure. And, just in case one may still be inclined to suspect her of some defects or lacks, one is told that she just got married to a member of her unit, whom she dated secretly while they were serving together, and left her unit to become a trainer for other women, a currently much less transgressive role for women in the Israeli military.

In light of its transgressive side, the production of violent women bodies is, on an Arendtean account, an action that breaks through and goes beyond the boundaries set for it by an ethico-political justification that limits its ends to women bodies that are capable of self-defense. An action of this kind, an excessive action, could be quite problematic from an Arendtean point of view. Yet would this specific excessive action, the action that is the production of violent women bodies, be problematic from an Arendtean point of view? In order to answer these questions, it is necessary to rethink some standard feminist understandings.

FEMINIST MODALITIES

Under a fairly standard feminist analysis, the everyday kinds of violence that women experience, usually at the hands of men, are systemic rather than random, in the sense that it is the matrix of domination and submission within which women and men become what they are and interact that makes such experiences possible. For feminists, this is why violent actions that target women are political and why it makes sense to think of the response to them as political, including a violent response such as self-defense.

Were Arendt to analyze the standard feminist position, she would have pointed out that feminists, like members of the social movements of the 1960s, confuse and conflate *authority, force, strength, violence,* and *power,* terms that she believed to be rather distinct. The resulting elisions, according to Arendt, lead to insensitivity about the complexity of human affairs. She says,

> What is involved is not simply a matter of careless speech. Behind the apparent confusion is a firm conviction in whose light all distinctions would be, at best, of minor importance: the conviction that the most crucial political issue is, and has always been, the question of Who rules Whom? Power, strength, force, authority, violence—these are but words to indicate means by which man rules over man; they are held to be synonyms because they have the same function. It is only after one ceases to reduce public affairs to the business of domination that the original data in the realm of human affairs will appear, or rather, reappear, in their authentic diversity.[28]

If one follows Arendt here, one could not politicize self-defense in the standard feminist way because one could not think of the systemic relationship of women and men as political, if one were to think of it as constituting a matrix of domination and submission. Indeed, it is exactly this description of the relationship that would disqualify it from being thought of by Arendt as political. But, as critical as Arendt would have been of the standard feminist position, her own sense of what power is makes it possible, nonetheless, to think of women's self-defense as political, yet ironically, because this is something Arendt would have not liked at all,[29] only if it is a feminist project. On Arendtean grounds, insofar as feminists are people who get together in order to act in concert politically, as did, for example, members of the French Résistance when they came together to fight the Nazi regime,[30] their taking on, as feminists have done and still do, women's self-defense as a project politicizes it. Because, as a feminist project, women's self-defense involves the production of violent women bodies, this production too can be taken as political.

As a political action the production of violent women bodies can be motivated by women's self-defense needs but cannot be bound to these needs. Were it so bound, it would not be free, and therefore, for Arendt, it would not be an action at all. In addition, were it so bound, it would be motivated solely by self-interest, which for Arendt undermines political action because it undermines a promised principled solidarity that connects people who are quite different from each other and through this connection makes it possible for all of them to act politically. Arendt writes about self-interest,

> Some experiences plus a little reflection teach . . . that it goes against the very nature of self-interest to be enlightened. . . . The self qua self cannot reckon in terms of long range interest. . . . Self-interest, when asked to yield to "true" interest—that is, the interest of the world as distinguished from that of the self—

will always reply, Near is my shirt but nearer is my skin. That may not be particularly reasonable, but it is quite realistic; it is not a very noble but adequate response to the time discrepancy between men's private lives and the altogether different life expectancy of the public world.[31]

For Arendt, what political action should be about and cannot be about when action is bound and self-interested is an interruption of the status quo, which Arendt saw as "the function . . . of all action, as distinguished from mere behavior, to interrupt what otherwise would have proceeded automatically and therefore predictably."[32] If what political action is about is the interruption of the status quo, then it seems that there is no need to worry about the transgressive excess of the feminist production of violent women bodies, about these bodies breaking through the boundaries that are set by an ethico-political justification that limits them to self-defense capabilities and becoming what they are not supposed to be. In Arendtean terms, it seems that transgressive excess can be taken as an indicator that testifies to the political nature of the feminist production of violent women bodies. If this production had not resulted in transgressive bodies, then it would have been problematic from an Arendtean point of view.

COMPLICATIONS

It is necessary to add a word of caution. To the extent that bodies are produced as implements of violence, they may take on implemental characteristics. According to Arendt, these characteristics are discernible when power confronts violence. As she points out, "Those who oppose violence with mere power . . . soon find out that they are confronted not by men but by men's artifacts, whose inhumanity and destructive effectiveness increase in proportion to the distance separating the opponents."[33]

Feminists who take on the production of violent women bodies have to stay aware of this. A feminist cannot merely celebrate the transgressive excess that she creates through the production of her own or other violent women bodies. She must concern herself with quite complex questions about the possibility that, as women's bodies become habituated to violent action, they may act in ways that "inhumanely" and "destructively" transgress the boundaries that are specified by an ethico-political justification for the action that they are undertaking. This is a possibility that cannot be dismissed as too marginal to worry about, not in light of the extensive evidence regarding the enormity of past and present abusive or cruel violence in which women too have partaken. Women have acted violently not merely because they are not in control but also because, like men of the same socioculture, they too can find something attractive about violence.

Arendt was aware of this. In her introduction to J. Glenn Gray's *The War-riors: Reflections on Men in Battle,* Arendt cites one of Gray's anecdotal sto-ries intended to show that war can fascinate and seduce. The anecdote is about a woman, and Arendt describes Gray's use of it as follows,

> [Gray's book] makes opposition to war forceful and convincing by not denying the realities and by not just warning us but making us understand why "there is in many today as great a fear of a sterile and unexciting peace as of a great war." To make his point, [Gray] tells the story of a Frenchwoman whom he had known in the years of dangers and sufferings and then met again in peace and com-fortable circumstances. [The woman] said [to Gray]: "Anything is better than to have nothing at all happen day after day. You know that I do not love war or want it to return. But, at least it made me feel alive, as I have not felt before or since." Gray comments: "Peace exposed a void in them that war's excitement had enabled them to keep covered up," and he warns of "the emptiness within us," of the exultation of those who feel bound "to something greater than the self." Could boredom be more terrifying than all war's terrors?[34]

I wanted to end with Gray's/Arendt's suggestive question regarding the possibility that war, as horrible as it might be, also offers an avenue of escape from the ordinariness of the experience of the self under modern/postmod-ern conditions because it is a humbling question with wide implications even for feminists who, I do think, can make ethico-political sense of women's martial and self-defense training. I do not find ending on such a question problematic, for, given that what is at issue is the production and maintenance of violent bodies, I prefer to have no clear resolution that would relieve me from having to return to my doubts about the issue, in-cluding, of course, my doubts about what I am doing as I continue my mar-tial arts training.

At the same time, though, I do not mean to deny the importance of women's feminist martial arts and self-defense training—quite the contrary. Especially with the direction that it seems to be taking now, with an empha-sis not only on skills but also, in the spirit of the Southeast Asian traditional martial arts, whose development was entwined with Buddhism, on healing and compassion, feminist martial arts and self-defense training is maturing and offers women a path that is more complex and internally puzzling than it did in its early years when it conceived of itself as unproblematic.

At the 2000 Special Training event of the National Women's Martial Arts Federation, close to 100 girls between the ages of six and eighteen, white belts to black belts, performed, exhibiting what they already know. This was the best recommendation I have ever been presented with for women's fem-inist martial arts and self-defense training. Surely, I will continue to have questions, but I will also continue to train.

NOTES

Versions of this essay have been read at Mount Holyoke College and Binghamton University, and I want to thank people at the readings for their comments. I also want to thank Lisa Tessman, Janet Aalfs, and Mary Jane Treacy.

1. Following Michelle Foucault's work on the history of sexuality—*The History of Sexuality, Volume 1: An Introduction* (New York: Random House, 1978 [published in French in 1976]); *The History of Sexuality, Volume 2: The Uses of Pleasure* (New York: Random House, 1985 [published in French in 1984]); *The History of Sexuality, Volume 3: The Care of the Self* (New York: Random House, 1986 [published in French in 1984]); and other work on the body—such as that of Susan Bordo, *Unbearable Weight: Feminism, Western Culture, and the Body* (Berkeley: University of California Press, 1993); Judy Butler, *Bodies that Matter* (New York: Routledge, 1993); Elizabeth Grosz, *Volatile Bodies: Toward a Corporeal Feminism* (Bloomington: Indiana University Press, 1994); and Thomas Laqueur, *Making Sex: Body and Gender from the Greeks to Freud* (Cambridge: Harvard University Press, 1990)—I take the social construction of the body quite seriously and especially its construction by micropractices that habituate. See also Joanna Bourke, *An Intimate History of Killing: Face to Face Killing in 20th Century Warfare* (New York: Basic Books, 2000), 1–32.

2. For the development and complexity of this, see Anita Shapira, "Zionism and Force—The Ethos and Reality," in *Walk on the Horizon* (Tel-Aviv: Am Oved, 1989), 23–71; as well as Shapira, *The Dove's Sword* (Tel-Aviv: Am Oved, 1992), both in Hebrew. See also Bat-Ami Bar On, "Sexuality, the Family, and Nationalism," in *Feminism and Families,* ed. Hilde Nelson (New York: Routledge, 1997), 221–34.

3. There is a lot of repetition in play, and a fair amount of it was built into premilitary training. But neither involves the rigorous kind of military drilling into standardization that armies have offered ever since Maurice of Nassau developed drilling for his armies in the late sixteenth century. See William H. McNeill, *The Pursuit of Power* (Chicago: University of Chicago Press, 1982), 117–43. See also Bourke, *An Intimate History of Killing,* 57–90.

4. There is some evidence for the thinness of the line in literature concerned with soldier training and how soldiers are made to fit with technology through constant simulation. See Chris Hables Gray, *Postmodern War: The New Politics of Conflict* (New York: Guilford, 1997); Manuel de Landa, *War in the Age of Intelligent Machines* (New York: Zone, 1991); and Les Levidow and Kevin Robins, eds., *Cyborg Worlds: The Military Information Society* (London: Free Association Books, 1989). Another sort of evidence can be found in feminist literature about the relationship between soldiering and violence against women. See Cynthia Enloe, "All the Men Are in the Militias, All the Women Are Victims: The Politics of Masculinity and Femininity in Nationalist Wars," in *The Women and War Reader,* ed. Lois Ann Lorentzen and Jennifer Turpin (New York: New York University Press, 1998), 50–62; as well as selections in Enloe, *Maneuvers: The International Politics of Militarizing Women's Lives* (Berkeley: University of California Press, 2000); and Simona Sharoni, "Homefront as Battleground: Gender, Military Occupation, and Violence against Women," in *Women and the Israeli Occupation: The Politics of Change,* ed. Tamar Mayer (New York: Routledge, 1994), 121–37.

5. From its beginning, the feminist discussion of the everyday kinds of violence experienced by women brought to light processes of socializing boys to be boys and later adult men. See, for example, Susan Brownmiller, *Against Our Will: Men, Women, and Rape* (New York: Simon and Schuster, 1975). Sarah Ruddick's discussion of the masculinity of war and her fear of masculinizing women who join militaries is among the most revealing in this context. See Ruddick, *Maternal Thinking: Toward a Politics of Peace* (Boston: Beacon, 1989).

6. Arendt herself notes that few political theorists have attended to the issue of violence. Most feminist philosophical work on the subject of violence tends to pacifism. Examples include Ruddick's *Maternal Thinking* and most of the essays in *Hypatia's* special issue on peace (vol. 9, no. 2, Spring 1994), which was edited by Karen J. Warren and Duane L. Cady. Other women's philosophical discussions of violence include G. E. M. Anscombe, "War and Murder" (1961), in *Ethics, Religion and Politics: Collected Philosophical Papers Volume III* (Minneapolis: University of Minnesota, 1981), 51–61; Judith Jarvis Thomas, "Self-Defense and Rights" (1976), in *Rights, Restitution, and Risk: Essays in Moral Theory,* ed. Willima Parent (Cambridge, Mass.: Harvard University Press, 1986), 33–48; and Annette C. Baier, "Violent Demonstrations" (1991), in *Moral Prejudices: Essays on Ethics* (Cambridge: Harvard University Press, 1995), 203–21.

7. Hannah Arendt, *On Violence* (San Diego: Harcourt Brace, 1969).

8. For Arendt's most elaborate discussion of what she takes as action, see *The Human Condition* (Chicago: University of Chicago Press, 1958).

9. On Arendt and the relationship between ethics and politics, see Seyla Benhabib, "Judgment and the Moral Foundations of Politics in Arendt's Thought," *Political Theory* 16, no. 1 (February 1988): 29–51; and Suzanne Duvall Jacobity, "The Public, the Private, the Moral: Hannah Arendt and Political Morality," *International Political Science Review* 12, no. 1 (1991): 281–93.

10. Arendt, *On Violence,* 79.

11. Arendt, *On Violence,* 70.

12. Arendt, *On Violence,* 54–55.

13. For a discussion of Arendt's concept of power, see Jürgen Habermas, "Hannah Arendt's Communication Concept of Power," *Social Research* 44, no. 1 (Spring 1977): 3–24.

14. Arendt, *On Violence,* 56.

15. For discussions of this strand in Arendt's work, see Reuben Garner, "Adolph Eichmann: The Making of a Totalitarian Bureaucrat," in his *The Realm of Humanitas: Responses to the Writings of Hannah Arendt* (New York: Peter Lang, 1990), 67–100; and Alan Milchman and Alan Rosenberg, "Hannah Arendt and the Etiology of the Desk Killer: The Holocaust as Portent," *History of European Ideas* 14, no. 2 (1992): 213–26.

16. Arendt, *On Violence,* 85. The example of the World Trade Organization protests is quite interesting here because it seems to point out what avenues are left now for "authentic" political action.

17. For discussions of Arendt's ideas regarding democracy, see George Kateb, "Arendt and Representative Democracy," *Sulmagundi* 60 (Spring/Summer 1983): 20–59; and John F. Sitton, "Hannah Arendt's Argument for Council Democracy," *Polity* 20, no. 1 (Fall 1987): 80–100.

18. Arendt, *On Violence,* 6.

19. In these comments Arendt is most patronizing, as well as racist. For a discussion of this, see Anne Norton, "Hearts of Darkness: Africa and African Americans in the Writings of Hannah Arendt," in *Feminist Interpretations of Hannah Arendt*, ed. Bonnie Honig (University Park: University of Pennsylvania Press, 1995), 247–62.

20. Arendt, *On Violence*, 53.

21. Arendt, *On Violence*, 52.

22. From what she says in *On Violence* it is quite obvious that she did not approve of all the implements of violence that could be devised. Some of her comments in *The Human Condition* are quite similar and suggest a suspicion of technoscience cut loose and run amok as too destructive. Still, Arendt did not disapprove of all implements of violence either.

23. Arendt, *On Violence*, 52.

24. For examples, see Noreen Connell and Cassandra Wilson, eds., *Rape: The First Sourcebook for Women* (New York: New American Library, 1974); and Frédérique Delacoste and Felice Newman, eds., *Fight Back: Feminist Resistance to Male Violence* (Minneapolis: Cleis, 1981). For a discussion, see Martha McCaughey, *Real Knockouts: The Physical Feminism of Self-Defense* (New York: New York University Press, 1997).

25. Diane Griffin Crowder, "Lesbians and the (Re/De)Construction of the Female Body," in *Reading the Social Body*, ed. Catherine B. Burroughs and Jeffrey David Ehrenreich (Iowa City: University of Iowa Press, 1993), 72. See also Judith Halberstam, *Female Masculinity* (Durham, N.C.: Duke University Press, 1998); and Leslie Heywood, *Bodymakers: A Cultural Anatomy of Women's Body Building* (New Brunswick, N.J.: Rutgers University Press, 1998).

26. See, in contradistinction, Iris Marion Young, "Throwing like a Girl: A Phenomenology of Feminine Body Comportment, Motility, and Spatiality," *Human Studies* 3 (1980): 137–56; and Sandra Lee Bartky, "Shame and Gender," in her *Femininity and Domination: Studies in the Phenomenology of Oppression* (New York: Routledge, 1990), 83–98.

27. "The Blond Arab-Stormer," *Yediot Achronot* (in Hebrew), 22 October 1995: 10.

28. Arendt, *On Violence*, 43–44.

29. Arendt objected to feminism because she took it to be a movement limited to the interests of a group rather then "caring for the world," one of Arendt's most important criteria for political participation. See Elizabeth Young-Bruehl's comment on this in *Hannah Arendt: For Love of the World* (New Haven, Conn.: Yale University Press, 1982), 273.

30. I am using this example given Arendt's discussion of this in her preface to *Between Past and Future: Eight Exercises in Political Thought* (New York: Viking, 1961), 3–15.

31. Arendt, *On Violence*, 78.

32. Arendt, *On Violence*, 30–31.

33. Arendt, *On Violence*, 53.

34. Hannah Arendt, "Introduction," in *The Warriors: Reflections on Men in Battle*, J. Glenn Gray (New York: Harper, 1966), xii.

III

CHARACTER AND ITS VIRTUES

6

Critical Virtue Ethics: Understanding Oppression as Morally Damaging

Lisa Tessman

I believe that a critically revised yet still Aristotelian-based virtue ethics has something potentially useful to offer to those engaged in analyzing oppression and creating liberatory projects. I take it that oppression is a form of harm that can be characterized in many ways. Here I will characterize it by using the language of a virtue ethics framework: the oppressed are harmed in that they are disenabled from living the best possible lives, barred from attaining "human flourishing." If this were not the case, namely, if one could fully flourish under conditions of oppression, or even more implausibly, if oppression enabled flourishing, there would be no reason to resist being oppressed and nothing morally objectionable about oppression. Implicit in an objection to oppression, then, is an acknowledgment that oppression interferes with flourishing. What I will suggest in this chapter is that a critical virtue ethics can help clarify one of the ways in which oppression interferes with flourishing; specifically, it helps clarify an aspect of oppression that can be called "moral damage." I will further argue that this clarification is important for the success of liberatory struggles.

Although I will not attempt to give a positive definition of flourishing, I would like to point out that without some working notion of what is a greater rather than a lesser degree of flourishing or, put differently, a better rather than a worse sort of life, one cannot object to oppression based on what it does to a person who is subjected to it. To object to some specific forms of oppression one must be able to claim, for instance, that one lives better when one is not in fear of police brutality than when one is; that it is preferable for one to believe that one deserves love than for one to believe that one is beaten because one is bad; that self-chosen, meaningful work contributes more to flourishing than mind-numbing, repetitive labor does;

that a good life is not marked by the overwhelming loss of loved ones through racial or ethnic persecution; that the disintegration of self that occurs under torture destroys rather than enhances one's life.

It is not simply that oppression interferes with flourishing in ways such as those just mentioned but that it does so systemically and in a targeted way; that is, oppression operates by systemically interfering with the possibility of flourishing for members of specific social groups. The most obvious site of this interference is in the systemic barriers that make it difficult or impossible for those who are oppressed to gain or be granted the "external" goods— including freedom, material resources, political power, and respect or social recognition of personhood—that are needed to live well. But according to an Aristotelian or virtue ethics model, there is an additional way in which one can be prevented from flourishing: one can fail to fully develop and exercise the virtues; one's own character can stand in the way of the good life. Thus, I would like to explore the ways in which oppression may interfere with flourishing, not only through the denial of external goods (which, I would contend, remains the most important aspect of oppression) but also by structurally diminishing the possibilities for the development of virtues.

However, characterizing the oppressed as lacking in virtues—or put differently, as morally damaged—can certainly be problematic. To begin with, it seems that it is primarily the oppressors rather than the oppressed who should be understood as morally damaged; after all, the character traits that allow one to actively dominate others, or even to be passively satisfied with benefiting unfairly from overprivilege, could accurately be described as character flaws or vices. Though I believe that in fact both oppressors and oppressed are morally damaged and thus prevented in this way from what could truly be called a flourishing life, here I will not be exploring how members of oppressor groups are damaged by enacting their dominator roles. My examination of the question of moral damage in the oppressed is not intended to deny that there are vices specific to those who dominate. I focus on the damage done to the oppressed because I am interested specifically in thinking about how this damage hinders members of oppressed communities from effectively resisting.

But a second, more serious, concern presents what may turn out to be a good reason for refraining from the project of investigating how the oppressed are morally damaged. Portraying a group as flawed exposes that group to the danger that the shortcomings will be used against them, as evidence, perhaps, of an inherent or at least permanent or semipermanent inferiority. Thus, when analyzing the problems that face an oppressed people, it is crucial to avoid the mistake of characterizing those people *as* the problem, a thought that is captured in W. E. B. Du Bois's repeated posing of the question, "How does it feel to be a problem?"[1] Following Du Bois, Lewis Gordon remarks that "we must study even dehumanized human subjects in

a humanistic way in order to recognize the dehumanizing practices that be-
siege them."[2] While it is indeed my aim here to theorize about dehumanization without *engaging* in dehumanization, it may not be enough to have
good intentions: even when one's goal is to identify the systemic sources of
moral damage, and even when one emphasizes that finding moral damage
in the oppressed only serves to further demonstrate the injustices of oppression, in a context of entrenched prejudices one's words can easily be trans-
formed into precisely what Du Bois meant to caution against: turning those
who suffer from a problem into the problem itself. And yet, simply denying
damage—perhaps even taking "vices" of the oppressed and glorifying them
as virtues[3]—can be problematic, too. So, despite the strategic dangers of exposing moral damage in the oppressed, in the end I do believe that ignoring
such damage leads to a misrepresentation of how oppression is maintained,
and relying on this misrepresentation can diminish the capacity of oppressed
groups to pursue liberatory projects.

ARISTOTLE ON HUMAN FLOURISHING AND THE VIRTUES

I will begin by saying a few words about the Aristotelian or more generally
virtue-based approach to understanding what enables a good or flourishing
life. However, any Aristotelian model will need to be critically revised in order to be useful for understanding oppression.

For Aristotle, certain "external" goods are necessary for flourishing,[4] but he
envisions these goods or the lack thereof as resulting from accidental or natural events such as being born of high or low status, having friends or children who die, or encountering misfortunes in old age that ruin one's pros-
perity. An analysis of oppression as a structural phenomenon requires seeing
social or systemic forces as responsible for the fact that members of some social groups are deprived of these "external resources." Hence it requires expanding Aristotle's list of the things that typically interfere with flourishing.
The list should include, for instance, resources that are distributed unfairly in
an oppressive system, such as housing, education, health care, or, more generally, income and wealth. There are also resources that are not the sorts of
things that can be captured under what Iris Young calls the "distributive paradigm";[5] some of the forces of oppression and domination cannot be remedied simply by instituting a fairer system of distribution. Young points out,
for instance, that the oppressed may be exploited, marginalized, made powerless, subjected to cultural imperialism, and/or targeted for violence;[6] all of
these could be described as ways in which oppression creates external conditions that prevent flourishing.

But despite Aristotle's acknowledgment that certain external conditions must
be obtained for a person to flourish, his primary focus is on a consideration

of the features of character that enable flourishing. Because, for him, the "human good [is] an activity of soul in accordance with virtue,"[7] it is only the virtuous man who attains this good. That is, Aristotle links moral excellence with living the good life; one cannot be said to have reached *eudaimonia* without a virtuous character.

It is difficult, at first glance, to see how the claim that one must be virtuous to attain the good life will be helpful for understanding *oppression* as interfering with flourishing. Instead, the claim seems to place the blame on oppressed people themselves for being unable to flourish: the inability is based on their own lack of virtue! In a chorus of victim blaming one hears that, for instance, women are overly emotional, blacks are prone to violence, Jews are stingy, the poor lack self-discipline, and so on and that these vices are what bring on the particular hardships faced by members of these groups.

In order *not* to echo a victim-blaming refrain, one needs both to revise the table of the virtues (so, for instance, lack of emotion can be seen as a vice rather than a virtue) and to cease assigning virtues or vices to social groups based on pernicious stereotypes. Just as importantly, however, one also needs to assert that the failure to develop the virtues can itself have structural or systemic sources rather than, for instance, sources in what is inherent, biologically given, and unchangeable. That is, there is injustice already at work in the formation of character; the fact that something is based on character does not imply that it is not also rooted in an oppressive social system.

What Aristotle lacks is any way of seeing that the social and political positioning of people such that they have unequal chances for developing the virtues is itself an injustice. Clearly, for him, some people do have a better chance of being virtuous than others; to begin with, one must be a citizen male and must have the sort of leisure time necessary for practicing the virtues, and all of this can take place only within a correctly constituted and good polis, and even then, one does not fully develop all virtues unless one is ruling and thereby able to develop the virtues associated exclusively with ruling.[8] But there is, for Aristotle, no injustice in this inegalitarian state of affairs wherein some are better positioned than others for becoming virtuous; as long as all those who are equals are treated equally, it is perfectly just that unequals be treated unequally and be given unequal opportunities for developing the virtues.[9]

PSYCHIC DAMAGE, MORAL DAMAGE, AND RESPONSIBILITY

But let us suppose, contrary to Aristotle, not only that people are unequally situated for becoming virtuous but that there is injustice in this arrangement. This is the position taken by Claudia Card in *The Unnatural Lottery,* in which, rejecting the Kantian assumption that "the same basic character development is accessible to everyone,"[10] she observes that "different combinations of circumstances . . . provide opportunities for, stimulate, nurture, or discourage the development of different virtues and vices, strengths and weaknesses of character."[11] Focusing on the circumstances of various groups of oppressed people and making use of empirical work such as that of Carol Gilligan, she explores the ways in which such circumstances may give rise both to special insights and to forms of damage, noting that "a challenge for feminist moral philosophers has been to distinguish the insights from the damage."[12] The sorts of traits that she has in mind when speaking of damage include, for the oppressed, "low self-esteem, ingratiation, affiliation with abusers, . . . a tendency to dissemble, [and] fear of being conspicuous."[13] These character traits typically develop as survival mechanisms under oppressive circumstances. For instance, Card suggests that because of women's "political inability to end bad relationships, we have not learned to discriminate well between good ones and bad ones," which contributes to women having a tendency to focus on maintaining relationships—no matter what—rather than a tendency to value separation and autonomy.[14]

The moral damage that Card describes bears a relationship to what has commonly been understood as the "psychic damage" suffered by the oppressed. There is a fairly long history in the United States of blacks being portrayed (and in some cases portraying themselves) as psychically damaged, a history that I will discuss at more length in the next section. Additionally, beginning early in the second wave of the women's liberation movement, feminists have described women's "psychological oppression."[15] One way in which psychic damage comes about is from the internalization of oppression; the oppressed may come to believe about themselves, for instance, that it is their own inferiority that accounts for their subordinate position. As Sandra Bartky writes, "The psychologically oppressed become their own oppressors; they come to exercise harsh dominion over their own self-esteem."[16] When conceived as an internalization of external messages or forces, the psychic states characteristic of the psychologically oppressed are clearly a product of systemic—social, political, and economic—phenomena, though they certainly may be perceived as having their origins in internal, even biological deficiencies. Indeed, psychological oppression helps keep the oppressed subordinated in part by obscuring the systemic sources of their troublesome psychological traits, thus making the oppressed appear, even to themselves, responsible for their own condition.

The sense that one is responsible for one's own damaged state—and perhaps even for one's own subordination, as some kinds of damage help keep one subordinated—is only compounded when one is described not only as *psychologically* damaged but also as *morally* damaged. Even while it might be clear that someone or something else is responsible for inflicting psychic pain on me, if I am described as having *character* flaws, it seems that I am morally responsible for my deficiency, not to mention for any reprehensible actions that proceed from my flawed character.

Yet, in a virtue ethics framework, any psychological trait that can be labeled "damage" will in fact count as a moral trait, that is, a character trait, precisely because in calling it a form of damage one is making a normative judgment about it, in this case a negative judgment based on the trait's tendency to interfere with flourishing. So while some psychological traits may be morally neutral (and *too* much of the personal will become political if *all* psychological traits must be normatively evaluated!), a damaged psyche represents a lack of a virtue (if not the presence of a vice), a lack of a trait that could help one toward flourishing. For instance, all of the following are possible forms of both psychic and moral damage: a tendency to feel guilt or resignation instead of anger when one is wronged, a disposition to feel persistent hopelessness, a habit of manipulating or lying to others, a lack of self-confidence.

Thus, a virtue ethics framework, in connecting living a good life with moral excellence, will count psychic damage that interferes with flourishing as moral damage. However, this shift from characterizing the oppressed as psychically hurt or damaged to characterizing them as morally damaged is likely to meet resistance because it amplifies disturbing questions of moral responsibility, burdening the victim of oppression with blame. Some of these questions can be resolved by applying, as Claudia Card does, the concept of moral luck.[17]

Moral luck is that which is not within an agent's own control and yet affects the agent in a morally relevant way by, for instance, influencing character, decisions, or actions. The concept of moral luck implies, as Margaret Urban Walker puts it, that *"responsibilities outrun control,"*[18] that is, one can be morally responsible, though in complex ways, for more than just that over which one has complete control. While moral luck is always outside of the agent's own control, its source can vary. Card's interest is in luck that issues from what she calls the "unnatural lottery," namely, circumstances that are tied to social systems and that tend to affect people as members of social groups. This "systemic luck," as I will call it, includes the luck—in this case bad luck—of being subject to oppression. Card argues that one of the types of bad luck that oppressive circumstances tend to make one encounter is bad constitutive luck, where "constitutive luck" refers to luck that affects the formation of character.[19] That is, according to Card, oppression—when it takes the form of bad, constitutive, systemic moral luck—results in moral damage, damage to one's character. Oppression makes it more difficult to develop certain virtues.

The tendency toward "blaming the victim" is somewhat, though not completely, undermined by the understanding that having moral responsibility for something—such as one's own character—does not imply that one had or has complete control over it. Thus, characterizing the moral damage of the oppressed as a product of bad, constitutive, systemic moral luck conveys the notion of a different, more complex relationship of responsibility for that damage. This characterization of moral damage implicates oppressive systems as the sources of the bad constitutive moral luck that adversely affects the characters of the oppressed, but it also does not deny that the people who are morally damaged in this way retain moral responsibility for themselves, despite their lack of complete control in the formation of their own character.

I would argue that this complex sense of having and not having moral responsibility for one's own character is a useful one. It allows the oppressed person to preserve moral agency by retaining moral responsibility, and yet it does not "blame" the oppressed agent in a way that would simultaneously excuse all systemic or oppressive forces from responsibility. For example, consider a case of rape, which of course is a prime site for victim blaming: many girls and women have been socialized to have character traits that potentially contribute to their vulnerability to rape, traits such as passivity, fear of fighting back, and lack of clarity and/or sense of legitimacy about their own sexual desires.[20] If a woman chooses a strategy of submitting to an attempted rape rather than taking what she perceives to be the risks of resisting it, she will typically be blamed for the rape. The most obvious rebuttal here is that the rapist is the one responsible for the rape (and, of course, one could talk about the rapist as a morally damaged person). But there is also a second point to be made: one can implicate the gender system that contributed to the woman's vulnerability by affecting the formation of her character into someone who was afraid or unable to fight back, that is, into someone who was in this specific way morally damaged. In this case, one can recognize the moral wrongdoing of an oppressive system for being the source of moral damage without portraying the morally damaged, oppressed person as lacking in agency just because she lacks complete control over the constitution of her character. The woman is still morally responsible for her own character and her own choice, for, as the concept of moral luck implies, we can be moral agents responsible for some things over which we do not have control.

Nevertheless, even if it is possible to make *conceptual* sense of why a morally damaged character in an oppressed person should not be taken as evidence that the oppressed are to blame for their own oppression, in fact, historically, images of psychic and moral damage in the oppressed have been taken and continue to be taken in exactly this way, thus making it *strategically* risky to try to explore psychic or moral damage for liberatory purposes. A short review of a piece of this history will be helpful here, so I will turn to Daryl Michael Scott's historical account of the "image of the damaged black psyche," which presents a clear-cut case of damage imagery being used to the detriment of an oppressed group.

IMAGES OF THE "DAMAGED BLACK PSYCHE"

Scott's *Contempt and Pity: Social Policy and the Image of the Damaged Black Psyche, 1880–1996* chronicles the changing historical contexts in which damage imagery has been employed by social scientists studying and reporting on black Americans. He contends that despite the association of the use of damage imagery with conservatives and blatant racists, such imagery has actually been used by both racial liberals and conservatives, often at cross-purposes. He argues, however, that this entire range of uses of damage imagery should be regarded with suspicion; he writes, "I believe that depicting black folk as pathological has not served the community's best interest. Again and again, contempt has proven to be the flip side of pity. And through it all, biological and cultural notions of black inferiority have lived on, worsening the plight of black people."[21]

Scott's focus is on *psychic* damage, for his thesis is that in the late nineteenth century, "as personality replaced moral character as the key to success" and psychological well-being surfaced as an issue worthy of attention, it became possible to conceive of a person as being wronged by being hurt psychologically.[22] As this "therapeutic ethos" grew in strength even more after World War II, there began to be a humanitarian concern for the psychological health of subordinate groups. Scott explains that "liberals used damage imagery to play upon the sympathies of the white middle class. Oppression was wrong, liberals suggested, because it damaged personalities, and changes had to be made to protect and promote the well-being of African Americans."[23] This liberal use of damage imagery played a primary role in, for instance, the argument against segregation used in *Brown v. Board of Education,* in which Chief Justice Warren opined that "segregated children suffered damage to their psyches that made an equal education impossible."[24] However, argues Scott, the liberal use of damage imagery depended on evoking pity, an emotion that presupposes one's own superiority to the object of pity:

> Liberals proceeded as if most white Americans would have been willing to grant black people equal rights and services only if they were made to appear psychologically damaged and granted a special status as victims. In so doing, they militated against their efforts to eliminate white supremacy. As they assaulted its manifestations in the law, they reinforced the belief system that made whites feel superior in the first place.[25]

While the pity of white liberals presents a significant drawback to employing damage imagery for bringing about policy change, a further problem emerged when liberals split around the question of what sorts of changes were needed to address the damage. By the late 1950s social scientists theorizing about the "underclass"—a term introduced by Gunner Myrdal to refer to an economic, and not a specifically racial, group[26]—were divided into the "pathologists," who focused on curing individual pathological responses to poverty, and the "structuralists," who insisted that fundamental changes in social, economic, and political institutions would effectively end the phenomenon of psychic damage.[27] Although for a time it seemed that these two schools advocated changes that were at least compatible with each other, their incompatibility emerged with Oscar Lewis's introduction in 1959 of the "culture of poverty" theory,[28] according to which the poor developed a pathological culture that was passed down through the generations and became self-sustaining.[29] Whereas pathologists had previously been able to see institutional changes as helpful for addressing individuals' suffering, the "culture of poverty" theory suggested that, because the pathology would perpetuate itself regardless of changes in social structure, such changes would be misguided. As Stephen Steinberg has noted, for advocates of the "culture of poverty" thesis, "the aim of social policy becomes one of reforming the poor rather than changing society. That is, instead of instituting the sweeping changes that could redistribute income, the focus of social policy becomes indoctrinating the poor with middle-class values."[30] This conservative side of the pathologists' position alarmed the structuralists, who at that point "recognized that notions of severe damage, particularly permanent damage, cast doubt on the efficacy or desirability of state intervention."[31]

As the term *underclass* became more and more automatically understood to refer to a *black* underclass, and as it became clearer that portraying this underclass as pathological would fuel the conservative claim that blacks had no one but themselves to blame for their plight and therefore had no basis for claiming special treatment, reparations, or assistance from social programs, it became strategically more dangerous to attempt to use damage imagery to bring about progressive, antiracist change. Nevertheless, in 1965 Daniel Patrick Moynihan, in his *The Negro Family: The Case for National Action* (otherwise known as the Moynihan Report), tried to support a plan of action—to be initiated by President Johnson as preferential treatment programs—by relying on damage imagery. However, he made the same assumption as Lewis had in his "culture of poverty" theory, namely, that the pathological condition of blacks was being perpetuated by blacks themselves and would continue regardless of structural changes. Although he conceded that "not every instance of social pathology afflicting the Negro community can be traced to the weakness of family structure," he did argue that, "nonetheless, at the center of the tangle of pathology is the weakness of the family structure. Once or twice removed, it will be found to be the principal source of most of the aberrant, inadequate, or anti-social behavior that did not establish, but now serves to perpetuate the cycle of poverty and deprivation."[32] Moynihan contended that it was because of bad character formation in black families that there existed within the black community high rates of crime and delinquency, welfare dependency, unemployment, poor academic achievement, and, in turn, more "unstable"—which largely meant no more than "female-headed"—black families.

Moynihan recognized that white racism was originally responsible for creating the situation that blacks were in and even attributed the development of the black family structure to injustices perpetrated by whites under slavery and reconstruction; however, he did not believe that white racism had a significant role in perpetuating the situation of inequality—all responsibility for that had been shifted to blacks themselves. Thus Moynihan concluded, "Three centuries of injustice have brought about deep-seated structural distortions in the life of the Negro American. At this point, the present tangle of pathology is capable of perpetuating itself without assistance from the white world."[33]

Although it was probably not Moynihan's intention, the content of the Moynihan Report served as perfect evidence to bolster the conservative, racist image of blacks as inferior, an image that was used, for instance, to explain the behavior of blacks in the Watts riot. Scott points out that, "released at the moment of the riots, the Moynihan Report was viewed by conservatives as an expression of their own views on black social and personal pathology."[34] That is, damage imagery, intended by liberals to support antiracist measures and improve the condition of blacks, had quite the opposite effect. Furthermore, even if it had not been co-opted for straightforwardly conservative purposes, it still would have retained a paternalistic edge. As Scott puts it, "The racial liberals who sought to manipulate the paternalistic tendencies of whites may not have been racists and the dupes of racists, but many were all too willing to exchange black dignity for something other than justice, for social policies that reinforced white America's age-old belief in black inferiority."[35] Thus, in the wake of the Moynihan Report, there arose a near consensus on the Left to avoid all damage imagery and in fact to condemn its use as racist.

CONTEMPORARY NEOCONSERVATIVES AND THE RACIALIZED DISCOURSE ON CHARACTER

The dangers of trying to utilize damage imagery in liberatory projects have only intensified since the 1960s because, more recently, conservatives—or to be precise, neoconservatives—have reinvigorated such imagery and put it to use in their attacks on affirmative action and, more generally, in their arguments against government or social responsibility for improving the conditions that many blacks face. Governmental programs aimed at helping blacks are, they claim, the primary source of the new damaged black psyche; according to them, preferential treatment is actually causing, rather than ameliorating, psychic problems such as low self-esteem and is actually giving rise to character deficiencies such as "criminality" and "dependency."[36] Some neoconservatives point to what they see as the failures of governmental aid programs as evidence that insufficient attention has been given to what they see as the root of the problem: character flaws. Glenn Loury, for instance, laments the fact that other blacks do not share his own conviction that Moynihan had been right all along; Loury complains that thirty years after the Moynihan Report, "to invoke such terms as 'values,' 'character,' or 'social pathology' in speaking about the poor (black or otherwise) is still to invite the charge of blaming the victim or, if the speaker is black, of being an Uncle Tom."[37] Loury even goes on to express his disapproval of the fact that Moynihan himself has retreated from his former position and is no longer willing to condemn female-headed households or to show sufficient respect for "old-fashioned virtues."[38]

This neoconservative talk of "family values" along with the rise of other segments of the right wing such as the religious Right have shifted the language used in the discourse on damage; during much of the twentieth century concern with damage was represented primarily as an issue of psychological health, but there is now a movement back toward an explicit focus on character and moral virtue. Unfortunately, because a focus on character is almost entirely associated with the right wing, and because this discourse consists principally of the defamation of the characters of people of color, gays and lesbians, women, and poor people, it is extremely hard to imagine a critical or liberatory application of an analysis of character.

James Wilson, a neoconservative political scientist and policy adviser, provides in his 1991 book, *On Character,* a particularly clear example of this neoconservative discourse on character. In his schema, social problems are attributed to individual character deficiencies, and these character deficiencies are racialized. Wilson's thesis is that "a variety of public problems can only be understood—and perhaps addressed—if they are seen as arising out of a defect in character formation."[39] The public policy questions that he sees as most tied to character include crime and welfare. He identifies "a persistent and wanton proclivity to criminality" as that which "almost any of us would regard as a defect in character."[40] Welfare dependency can also be explained, according to Wilson, as a matter of character deficiency: Those on welfare have the wrong values and therefore do not feel appropriate shame at the dependency itself or at the actions—such as having children out of wedlock—that may have led to it. While Wilson argues that there has been a moral decline in the United States in general ever since, as he puts it, an "ethos of self-control" began to be replaced by "an ethos of self-expression,"[41] not surprisingly he remarks that "black Americans have been especially vulnerable" to this degenerate ethos.[42]

But perhaps even more disturbing than Wilson's explicit claim that black Americans have culturally acquired defective characters—a blatant reiteration

of the "culture of poverty" theory—is the fact that in the current political climate he actually has no need to make this *explicit* reference to blacks in a discussion of either crime or welfare; both are code words with so thoroughly
racialized meanings that a discourse on the degenerate character of criminals
or welfare recipients functions as a masquerade for a more directly racist—
and less socially acceptable—discourse in which blacks are directly cited as
the prime example of a morally deficient population. In the context of a racist
society in which blacks are stereotypically associated with both crime and
welfare, a complicated racial project actually takes place through a color-
blind discourse purportedly about crime reduction or about welfare reform.
In the course of this project, an image of "the criminal" and "the welfare recipient" as morally degenerate characters is formed, and the vices of these
characters are associated with blacks in general (particularly black men in the
case of crime and black women in the case of welfare), who already stand as
the stereotypical criminal and welfare recipient. Both the criminal and the
welfare recipient embody socially despised characteristics, characteristics that
are attributed not just to specific, actual people who commit crimes or receive
public assistance, and not even just to "criminals" and "welfare recipients" in
some generalized way, but, rather, to *blacks* in this generalized way, for in the
imagination shaped by this racialized discourse, blacks stand in for both the
(generalized) criminal and the (generalized) welfare recipient. Public fear (in
the case of crime) and resentment (in the case of welfare) are generated toward these morally degenerate characters and thus toward blacks in general.
And finally, public policy that addresses that fear and resentment seems reasonable and justified; if it involves harsh treatment of the criminal or the welfare recipient, such treatment is justified because it was brought on by those
characters' own moral degeneracy and furthermore is necessary to protect the
upstanding members of society against violence or against having to support
the undeserving with their own hard-earned money.[43]

There are clear policy implications to portraying blacks—with excep-
tions made for the middle class—as the morally degenerate exemplars of
such vices as criminality and dependency, for in the current conservative
context such a portrayal is not used to show the injustices of racism and
other structural forms of oppression but, rather, is used to demonstrate
that the moral deficiencies either inhere in blacks or actually result from
governmental attempts to end inequalities. Either way, the implication is
that there are no injustices to blacks as a group that need to be rectified.
Shelby Steele, for instance, makes this position explicit; by contrasting
psychological and moral problems—which he locates in the individual—
with social or systemic problems, he is able to site the source of blacks'
problems within individual blacks, claiming that "if conditions have wors-
ened for most of us as racism has receded, then much of the problem must
be of our own making."[44]

CRITICAL ATTENTION TO MORAL DAMAGE

In this increasingly conservative climate (and a climate in which it is only the conservatives who are talking about character), it becomes more likely, regardless of the intention of the theorist, that an examination of the ways in which oppression produces damaged people will be used against the oppressed group and against the notion that structural changes must (still) be fought for. It thus becomes risky *in practice* to raise the issue of moral damage with the intention of using it for liberatory ends, and it remains risky even if one can make a *conceptual* distinction among different ways of attending to moral damage. Indeed, the conceptual distinction is not hard to make; one can distinguish between the conservative victim-blaming stance, the liberal pity-evoking approach, and a critical position. One can point out that (unlike the conservative position) the critical position locates the source of moral damage in the continuing force of systems of oppression and rejects the individualist and voluntarist notion that one can simply will one's own character to change; and (unlike the liberal position) a more radical critical position is not concerned with appealing to the sympathy of the mainstream for reforms that will ameliorate damaging conditions but, rather, is primarily concerned with understanding moral damage in order to develop collective practices within communities of resistance that will effectively address or repair the damage, both for the sake of the individuals who suffer from the damage and for the sake of better enabling members of the community to pursue liberatory projects, especially those projects that aim at fundamentally transforming the structures of society.[45] However, these distinctions among various approaches to understanding moral damage notwithstanding, in light of the empirical evidence of how damage imagery has functioned in the political arena (historically and in contemporary times), one might be led, for purely strategic reasons, to simply refuse to discuss the ways in which moral damage may be a significant aspect of oppression.

I am very wary of the conservative context that is currently shaping the use of the concept of moral damage; I am also very wary of the liberal use of damage imagery to evoke pity or sympathy from dominant groups in an attempt to have them show concern for the oppressed. But I worry about potentially radical communities of resistance basing their agendas so strongly on the fear of the co-optation of their projects by either conservatives or liberals. Specifically, I worry when radicals become unable to attend to questions of moral damage simply because conservatives have poisoned the issue by declaring that the continuing subordination of, for instance, blacks is due to their character deficiencies *rather than* due to institutionalized racism. Stephen Steinberg, for instance, seems to think that one cannot simultaneously attend to moral damage *and* work to change structural causes of oppression. Because he takes *any* sort of attention to character to indicate an allegiance to the conservative victim-blaming stance, he leaves no conceptual space for a radical version of a character-based ethics. It is out of this conceptual vacuum that Steinberg is forced, for instance, to understand Cornel West's concern with "the profound sense of psychological depression, personal worthlessness, and social despair . . . widespread in black America" to necessarily imply—despite ample evidence to the contrary—that West does not locate the problem in systemic racism;[46] Steinberg goes so far as to charge West with "substitut[ing] a vapid and utterly inconsequential 'politics of conversion' for a genuine political solution."[47]

But Steinberg's own solution is one that does not pay attention to the difficulty of repairing damage, suggesting instead that damage will be undone automatically when conditions change. Insisting on structural explanations for all differences of character between social groups, he argues that character change will correspond neatly to structural changes, claiming that "individuals and groups who encounter a favorable structure of opportunity respond accordingly, and exhibit high motivation, zeal for work, and other virtues that we associate with success."[48] Steinberg starts from an assertion of the fact that an oppressive system causes damage—an important assertion to make, given the conservatives' denial of it—but infers from this that removal of the oppressive forces will simultaneously undo the damage. While it may very well be that favorable external conditions are necessary—or at least very helpful—for the development of certain virtues, it does not follow that such conditions are sufficient, especially once damage has already been done. It therefore does not follow that it is sufficient for the Left to focus *exclusively* on structural changes. If Steinberg were right that changing external conditions alone would undo moral damage, there would be no need for liberatory struggles to include any attention to the issue of moral damage. But, unfortunately, as Sandra Bartky has so starkly pointed out, "one of the evils of a system of oppression is that it may damage people in ways that cannot always be undone."[49]

I would like to suggest that radicals do need to examine moral damage for purposes other than those of the conservatives and the liberals and, thus, that a critical virtue ethics framework is useful because it makes conceptual space for such an examination. Without looking at moral damage, it may not be possible to formulate good strategies of resistance; that is, moral damage among its members may interfere with a community's ability to work to bring about structural changes. Feelings of hopelessness and an internalized belief in one's own inferiority are examples of forms of damage that may retard resistance. But there are others. For instance, one effect of oppression is that it can produce in the oppressed desires that conflict with liberatory aims or principles. Bartky illustrates this conflict with an example of a woman who has masochistic desires and finds herself eroticizing the exercise of power, even while this woman's own feminist principles lead her to oppose the relationships of domination and subordination to which these desires are tied. The production of the masochistic desires can be seen as a form of moral damage, for it creates a character that is morally problematic from the point of view of the woman's own liberatory principles.[50] Such moral damage is pervasive under oppression, as one is likely to have desires that are not consistent with liberatory principles simply because one's desires will have been shaped within and under the influence of capitalist, misogynist, racist systems.[51]

A further reason for communities of resistance—such as feminist communities—to attend to moral damage is that the damage may lead one to act oppressively toward others. Card's attention to the question of moral responsibility under oppression is motivated in part by her insistence that "although it is morally problematic for beneficiaries of oppression to hold its victims responsible for bad conduct," particularly when such conduct was chosen by a self who was morally damaged by oppression, "victims have responsibilities of their own to peers and descendants."[52] She is thinking, here, of the ways in which "women's oppression and childhood abuse are intertwined historically," such that "both are morally damaging, and the damage of one can apparently lead to that of the other."[53] Thus there are cases, for Card, in which it would be inappropriate to "blame" someone for acting out of a morally damaged character but in which one still must be able to demand that the person take responsibility for her character and her actions. Card writes, "Overcoming and resisting our own oppression require us to *take* responsibility for situations for which others could not reasonably hold us responsible . . . , despite our complicity."[54]

CONCLUSION

By recognizing the simple point that even Aristotle acknowledges, namely, that flourishing requires external goods as well as the right character, a critical virtue ethics can maintain, contrary to the conservative understanding of the role of character, that social, political, and economic systems create the most formidable barriers to members of oppressed groups being able to flourish. But there is room, after seeing the need for structural changes, to examine how lacking the opportunity to develop the virtues—that is, being morally damaged—actually prevents one both from living aspects of a good life and from carrying out liberatory projects. A critical virtue ethics will thus need to be able to identify moral damage and to distinguish the traits that constitute damage from the traits that may be virtues—virtues that help one both to flourish as much as possible under difficult conditions and to fight oppression, working to bring about radical transformation of all of the structural features of a society that contribute to it.

In order for a critical virtue ethics to approach the task of sorting through the list of potential virtues and vices and making practical use of such a sorting, two kinds of projects will need to be undertaken. The perhaps simpler project requires pursuing the largely empirical questions of how to repair damage and foster desired character traits (virtues) once these have been identified. This project may require, in addition to the efforts of ethical theorists, the work of social scientists (wary as one must be of how oppressed groups have been dealt with by social science) who can research questions of how the self learns new habits of desire, emotion, and action. Most importantly, however, will be those people working together in activist communities who can be the ones to develop political practices that will bring about personal or characterological transformations along with structural changes, with the assumption that character will not necessarily change automatically hand in hand with structural changes. But because character traits do tend to be constructed and reconstructed socially, it may be through collective practices that there will be the most potential to reverse moral damage. To give just one such example, consider the women's martial arts movement, which since the beginning of the second wave of the women's liberation movement has been politicized because it is linked to work against violence against women. This movement has consisted not only in women training in self-defense and martial arts (and thus learning a set of skills, a discipline, and an art form) but also in these women developing certain traits associated with this training, traits such as a sense of self-worth, assertiveness, resistance to violation, physical courage, and integrity of the body/self.[55] Indeed, there have been many attempts within the feminist movement, with its commitment to making the personal political, to link personal transformation with fundamental changes in social and political systems (though these personal transformations have not always proceeded successfully, and some—perhaps misguided ones—may actually have constituted further damage).[56]

But the project that is philosophically much more complicated involves the normative evaluation of character, that is, judging which character traits will count as virtues and which as vices, which in turn seems to require that one have a working conception of what it is to flourish. Thus, it seems that the development of a critical virtue ethics will lead one into having to justify one's use of a particular account or accounts of human flourishing. Here one will have a range of thorny possibilities stretching between two poles: the first pole is marked by the endorsement of a universal account of human flourishing, and the second consists of a relativist or subjectivist acceptance of just about any version of flourishing that someone claims fits a certain version of the good life.[57]

I find both poles to be problematic. Fortunately, I do not believe that engaging in critical thinking about potential virtues requires choosing between the poles. Instead, I find that the normative work of evaluating character demands the same kind of endorsement of values that the normative work of maintaining political commitments does. That is, each potential virtue or vice must be considered in light of one's other commitments. In the context of feminist or other communities whose commitments are to fighting oppression, investigation of any character trait takes the form of asking about its consistency with the liberatory aims of the community, rather than asking about whether the trait is universally one that contributes to (some universal version of) human flourishing. Does the character trait help its bearer to engage in liberatory struggles? Or, alternatively, does the character trait help its bearer to live well now (or to contribute to others' living well now), in the context of continuing oppression, where living well is itself understood in part by the same liberatory values that one wishes ultimately to be able to live out more fully?[58]

Any political commitment—whether one manifests it in theoretical arguments or in practice through activism—requires an implicit endorsement of some understanding of the good; one would not struggle for social changes if one did not believe the changes to be for the good. My claim here is that developing a critical virtue ethics requires a universal account of human flourishing to no greater extent than committing to a particular form of social or political changes does. But because conceptions of human flourishing and their corresponding virtues are not always made explicit or visible within communities that work for liberatory changes, it is worth engaging specifically in thinking about what sort of character traits are consistent with and supportive of the sorts of changes the community strives for.

There is good reason to expect that the virtues of such communities—the virtues associated with fighting oppression—will differ from (though may overlap with) mainstream tables of the virtues because there will be differences in the values of the community, as well as differences in the kinds of practices demanded of members of the community. One might argue that a mainstream account of the virtues is wrong in precisely the same way that one would argue that the status quo social arrangements that correspond to those virtues are wrong. For instance, the "virtue" of being able to command others with authority will be rejected as long as one rejects a hierarchical social arrangement in which some give orders and others obey. More radical virtues might include things like courage for taking on the hardest battles and paying the consequences—anything from going to jail, to losing a job, to being socially ostracized; propensity for visionary imagination; endurance; empathy or compassion; the capacity for solidarity; "proper" anger, such as anger at injustice; an aesthetics according to which one finds socially rejected bodies to be beautiful; the ability to be drawn to rather than repelled by or fearful of social difference; and a habit of warding off indifference. Each of these potential virtues would need to be investigated more carefully and in relation to particular communities that are engaged in liberatory struggles. Of course, developing a demanding table of the virtues carries its own danger: armed with a portrait of the "good radical" or the "good feminist" as the one who is characterologically well equipped to fight the good fight, one could easily develop a terrible self-righteousness, a trait that is not, I take it, a virtue.

NOTES

Portions of this essay were presented at the 1998 Radical Philosophy Association Conference and at the 1999 Feminist Ethics Revisited Conference, where I received valuable responses from participants. Special thanks go to Bat-Ami Bar On for her comments on drafts of the essay.

1. W. E. B. Du Bois, *The Souls of Black Folk* (New York: Signet Classic, 1969 [1903]), 43.

2. Lewis Gordon, "A Short History of the 'Critical' in Critical Race Theory," *APA Newsletters* 98, no. 2 (1999): 24.

3. I would not argue that it is never useful to perform this transvaluation, only that one should not do so in a way that makes one unable to ever treat damage as damage. Douglas Glasgow, for instance, performs what might be a useful transvaluation. Using the term *survival culture* to describe the so-called black underclass in positive terms, he argues that the character traits of this culture should be considered virtues given their utility in the situation. He writes, "Notwithstanding its reactive origin, survival culture is not a passive adaptation to encapsulation but a very active—at times devious, innovative, and extremely resistive—response to rejection and destruction. It is useful and necessary to young Blacks in their present situation" (Glasgow, *The Black Underclass* [New York: Vintage Books, 1981], 25).

4. Aristotle, *Nicomachean Ethics*, trans. W. D. Ross, in *The Basic Works of Aristotle*, ed. Richard McKeon (New York: Random House, 1941), 1099a31–1099b8, 1101a14–16.

5. Iris Marion Young, *Justice and the Politics of Difference* (Princeton, N.J.: Princeton University Press, 1990), chapter 1.

6. Young, *Justice and the Politics of Difference*, chapter 2.

7. Aristotle, *Nicomachean Ethics*, 1098a17–18.

8. Aristotle, *Politics*, trans. Benjamin Jowett, in *The Basic Works of Aristotle*, ed. Richard McKeon (New York: Random House, 1941), book 2, chapters 4–5.

9. Aristotle, *Politics*, 1280a10–15.

10. Claudia Card, *The Unnatural Lottery: Character and Moral Luck* (Philadelphia: Temple University Press, 1996), 4.

11. Card, *The Unnatural Lottery*, ix.

12. Card, *The Unnatural Lottery*, 8.

13. Card, *The Unnatural Lottery*, 53.

14. Card, *The Unnatural Lottery*, 64.

15. One of the sections in Robin Morgan's 1970 collection *Sisterhood Is Powerful* is entitled "The Invisible Woman: Psychological and Sexual Repression" (New York:

Random House, 1970); Sandra Lee Bartky's "On Psychological Oppression" (1979) (in her *Femininity and Domination* [New York: Routledge, 1990]) draws parallels between the psychological oppression of women and what Frantz Fanon refers to as the "psychic alienation of the black man" (*Black Skins, White Masks* [New York: Grove Press, 1967], 12).

16. Bartky, *Femininity and Domination*, 22.

17. The term comes from Bernard Williams and Thomas Nagel's (1976) symposium on the topic. See Bernard Williams, "Moral Luck," in his *Moral Luck* (New York: Cambridge University Press, 1981); and Thomas Nagel, "Moral Luck," in his *Moral Questions* (New York: Cambridge University Press, 1979).

18. Margaret Urban Walker, "Moral Luck and the Virtues of Impure Agency," in *Moral Luck*, ed. Daniel Statman (Albany: State University of New York Press, 1993), 241.

19. The term *constitutive luck* comes from Williams, "Moral Luck."

20. On this last point, see Deborah Tolman and Tracy Higgins, "How Being a Good Girl Can Be Bad for Girls," in *"Bad Girls"/"Good Girls": Women, Sex, and Power in the Nineties*, ed. Nan Bauer Maglin and Donna Perry (New Brunswick, N.J.: Rutgers University Press, 1996).

21. Daryl Michael Scott, *Contempt and Pity: Social Policy and the Image of the Damaged Black Psyche, 1880–1996* (Chapel Hill: University of North Carolina Press, 1997), xviii.

22. Scott, *Contempt and Pity*, xiii.

23. Scott, *Contempt and Pity*, xiii.

24. Scott, *Contempt and Pity*, 135.

25. Scott, *Contempt and Pity*, xiii.

26. Gunner Myrdal, *Challenge to Affluence* (New York: Pantheon, 1962).

27. Scott, *Contempt and Pity*, chapter 8.

28. Oscar Lewis, *The Children of Sanchez* (New York: Random House, 1961).

29. Scott, *Contempt and Pity*, 142.

30. Stephen Steinberg, *The Ethnic Myth: Race, Ethnicity, and Class in America* (Boston: Beacon Press, 1981), 109.

31. Scott, *Contempt and Pity*, 143.

32. Daniel P. Moynihan, *The Negro Family: The Case for National Action* (Washington, D.C.: Office of Policy Planning and Research, U.S. Department of Labor, 1965), 30.

33. Moynihan, *The Negro Family*, 47.

34. Scott, *Contempt and Pity*, 157.

35. Scott, *Contempt and Pity*, 185.

36. Scott, *Contempt and Pity*, chapter 10.

37. Glenn Loury, *One by One from the Inside Out: Essays and Reviews on Race and Responsibility in America* (New York: Simon and Schuster, 1995), 258.

38. Loury, *One by One from the Inside Out*, 260.

39. James Wilson, *On Character* (Washington, D.C.: American Enterprise Institute for Public Policy Research, 1991), 11.

40. Wilson, *On Character*, 5. Wilson defines criminality itself as a character trait; he takes criminality to be "not an occasional violation of the law but a persistent and high rate of participation in illegal or disorderly actions. Criminality in this sense refers to a personality disposition—a character trait—that makes some people less

likely than others to resist the temptations presented by criminal opportunities, less likely because they are impulsive or self-centered" (*On Character,* 43).

41. Wilson, *On Character,* 28.

42. Wilson, *On Character,* 35.

43. For a discussion of the association of blacks with crime, see Angela Davis, "Race and Criminalization: Black Americans and the Punishment Industry," in *The House that Race Built,* ed. Wahneema Lubiano (New York: Random House, 1997), 264–79. For an example of the racialized discourse on welfare, see Patricia Williams's commentary on the *Washington Post,* which "ran an eight-day series on the trials and tribulations of a welfare mother named RosaLee who seemingly had committed every sin the Bible could think of, including, of course, having many children by many different men, setting up her boyfriend to be killed, spreading AIDS, teaching her children to steal, and cheating the welfare system" (*The Rooster's Egg: On the Persistence of Prejudice* [Cambridge: Harvard University Press, 1995], 8). As Williams points out, such discourse—and the examples of it are plentiful in the mainstream media—gives the false impression that cases such as those of RosaLee are typical ones, portraying the case "as generally representative of a 'culture' of black pathology whose cure could only come from blacks themselves" (Williams, *The Rooster's Egg,* 8).

44. Shelby Steele, *The Content of Our Character: A New Vision of Race in America* (New York: St. Martin's Press, 1990), 15.

45. A critical approach might involve attempting to answer a question that Card poses: "How is it possible for us as damaged agents to liberate ourselves from the damage?" (*The Unnatural Lottery,* 41).

46. Cornel West, *Race Matters* (Boston: Beacon Press, 1993), 12–13.

47. Stephen Steinberg, *Turning Back: The Retreat from Racial Justice in American Thought and Policy* (Boston: Beacon Press, 1995), 132.

48. Steinberg, *Turning Back,* 14.

49. Sandra Bartky, "Feminine Masochism and the Politics of Personal Transformation," in her *Femininity and Domination* (New York: Routledge, 1990), 58.

50. Bartky, "Feminine Masochism and the Politics of Personal Transformation."

51. Alison Jaggar makes a related point in "Love and Knowledge": "Within a hierarchical society, the norms and values that predominate tend to serve the interests of the dominant group. Within capitalist, white supremacist, and male-dominant society, the predominant values will tend to serve the interests of rich white men. Consequently, we are all likely to develop an emotional constitution quite inappropriate for feminism" ("Love and Knowledge: Emotion in Feminist Epistemology," in *Gender/Body/Knowledge,* ed. Alison Jaggar and Susan Bordo [New Brunswick, N.J.: Rutgers University Press, 1989], 159).

52. Card, *The Unnatural Lottery,* 41.

53. Card, *The Unnatural Lottery,* 41.

54. Card, *The Unnatural Lottery,* 41.

55. One source for further information is the website of the National Women's Martial Arts Federation, which also has links to many women's/feminist martial arts schools: <http://www.nwmaf.org/home.html>. See also Bat-Ami Bar On's "Violent Bodies" (in this volume) for a consideration of what may be problematic about the sorts of habits learned by women training in the martial arts.

56. As I have argued elsewhere (Lisa Tessman, "Moral Luck in the Politics of Personal Transformation," *Social Theory and Practice* 26, no. 3 [Fall 2000]: 375–95), feminist "politics of personal transformation" have not sufficiently taken into account the ways in which moral luck complicates the possibilities for effectively changing character; many feminist political projects have overestimated the degree of control that one can have in bringing about personal transformation.

57. Martha Nussbaum does not shy away from the first pole, endorsing what she believes to be a universal account of human flourishing. Her approach, which she calls the "capabilities approach," lists human capabilities (that is, opportunities for functioning) for which she believes all nations should provide support, and Nussbaum uses the list to argue that governments should be politically pressured to provide guarantees that each and every citizen shall be enabled with each of the capabilities. While many items on her list are quite broad and would be hard to reject (they also may be difficult to implement in practical ways without losing the universality that they do have), her overall aim is a liberal (and thus, I would argue, not universal, in that one might reject liberalism) one: she uses an account of human nature that assumes humans engage in choices as autonomous individuals (though highly influenced socially), and she privileges the preservation of an individual's capability to *choose* to develop and maintain certain human functions. Nussbaum thus believes that she allows for plurality despite the universality of her account of human functions, for no individual is required to develop a particular function. See Martha Nussbaum, *Women and Human Development: The Capabilities Approach* (New York: Cambridge University Press, 1999).

58. It is this kind of inquiry that I attempt to carry out with respect to the character trait of loyalty in Lisa Tessman, "Dangerous Loyalties and Liberatory Politics," *Hypatia: A Journal of Feminist Philosophy* 13, no. 4 (Fall 1998): 18–39.

7

Feminist Ethics: Care as a Virtue

Margaret A. McLaren

Care ethics is alternately lauded as a breakthrough for feminist ethics and criticized for countering feminist aims by reinforcing feminine stereotypes.[1] This essay explores the question of whether or not care ethics can be a feminist ethic. I show how care ethics can be characterized as a feminine ethic and review some criticisms of care ethics. I test care ethics against Alison Jaggar's definition of feminist ethics. I argue that Carol Gilligan's care ethics falls short of being a feminist ethic. I then explore Joan Tronto's notion of extending care into the political realm. While I agree with this extension of care ethics, I argue that Tronto's analysis does not radically undermine traditional moral theory or liberal politics. Contrary to Tronto, I argue that care ethics works best when understood within a virtue ethic framework. Furthermore, I argue that virtue ethics is the most promising framework from which to approach feminist ethics. I conclude with some suggestions about future directions for feminist virtue theory.

CARE ETHICS

Here I use "care ethics" to refer to contemporary approaches to moral theory that focus on care as a significant category. The two most prominent proponents of care ethics are Carol Gilligan and Nel Noddings. Care ethics is a relatively recent phenomenon; each author published a major text developing care ethics in the early 1980s. Gilligan's *In a Different Voice: Psychological Theory and Women's Development* and Noddings's *Caring: A Feminine Approach to Ethics and Moral Education* define the terrain of care ethics. Both Gilligan and Noddings claim that the moral reasoning of women differs from that of men. Noddings says, "It is well known that many women—perhaps most women—do not approach moral problems as problems of principle, reasoning, and judgment."[2] And Gilligan notes, "The psychology of women that has consistently been described as distinctive in its greater orientation toward relationships and interdependence implies a more contextual mode of judgment and a different moral understanding."[3] Gilligan and Noddings each explore what women's moral reasoning may have to offer to moral theory. Care is a central moral category for both Gilligan and Noddings. As the title of her book implies, Noddings expresses a feminine view of caring. She proposes a view of caring that is "rooted in receptivity, relatedness, and responsiveness."[4] She advocates a view of ethics that takes as basic the relation between the one caring and the one cared for. Gilligan uses empirical studies to demonstrate that women may, indeed, discuss moral problems "in a different voice." She uses the results of these empirical studies to challenge the prevailing theories of moral development. While both Noddings and Gilligan present interesting arguments for care ethics, here I focus on the work of Carol Gilligan. Her *In a Different Voice* has had a tremendous impact on moral theory.[5]

Gilligan's model of moral development directly challenges Lawrence Kohlberg's model.[6] Kohlberg's model of moral development, like Immanuel Kant's moral theory, views invoking universal principles as the highest form of moral reasoning. This focus on universal principles and the correlative atomistic, rational, rights-bearing subject has been criticized by many feminists as masculinist.[7] Gilligan challenges the paradigmatic model of deontological moral theory. Deontological moral theory emphasizes universal principles, assumes a self that is isolated from others and abstracted from context, privileges reason and rationality over emotion, and relies on hypothetical rather than actual situations. Gilligan advocates, instead of the traditional moral theory based on abstract universal principles and an atomistic rights-bearing self, an ethics of care based on responsiveness to others, responsibility, and a relational self.

Since the 1970s, Harvard psychologist Lawrence Kohlberg's model of moral development has provided a standard scale by which to judge an individual's moral maturity. On Kohlberg's scale women have consistently ranked below men regarding their level of moral maturity. Rather than assuming women's inferiority, Gilligan reframes the question from, "What is wrong with women that prohibits them from ranking higher on this scale of development?" to "What is wrong with this scale of development that prohibits women from ranking higher?" Her studies reveal that women may speak in a "different voice" than men when discussing moral issues. She proposes an alternative model of moral development. On this alternative model, care and responsiveness to others are neither morally neutral nor moral failings but, rather, are viewed as valuable. By revaluing these stereotypical feminine traits, Gilligan exposes male bias in theory construction. Thus, care ethics contributes to exposing the masculine bias in the construction of moral theory.

This male bias appears not only in Kohlberg's scale of moral development but also in traditional moral theory. Many feminists have challenged the assumption of the atomistic self implicit in deontological moral theory and liberal political theory.[8] The traditional view of autonomy assumes that individuals are independent and equal with respect to moral decision making. This conception of autonomy as separation inherent in modern moral philosophy devalues interdependence and the caring work of mothering.[9] Furthermore, as in social contract theory, this conception of moral autonomy assumes that individuals come together voluntarily as equals. This voluntarism ignores the fact that many of our relationships are unchosen, for instance, familial relationships. Moreover, many relationships are characterized by inequality, paradigmatically the relationships between parents and minor children but also any relationship in which one person is dependent or vulnerable, such as in the case of the elderly or the sick. Gilligan's theory, on the other hand, revalues activities of care traditionally associated with women. But it is precisely this revaluation of activities traditionally associated with women that poses a problem for care ethics.

In spite of its significant challenge to male bias in moral and psychological theory, care ethics has several flaws. Critics argue that (1) it is essentialist, (2) its general claims about women result in false universalization, (3) it draws on and reinforces stereotypes of feminine qualities that have been formed under conditions of oppression, and (4) it does not take considerations of justice into account.[10] The first three criticisms stem from the association of women with the ethic of care. The presumed essentialism implicit in Gilligan's theory is challenged by other psychologists who find little or no gender difference in moral reasoning in their own research.[11] The charge of false universalization arises because Gilligan talks of women's moral reasoning with no attention to differences in class, race, ethnicity, or sexual orientation.[12] The third criticism, that care ethics reinforces stereotypically feminine attributes that have been formed under conditions of oppression, serves as a final caution regarding the uncritical association of women with care ethics.[13] This third criticism characterizes care ethics as a feminine ethics. I discuss this further in the next section.

As noted above, there are several problems with Gilligan's care ethics. She bases care ethics on women's moral experience without attention to differences among women and similarities between men and women or acknowledging the social and political circumstances, such as gender oppression, of women's experience. In her attempt to revalue activities of care traditionally associated with women, Gilligan reinscribes the feminine stereotypes that perpetuate women's oppression. Thus, care ethics as articulated by Gilligan can be characterized as a feminine ethic. As a feminine ethic, care ethics needs to be approached cautiously by feminists.

Despite the problems with Gilligan's care ethics, it has been extremely useful for feminists. Contemporary feminists have extended, applied, and criticized Gilligan's work in interesting and important ways. Seyla Benhabib's notion of the concrete other provides an important corrective to the generalized other in deontological moral theories.[14] Marilyn Friedman's work on the importance of context to moral thinking and to the social self draws out some important philosophical implications of care ethics.[15] And Diana Meyers's conception of autonomy as a learned competency reformulates the traditional idea that autonomy is opposed to socialization.[16] As many feminists have argued, acknowledging interdependence, inequality, and vulnerability improves on the traditional contractarian model of ethics.[17] Activities of care are necessary for the reproduction of culture and human life. Feminist interventions in and extensions of care ethics address a wide range of issues: the role of context in moral reasoning, the undesirability of the impartial point of view, the conception of autonomy, the conception of the moral person, the relationship between care and justice, and the extension of care into the political realm.[18] Can care ethics contribute to a feminist ethics? I argue that it can, if viewed within a virtue ethics framework.

Care ethics provides a significant challenge to deontological ethics. It questions fundamental assumptions of deontology, such as the ontological separateness of the self, the superiority of universal reasoning, the exclusion of the emotions from moral reasoning, and the highly abstract and hypothetical nature of moral problems. Contemporary virtue theory poses a similar challenge to deontological ethics. Virtue theorists, too, question the fundamental assumptions of deontological moral theory regarding the nature of the self, the role of rationality and universality in moral reasoning, and the role of context and specificity regarding moral problems.

VIRTUE ETHICS AND FEMININE ETHICS

The tradition of virtue theory has a long history, beginning with the Pre-Socratics, championed by Aristotle, and continuing into the present with contemporary revivals of virtue theory espoused by philosophers such as Alasdair MacIntyre. While Aristotle and MacIntyre are more concerned with what I call the normative aspects of virtue theory, philosophers have also debated whether virtues are gender neutral or gender related.

As a feminine ethic, care ethics fits into the traditional view that men and women have separate virtues. Some philosophers, such as Kant, view women's virtues of compassion, sympathy, and benevolence as inferior to men's virtues of justice, rationality, courage, and temperance.[19] Some, for instance, Rousseau, view women's and men's virtues as different but complementary. Yet others, such as Mary Wollstonecraft and John Stuart Mill, argue that the virtues are gender neutral. Historically, viewing virtues as gender related has only served to contribute to women's oppression because the virtues associated with women have been seen as less important than those associated with men and because the virtues associated with women serve to reinforce women's connection with the private sphere.

I argue, however, that virtue theory can contribute positively to a feminist ethic. First, I highlight the aspects of virtue theory that I believe can positively contribute to a feminist ethic. Then I examine Kant's argument for feminine virtues and explore how the notion of feminine virtues serves to perpetuate the subordination of women. Third, I address feminist criticisms that the feminine virtues and care ethics are dangerous for women. I conclude that care may indeed be a *feminist* virtue worth cultivating.

As a normative theory, virtue theory has several attractive features. It emphasizes the concrete, particular aspect of moral situations. It assumes that the moral agent is embodied and part of a community.[20] It recognizes that practical judgment and moral perception play a role in moral reasoning. It holds that both the action and the intention behind it are important. It brings considerations of character to light. Finally, friendship plays a significant role in moral life.

In addition to these positive features, traditional virtue theory provides a standard of appropriateness as well as a normative framework. The standard of appropriateness is the mean—a virtue is always the mean between two extremes, for example, courage is the mean between foolhardiness and cowardice. The normative framework stems from the definition of virtue itself as that which promotes human flourishing. Although accounts of what promotes human flourishing have varied historically and from culture to culture, it is widely accepted, for instance, that genocide does not promote human flourishing.[21]

Let me elaborate on each of the claims made above regarding virtue theory as a normative theory. Here I focus on Aristotelian and neo-Aristotelian virtue theory, and I contrast this with a deontological Kantian model of moral theory.[22] Rather than relying on principles and rules the way that deontological moral theory does, virtue theory begins from the concrete, actual situation. The details of the situation are relevant for determining the proper moral action. This concreteness and specificity carries over into moral agency. Virtue theory posits an individual moral agent who has a particular moral identity, is a social and political being, has specific social roles, and is part of a particular historical and cultural context. Neo-Aristotelians, such as MacIntyre, emphasize the importance of community and social roles in establishing the appropriate moral response. This contrasts sharply with Kantian moral agents who function as better moral agents the more they rid themselves of empirical considerations, including their own emotions and inclinations. In contrast to Kant's devaluation of the role of the empirical in moral reasoning, virtue theory recognizes that moral perception, practical wisdom, and the emotions play important roles in moral deliberation.

Another attractive feature of virtue theory as a normative theory is that instead of focusing solely on the act, the way that utilitarianism does, or concerning itself only with intention, the way that Kant's deontology does, virtue theory considers both the action and the intention important. What one does and why one does it are both important to the formation of character. Character—the set of dispositions that results in part from repeated actions—provides another register by which to judge oneself and others as good or bad, praiseworthy or blameworthy. Last, but not least, of the positive features that virtue theory offers is the recognition that friendship is a significant moral category. Virtue theory recognizes that we do not exist alone in the world as abstracted and isolated moral agents. Moreover, it recognizes friendship as integral to living a virtuous life. I believe that virtue theory has much to offer feminist ethics as a framework for understanding moral life. Yet there are also good reasons for feminists to be skeptical of virtues for women. Historically the idea of women's virtues has served to perpetuate women's subordination and reinforce negative stereotypes of women.

One of the most notorious discussions of women and virtue is found in Immanuel Kant's *Observations on the Feeling of the Beautiful and the Sublime.*[23] Kant counts neatness, sensitivity to shame, modesty, and a heart for friendship as among women's virtues.[24] He also says that women are goodhearted and compassionate. One might consider this a reasonable list until it is set in the context of Kant's other remarks. According to Kant, women are capable only of the beautiful virtues, not the sublime and noble virtues of men. Beautiful virtues are, of course, inferior to sublime, noble virtues. Beautiful virtues are concerned with pleasantness, attractiveness, and charm (the best a woman can hope for is to be good company and attractive to the opposite sex). Most of the beautiful virtues are superficial. Many have to do with physical appearance including facial features, body type, and bodily adornment.

Even those virtues that may seem positive, such as a heart for friendship, goodheartedness, and compassion, appear less positive when set in the context of Kant's discussion. These virtues, like all women's virtues, stem from Kant's association of women with feeling and sense.[25] Feeling and sense are contrasted with deep understanding, thought, and reason. The former belong to women, the latter to men. In Kant's words, "Her [woman's] philosophy is not to reason, but to sense."[26] It hardly needs saying that reason is privileged in Kant's philosophy, while feeling and sense are devalued. Because women's virtues—the "beautiful virtues"—rely on sense rather than reason, women are incapable of acting from moral principles. For Kant, as for Kohlberg, acting from principle is the *sine qua non* of morality. Because women's virtues are inferior to men's and reinforce the woman's roles as caretaker and sexual object, it is easy to understand why feminists find gender-specific virtues problematic.

Critics focus on the ways that gender-specific virtues are dangerous to women, insofar as they support patriarchy and perpetuate women's subordination. Care ethics reinforces stereotypical "womanly virtues" because it draws on the idea of women as caretakers and nurturers. Two prominent feminist critics of care ethics, Claudia Card and Sarah Hoagland, both urge us to be cautious of women's virtues formed under the oppressive conditions of patriarchy.

In "Gender and Moral Luck" Claudia Card questions an uncritical view of care as a virtue. Noting that women in patriarchal societies exist under conditions of oppression, Card is skeptical that virtues developed under these conditions should be taken at face value. She suggests that care may simply be a coping mechanism for those with less power to survive by appeasing those with more power. She points out that care and connection may not always function as virtues. For instance, in the case of abusive relationships connection is extremely harmful. Furthermore, she notes that the oppression that women face can result in moral damage and that care may be a result of that moral damage, rather than a virtue. She also points out that the special goodness often attributed to women is usually connected to a presumed deficiency in their capacity for justice.[27] Card's critique reveals that Gilligan's theory leaves intact and unquestioned the unequal relations of power between women and men in patriarchal society.

Sarah Hoagland argues that the feminine virtues, such as altruism and self-sacrifice, preserve the relationship between dominance and subordination. Following Mary Daly, she calls the feminine virtues "virtues of subservience."[28] Hoagland concurs with Card that because the feminine virtues are formed under oppressive conditions, in a situation of unequal power between men and women, feminists should be wary of endorsing them. Developed under heteropatriarchy, the feminine virtues are part of women's survival skills. But these survival skills, developed by those with less power to appease those with more power, do not necessarily contribute to women's own good. In fact, a woman's care for others often comes at a great cost to herself. Hoagland extends Card's critique by suggesting that women have refined the feminine virtues in defense and resistance in order to gain some (limited) control from a subservient position. In order to exercise some control women may resort to manipulation, cunning, and deceit. In her words, "The feminine virtues, virtues which accrue to the less powerful, are developed as strategies for manipulating and gaining control in a relationship of dominance and subordination."[29] Obviously, the refinement of the feminine virtues only makes them less appealing, for they now sound like vices. As developed under heteropatriarchy, the feminine virtues perpetuate women's subordination and undermine female agency. As Hoagland says, "The feminine virtues do not serve us."[30]

FEMINIST ETHICS AND POLITICIZED CARE

Deriving feminist ethics from women's moral experience is inherently problematic. This is succinctly put by Alison Jaggar when she writes that "the feminine is not the feminist."[31] Taking Jaggar's characterization of feminist ethics as a starting point, I examine whether care ethics can be a feminist ethics. In "Feminist Ethics: Projects, Problems, Prospects," Jaggar makes the following claims. First, feminist ethics can be identified by its explicit commitment to challenging perceived male bias in ethics. Following from this it should articulate moral critiques of actions and practices that perpetuate women's subordination, prescribe morally justifiable ways of resisting such actions and practices, and envision morally desirable alternatives that will promote women's emancipation. Second, feminist ethics cannot assume that men and women are similarly situated. Third, it must understand individual actions in the context of broader social practices. Fourth, it must provide guidance on private life as well as critically examine the public/private distinction. And fifth, feminist ethics must treat women's moral experience respectfully but not uncritically.[32]

At first glance care ethics seems to fulfill many of the criteria set forth for feminist ethics. On a theoretical level it challenges perceived male bias in ethics by questioning many of the masculinist assumptions about moral reasoning. It does not assume that men and women are similarly situated, and it provides guidance on private life. However, as Card and Hoagland demonstrate, it falls short of understanding individual actions within the broader social context, and it fails to treat women's moral experience critically. Critics have convincingly shown that it reinforces feminine stereotypes. Furthermore, by representing women's experience as unified, it reinforces not just male bias but also racial, ethnic, class, and heterosexuality bias.

Care ethics does not provide moral critiques of actions that perpetuate women's subordination, nor does it prescribe morally justifiable ways of resisting such actions and practices. It may, however, be useful in envisioning morally desirable alternatives that will promote women's emancipation. One promising approach is a "politicized care," that is, extending care into the political realm.

In her book, *Moral Boundaries,* Joan Tronto argues that care can and should be extended to politics. She names the three major boundaries in contemporary moral thinking: (1) between morality and politics, (2) between public and private life, and (3) between lived experience and the impartial moral point of view. Tronto argues that moral theory is inextricable from political context. She believes that care has radical political potential and that it should be extended into the political realm. Tronto urges us to view care as a political ideal in order to raise the status of both care as a practice and those who do caring work. Currently caring work is devalued labor in spite of the fact that it is absolutely necessary labor. Although it is true at present that women in the contemporary United States do the majority of caring labor, Tronto holds that care itself is not gendered. Tronto defines care as "a species activity that includes everything that we do to maintain, continue and repair our 'world' so that we can live in it as well as possible."[33] I accept Tronto's definition with some reservations because, without the addition of some normative assumptions, it reinforces the status quo.[34] One would need to spell out in more detail what repairing our world entails. If caring simply maintains and continues the world, it does not challenge current social and political systems.[35]

Tronto explicitly rejects what she calls a "morality first" approach that views care as a virtue, arguing that this view leaves the boundary between morality and politics intact. On the contrary, I argue that understanding care within the framework of virtue theory can contribute to a feminist ethics. Tronto's definition of care as "maintaining, continuing, and repairing the world so that we can live in it as well as possible" meets the criteria for a virtue, that is, a social good that promotes human flourishing. Furthermore, I demonstrate that virtue theory can provide the normative framework that care ethics lacks.

CARE ETHICS AND VIRTUE ETHICS, OR WHY NOT VIRTUE?

As is discussed above, some feminists think that aligning care with virtue ethics is detrimental to women's interests. In one interpretation, care ethics can be viewed as a contemporary incarnation of the view that there are "womanly virtues" such as sympathy, gentleness, and so on. Typically, the virtues associated with women in this view are related to women's roles in the domestic sphere as caregiver, wife, and mother.[36] However, if we follow Tronto's suggestion and disassociate the activities of care from the gender of the carer, then it may be possible to retain the insights of care ethics without perpetuating feminine stereotypes.

The relationship between care and virtue is complicated, but I think that there are many benefits to placing care in the framework of virtue theory. Both virtue theory and care ethics challenge many of the assumptions of deontological moral theory and a liberal political framework. One of the advantages is that virtue theory can account for the overlap of the ethical and the political. It recognizes the overlap between moral and political and between public and private, and it eschews the impartiality usually associated with the moral point of view. In these respects, care ethics and virtue theory are similar. I argue, however, that care ethics is best viewed within the framework of virtue ethics because it provides an important normative framework that care ethics lacks.

As a normative theory, care ethics falls short in a number of ways. Its association with women serves to perpetuate feminine stereotypes while it occludes the diversity of women's lives. Its focus on responsibility to others and the particulars of the situation seems to relegate care to the private realm of an individual caring for other individuals, and this seems to exclude care from the public realm. Typical criticisms of care claim that, because care ethics does not advocate universal moral principles, its application is limited to the private realm of family and personal relationships. Typically, care has been contrasted to the notion of justice as found in deontological moral theory. Taking justice as paradigmatic of morality is part of what makes the public/private distinction so intractable in moral theory. Removing care from the justice framework and placing it in a virtue theory framework may help to blur the boundaries between public and private.

There are three commonalities between care ethics and virtue theory that make a comparison inviting. Both care and virtue hold that the self is a relational, social self; both urge attention to the particular moral situation; and both acknowledge that social and political contexts are significant for moral theory. Virtue theory sees moral agents as social and political, defined in part by their social roles. Gilligan, too, views the self as relational, defined in part through social roles and the web of relationships to others. This social self, which is embedded in a framework of social and cultural roles and institutions, has been extremely important in feminist theorizing.

The second significant commonality between virtue and care ethics is attention to the particulars of the situation and the grounding in a concrete ethical situation. In Aristotle's account in the *Nicomachean Ethics* the right thing to do depends on the situation.[37] Making the right decision requires practical wisdom, that is, the ability to make the correct judgment about the situation. Knowledge of particulars is necessary if one is to exercise practical wisdom. In her work Gilligan stresses actual over hypothetical dilemmas, and she argues that hypothetical dilemmas "divest moral actors from the history and psychology of their individual lives and separate the moral problem from the social contingencies of its possible occurrence."[38] Recent mainstream moral theory and feminist work reaffirm the importance of attention to the concrete in moral theory through increasing attention to an agent's social location, individual history, and the issues of moral perception and moral psychology.[39]

The third significant overlap between care ethics and virtue theory is the importance of social and political context. Although Aristotle's account has its limitations, most notably the view that men and women are unequal, it emphasizes social and political context and the importance of social institutions in promoting virtue. In virtue theory the virtues are seen as social goods to be fostered through social, political, and educational institutions. Virtue theory does not separate the ethical from the political; this overlap between the ethical and political is important to considerations of feminist ethics.[40]

Care ethics is less attentive to social and political context than virtue theory is. Gilligan's empirical research focuses on the particular situations experienced by her research subjects. As we have seen, though, her lack of attention to diversity among women with regard to ethnicity, race, class, and sexuality undermines the relevance of her conclusions regarding the empirical association of women with care ethics. Gilligan also fails to explore the political context in which care ethics arises. In spite of Gilligan's neglect, attention to social and political context is essential for any feminist ethics.

Virtue theory seems able, then, to fulfill several of the criteria for feminist ethics laid out by Jaggar. It places individual actions in the context of broader social practices; it blurs the distinction between public and private life; and it provides guidance in private life. Because virtue theory takes account of social location, it could and should account for men's and women's dissimilar social situations. However, there is not an explicit commitment to challenging male bias in ethics—in fact, it has often been criticized for perpetuating just such bias. Can a virtue theoretical approach contribute to overcoming women's subordination?

CONCLUSION: FEMINIST VIRTUE ETHICS

I conclude with some speculations about the possibility of a feminist virtue theory. Thus far I have examined care ethics in relation to virtue ethics. I have shown how both care ethics in its "feminine" form and virtues as conceptualized by Kant reinforce the stereotypically feminine view of women as sympathetic and benevolent nurturers. While holding women up as moral paragons is better than vilifying us, it relegates women to the private sphere and saddles us with the role of caretaker. Nonetheless, the philosophical work on care ethics contributes significantly to moral theory. In closing, I want to suggest three different ways that care can be useful to feminists. First, following Tronto, care can be applied to politics and perhaps lead to considerations of justice. Second, as I have shown, understanding care within a virtue ethics framework shores it up against some criticisms, thus strengthening care ethics as a moral theory. Finally, I suggest that care should be fostered as a feminist virtue.

Understood in its broadest sense care applies not just to particular persons but, as Tronto suggests, to the political realm as well. Why should care be limited to particular individuals? Some ecofeminists who expand on Gilligan's work argue that care should extend to include not just individual persons but also animals and even inanimate natural objects, such as rocks.[41] If we see care as a practice, as Tronto suggests, and if it is a practice directed toward maintaining, continuing, and repairing our world, including bodies, selves, and environment, then the scope of our care is not limited to individual persons or even groups of persons. Care can be directed toward politics and principles that make the world a better place.[42]

A politicized care such as Tronto suggests may even promote concern for justice. Care for others can lead to a concern for justice. Caring for particular others and understanding their context can make one keenly aware of systemic injustice. For example, when one cares for someone who is terminally ill, it may become clear that the quality of health care available varies according to socio-economic status. When care reaches its fullest expression, it must take into account the social circumstances that perpetuate any type of oppression, subordination, or domination.[43]

By placing care within a virtue ethics framework, my aim has been to disassociate it with women, clarify its possible relationships to justice, and pay heed to the importance of social and political context for any ethics. Indeed, one of the hallmarks of feminist ethics is that it is inseparable from social and political context. Understanding care within the context of virtue ethics demands that we pay attention to social and political conditions. Yet virtue ethics needs to be supplemented by a feminist politics and a conception of human flourishing that promotes equality. Viewing care in the framework of virtue theory may allow us to see both care and justice as social capacities that need to be sustained along with normative ideals,[44] as human capacities they need to be developed and sustained by social institutions that support them. These social institutions must, in turn, be regulated by normative ideals that promote gender equality and nondomination.

Reclaiming care as a feminist virtue recognizes the value of care in a world that desperately needs individuals to perform more than the moral minimum. I have argued that feminist ethics can benefit from virtue theory and that "appropriate care" should be counted among the feminist virtues. What would a feminist virtue theory look like? It would need to be committed to equality between men and women and, more broadly, committed to ending oppression in all its forms. Like Aristotle's virtue theory, feminist virtue theory would emphasize the contextual and situational aspects of moral and ethical situations while still condemning some things as wrong. Feminist virtue theory would recognize the significant role that moral perception and judgment and practical wisdom play in moral life. It would also acknowledge the importance of character and friendship. Feminist virtue theory would recognize the inseparability of the ethical and the political. Finally, feminist virtue theory would recognize the particular, the specific, the concrete aspects of moral life.

To this end, feminist virtue theorists would recognize that virtues are developed and sustained within particular social and institutional contexts and may even be specific to social roles and political purposes. For feminists the primary political goal is to end the subordination of all women.[45] I have argued that feminists should reclaim care as a virtue. What other virtues might be counted among the feminist virtues? In addition to care, feminists might want to include the virtue of feistiness, the virtue of self-respect, and the virtue of playfulness.[46] A list of other virtues particularly useful for feminists might include openness, self-awareness, and courage.

In spite of valid criticisms that care can be viewed as a *feminine* virtue formed under conditions of oppression, I suggest that care ought to be a *feminist* virtue. It is essential to helping us envision morally desirable alternatives that promote equality and emancipation.

NOTES

I thank the participants at the Feminist Ethics Revisited Conference for their questions and comments on an earlier version of this essay. Thank you to the editors of this book, Peggy DesAutels and Joanne Waugh, for their helpful suggestions. I am also grateful to the following friends and colleagues for their feedback on an earlier draft of this essay: Raja Halwani, Heike Amelung, Claudia Card, Tom Cook, Diane Erbe, Mark Juergens, Amelie Oksenberg Rorty, and Scott Rubarth.

1. Rosemary Tong's *Feminine and Feminist Ethics* (Belmont, Calif.: Wadsworth Publishing Co., 1993) provides a useful overview of this issue.

2. Nel Noddings, *Caring: A Feminine Approach to Ethics and Moral Education* (Berkeley: University of California Press, 1984), 28.

3. Carol Gilligan, *In a Different Voice: Psychological Theory and Women's Development* (Cambridge: Harvard University Press, 1982), 22.

4. Noddings, *Caring,* 2.

5. Although Nel Noddings has published a significant work dealing with care, her work has not been nearly as influential as Gilligan's. The impact of Gilligan's work is evident through the number of anthologies devoted to criticizing, extending, and applying her ideas. See, for example, Eva Feder Kittay and Diana T. Meyers, eds., *Women and Moral Theory* (Totowa, N.J.: Rowman and Littlefield Publishers, 1987); Mary Jean Larrabee, ed., *An Ethic of Care: Feminist and Interdisciplinary Perspectives* (New York: Routledge, 1993); and Eve Browning Cole and Susan Coultrap-McQuin, eds., *Explorations in Feminist Ethics: Theory and Practice* (Bloomington: University of Indiana Press, 1992). While all of these anthologies deal centrally or solely with Gilligan's care ethics, as far as I know there are no anthologies devoted specifically to Noddings's care ethics. There is some overlap in their positions, most notably taking care as the central moral category and identifying care reasoning with women, either explicitly or implicitly (both, however, do say that care reasoning is not limited to women but, in fact, can be used by men as well). Some of the criticisms addressed in the body of this chapter apply to both Gilligan's and Noddings's positions, notably the criticism that care is formed under conditions of oppression and therefore should not be seen as a virtue. Despite some commonalities, their positions differ significantly. One important difference in relation to this chapter is that Noddings discusses the relationship between virtue and care whereas Gilligan does not. However, Noddings is far from consistent in her position on the relationship between care and virtue. For example, she claims that she is in part advocating an ethic of virtue but not of the virtues (*Caring,* 80), and then she goes on to say that "caring is not in itself a virtue" (*Caring,* 96). Her position differs significantly from mine, as she makes no attempt to systematically examine the commonalities between virtue theory and care ethics and does not discuss the benefits of placing care ethics within a virtue ethics framework. Space does not permit me to address her argument more fully here. I have chosen to focus on Gilligan's care ethics because it has been taken up by feminist philosophers and ethicists in interesting and important ways.

6. See Lawrence Kohlberg, *Collected Papers on Moral Development and Moral Education* (Cambridge: Harvard University Moral Education Research Foundation, 1973).

7. See Seyla Benhabib, "The Generalized and the Concrete Other: The Kohlberg–Gilligan Controversy and Moral Theory"; Diana T. Meyers, "The Socialized Individual and Individual Autonomy: An Intersection between Philosophy and Psychology"; and Virginia Held, "Feminism and Moral Theory"—all in *Women and Moral Theory,* ed. Eva Feder Kittay and Diana T. Meyers.

8. See Benhabib, "The Generalized and the Concrete Other"; Meyers, "The Socialized Individual and Individual Autonomy"; and Held, "Feminism and Moral Theory." See also Susan Moller Okin, *Justice and Gender* (New York: Basic Books, 1989); and Marilyn Friedman, "The Social Self and the Partiality Debates," in *Feminist Ethics,* ed. Claudia Card (Lawrence: University Press of Kansas, 1991).

9. Here I follow Sara Ruddick, Virginia Held, and others who view mothering as an activity open to both men and women.

10. Much of the discussion surrounding care ethics has centered on whether it can take considerations of justice into account. Typically, care and justice have been viewed as being in opposition, with care being associated with partialism, feeling, and particular relationships, while justice is associated with impartiality, reason, and the public sphere. Some theorists have argued that this strict opposition no longer holds. Care is sometimes viewed as complementary to justice and sometimes viewed as supplementary to justice. In the complementary view, care and justice are both seen as valuable, but they have separate spheres. Care is relegated to the private realm of family and personal relationships, and justice is to be used in the public realm of politics and work. The complementary view is consistent with the view that care is gender related, for it views care, a feminine virtue, as appropriate for the domestic sphere. In the supplementary view, care and justice are both seen as valuable in the realms of public and private. In this view, one does not want to exclude considerations of justice from the private realm; for instance, in the case of domestic violence justice is required within the family. The supplementary view also recognizes that justice provides only moral minimalism in the public sphere and that care could rectify this. Dealing fully with the care/justice debate is beyond the scope of this chapter. However, rather than exploring whether care ethics can deal with considerations of justice, I am proposing an alternative—that we think of both care and justice as compatible virtues within a virtue theory framework.

11. See, for instance, John M. Broughton, "Women's Rationality and Men's Virtues: A Critique of Gender Dualism in Gilligan's Theory of Moral Development," 112–39; Lawrence J. Walker, "Sex Differences in the Development of Moral Reasoning: A Critical Review," 157–76); and Catherine G. Greeno and Eleanor E. Maccoby, "How Different Is the 'Different Voice'?" 193–98)—all in *An Ethic of Care: Feminist and Interdisciplinary Perspectives,* ed. Mary Jean Larrabee. It is important to distinguish between biological and sociological essentialism. Although Gilligan does make general claims about women, she never claims that gender difference is biologically based but, rather, that it is the result of socialization. Furthermore, although her studies show that women are far more likely to use care reasoning than men, she advocates that both men and women use both care and justice reasoning.

12. This valid criticism has been raised by several feminists; see, notably, Carol Stack, "The Culture of Gender: Women and Men of Color," in *An Ethic of Care: Feminist and Interdisciplinary Perspectives,* ed. Mary Jean Larrabee; Nancy Fraser and Linda Nicholson, "Social Criticism without Philosophy: An Encounter between Feminism and Postmodernism," in *Feminism/Postmodernism,* ed. Linda Nicholson (New York: Routledge, 1990); and Linda Kerber, "Some Cautionary Words for Historians," in *An Ethic of Care: Feminist and Interdisciplinary Perspectives,* ed. Mary Jean Larrabee.

13. For the best articulations of this position, see Claudia Card, "Gender and Moral Luck," in *Identity, Character, and Morality: Essays in Moral Psychology,* ed. Owen Flanagan and Amelie Oksenberg Rorty (Cambridge: MIT Press, 1990); Sarah Lucia Hoagland, *Lesbian Ethics: Toward New Value* (Palo Alto, Calif.: Institute of Lesbian Studies, 1988), especially chapter 2, 69–113; and Bill Puka, "The Liberation of Caring: A Different Voice for Gilligan's 'Different Voice,'" in *An Ethic of Care: Feminist and Interdisciplinary Perspectives,* ed. Mary Jean Larrabee.

14. See Benhabib, "The Generalized and the Concrete Other"; and *Situating the Self: Gender, Community and Postmodernism in Contemporary Ethics* (New York: Routledge, 1992), especially part 2.

15. See Friedman, "Care and Context in Moral Reasoning," in *Women and Moral Theory,* ed. Eva Feder Kittay and Diana T. Meyers; "Beyond Caring: The De-Moralization of Gender," in *An Ethic of Care: Feminist and Interdisciplinary Perspectives,* ed. Mary Jean Larrabee; "The Social Self and the Partiality Debates," in *Feminist Ethics,* ed. Claudia Card; and *What Are Friends For? Feminist Perspectives on Personal Relationships and Moral Theory* (New York: Cornell University Press, 1993), especially parts 1 and 2.

16. See Meyers, "The Socialized Individual and Individual Autonomy: An Intersection between Philosophy and Psychology," in *Women and Moral Theory,* ed. Eva Feder Kittay and Diana T. Meyers; and *Subjection and Subjectivity: Psychoanalytic Feminism and Moral Philosophy* (New York: Routledge, 1994), especially chapters 2 and 6.

17. For an elaboration of this point, see Virginia Held, "Non-Contractual Society: A Feminist View," in *Science, Morality and Feminist Theory,* ed. Marsha Hanen and Kai Nielsen (Calgary: University of Calgary Press, 1987).

18. See, for instance, the articles in Cole and Coultrap-McQuin, *Explorations in Feminist Ethics;* Kittay and Meyers, *Women and Moral Theory;* Card, *Feminist Ethics;* and Larrabee, *An Ethic of Care.*

19. Kant, for example, claimed that women were incapable of justice, and Jean-Jacques Rousseau felt that women and men had different but complementary virtues. See Kant, *Observations on the Feeling of the Beautiful and the Sublime,* trans. J. T. Goldthwait (Berkeley: University of California Press, 1960 [1764]); and Rousseau, *Emile* (London: J. M. Dent, 1993).

20. Not all accounts of virtue theory emphasize being in a community; here I am thinking particularly about communitarian and neo-Aristotelian versions of virtue ethics. My thanks go to Raja Halwani for pointing out that theories of virtue ethics differ in relation to the issue of community.

21. Recently there have been attempts to spell out an objective account of human flourishing as the ability to develop certain human capacities. See, for instance,

Martha Nussbaum, "Non-Relative Virtues: An Aristotelian Approach," in *The Quality of Life,* ed. Martha C. Nussbaum and Amartya Sen (New York: Oxford University Press, 1993).

22. For the sake of contrast, I focus on Kant's moral view as it is represented in *Critique of Practical Reason* and *Groundwork of the Metaphysics of Morals.* In these texts, Kant emphasizes the role of logic and reason in moral thinking and minimizes emotions and the empirical features of situations. Much recent work has been done that portrays a more balanced view of Kant and integrates some of his other work on moral theory, such as *The Doctrine of the Virtues.* For recent work that portrays a more balanced and sympathetic view of Kant's moral theory, see Onora O'Neill, Barbara Herman, Susan Wolf, and Marcia Baron.

23. The discussion is notorious (at least in feminist circles) because it portrays women as less capable of the higher moral virtues than men are. See especially section 3, "Of the Distinction of the Beautiful and Sublime in the Interrelations of the Two Sexes," in *Observations on the Feeling of the Beautiful and the Sublime.*

24. Kant, *Observations on the Feeling of the Beautiful and the Sublime,* 84–85.

25. Kant, *Observations on the Feeling of the Beautiful and the Sublime,* 79–81.

26. Kant, *Observations on the Feeling of the Beautiful and the Sublime,* 79.

27. One example of this is Kant's argument in *Observations on the Feeling of the Beautiful and the Sublime* addressed above. Another relevant example is Sigmund Freud, "Some Psychical Consequences of the Anatomical Distinction between the Sexes," in *The Standard Edition of the Complete Psychological Works of Sigmund Freud,* vol. 19, trans. and ed. James Strachey (London: The Hogarth Press, 1961).

28. See Mary Daly, *Gyn/Ecology: The Metaethics of Radical Feminism* (Boston: Beacon Press, 1978); and *Beyond God the Father: Toward a Philosophy of Women's Liberation* (Boston: Beacon Press, 1973).

29. Hoagland, *Lesbian Ethics,* 100.

30. Hoagland, *Lesbian Ethics,* 113.

31. Alison Jaggar, "Feminist Ethics: Projects, Problems, Prospects," in *Feminist Ethics,* ed. Claudia Card, 92.

32. Jaggar, "Feminist Ethics," 97.

33. Joan Tronto, *Moral Boundaries: A Political Argument for an Ethic of Care* (New York: Routledge, 1993), 103.

34. I owe this point to Heike Amelung.

35. See Ann Ferguson's review of Tronto's *Moral Boundaries* (in *Radical Philosophy Review of Books,* no. 13 [1996]) for an argument that Tronto's politicized care does not go far enough in spelling out the political and social institutions and conditions that would make an ethics of care feasible in the public realm.

36. This is true except for in the Scottish Enlightenment, when it was assumed that men also had these virtues. For a historical overview of moral sentiment theory that is persuasive in arguing that care is gender neutral, see Tronto, *Moral Boundaries,* 25–59.

37. This does not result in relativism because some things are always wrong, for example, adultery, murder, and theft.

38. Gilligan, *In a Different Voice,* 100.

39. See, for instance, Nancy Hartsock on feminist standpoint theory, Bernard Williams on individual moral history, and Owen Flanagan and Margaret Urban Walker on moral psychology.

40. See the introduction to *Daring to Be Good: Essays in Feminist Ethico-Politics* (New York: Routledge, 1998), edited by Bat-Ami Bar On and Ann Ferguson, for an overview of the ways feminists have been concerned with both politics and ethics.

41. See Karen Warren, "The Power and Promise of Ecological Feminism," *Environmental Ethics* 12 (Summer 1990): 125–46.

42. Some versions of care ethics do not allow for this expansion of care to include objects or principles. But care for a particular person or place (as in Warren's article) may lead to this broader understanding of care that I think is operative in Tronto's book. For example, if I have come to care for a particular place in nature, and this place is somehow threatened, I may get involved in environmental activism to save it. The relationship between caring for a particular person or place and more general concerns is contingent. I do not have the space to explore this issue more fully here.

43. Of course, there is no guarantee that the person doing the caring will automatically be led to considerations of justice. However, the last sentence in the paragraph is a normative claim: the fullest expression of care would need to include attention to social and political circumstances, such as the access to material goods.

44. Virtue theory can accommodate considerations of both justice and care. For an argument about how virtue ethics can include considerations of justice, see Alasdair MacIntyre, "Justice as a Virtue: Changing Conceptions," in his *After Virtue* (Notre Dame, Ind.: University of Notre Dame Press, 1984), 244–55.

45. Here I ascribe to the feminist view that oppressions are interlocking and that to work for the end to all women's oppression includes working to end all oppression, such as race, class, gender, and sexual oppression.

46. Here I am thinking of Claudia Card's introduction to *Feminist Ethics,* in which she advocates the feistiness of feminism; Robin Dillon's work on self-respect; and Maria Lugones's work on playful world traveling.

8

Angels, Rubbish Collectors, and Pursuers of Erotic Joy: The Image of the Ethical Woman

Barbara S. Andrew

> You may not know what I mean by the Angel in the House. I will describe her as shortly as I can. She was intensely sympathetic. She was immensely charming. She was utterly unselfish. She excelled in the difficult arts of family life. She sacrificed herself daily . . . in short she was so constituted that she never had a mind or a wish of her own, but preferred to sympathize always with the minds and wishes of others. Above all—I need not say it—she was pure.[1]

Virginia Woolf's image of the Angel in the House, a mere phantom, is only one of many images of femininity. It is a powerful image, however, representing a patriarchal construction of femininity and of discourse about how women should behave. Woolf challenges this construction in her attack on the Angel in the House and hence challenges what the reader expects of Woolf as a woman. The Angel in the House undermines self-expression, critique, and free thought, curtailing women's participation in intellectual endeavors.

The fantasy of female self-sacrifice and duplicity, of giving others one's own share and lying about one's thoughts, is still very much alive. It dominates even feminist discourse in subtle and pervasive ways. Feminist ethics of care and love are often criticized for reasserting the fantasy of the Angel in the House. While I find this to be an important criticism, I do not find the reassertion of the Angel in the House to be a primary goal (either unstated or assumed) of care ethics or feminist ethics of love.[2] However, the image of the Angel in the House impedes the care and justice debate. Care ethics, perhaps because of its founding texts, emphasizes mother–child relationships and ethical differences between men and women. While these are important

119

issues, they are not the only issues that a feminist ethic must address. A feminist ethic must search for liberation as well as connection to others.

An image or fantasy of the ideal ethical woman is important, perhaps even necessary, to feminist ethics, for it inspires both ethical imagination and action. Michel Foucault argues that ethics is about relationship to the self, especially one's attempt to make oneself into the best possible self. For Foucault, the relationship to the self has four components: ethical substance—the aspect of the self that moral conduct changes; the mode of subjectivation—the laws, codes, rules, or virtues by which people recognize their moral obligations; self-forming activity—"the means by which we can change ourselves in order to be ethical subjects"; and finally the telos—"the kind of being to which we aspire when we behave in a moral way."[3] These four components work together to mold or discipline subjectivity. The search for the best life, the most ethical life, is primarily a practice of making oneself into the best person one can by modeling oneself in conformity with the telos. For Foucault, all ethical systems discipline the self; self-discipline is definitional to ethical systems. Discipline, however, is not always domination. Instead, discipline can be a practice of self-constitution or molding the self to be free. Foucault advocates viewing the self as a work of art and promoting the most exuberant and fecund expression of self. My interest in this essay is in the telos of feminist ethics. The telos works with the rest of the ethic by providing an ideal image of the moral agent. While one exercises moral rules or participates in a set of practices to form oneself into an ethical self, one has this ideal in mind. An underlying concern, in my view, of much of the care and justice debate is the anxiety that care ethics' telos is the Angel in the House.

Ethics needs ideal images in order to inspire action. Feminist ethics particularly needs ideal images to encourage feminist political action and feminist moral questioning. Autonomy is often thought of as necessary to just political action. In this essay, I will define the concept of an ethical relationship and develop its analogy with autonomy. The analogy between relationship and autonomy helps to free care ethics from the telos of the Angel in the House. I will then turn to other potential ideal images for feminist ethics and suggest a telos: the creator of found art and pursuer of erotic joy.

ETHICAL RELATIONSHIP: CARE AS A VIRTUE AND A SOCIAL GOOD

Care ethics and feminist ethics of love elucidate ethical relationship. Relationship, like autonomy, is central to moral theory and moral judgment. Much of what is commonly referred to as justice ethics elucidates the idea of autonomy as a moral concept. Care ethics analogously explores and expands the ethical idea of relationship. This elucidation is one of the most important aspects of feminist ethics of care and love, but it is also one of the least explicitly theorized and criticized. Showing the significance of ethical relationship is an unrecognized goal of feminist ethics of care and love.

Care ethics elucidates the idea of relationship analogously to the ways in which justice ethics has defined and refined the concept of autonomy. According to most versions of justice ethics, the concept of autonomy works in two very different ways. First, one must be autonomous to make moral decisions. Second, just social conditions are those that allow one to be autonomous. In care ethics, relationship to the Other functions similarly to autonomy in justice ethics. First, one must recognize one's responsibility to respond to the Other. One must be caring in order to recognize that one is in a situation that calls for a moral response. Relationship to the Other is a basis for making moral judgments. Second, the social conditions that allow one to act responsibly to others, to love whom one chooses, to freely enter and exit relationships of intimacy, must be met. Just social conditions are those that allow one to care. Equal moral treatment requires that people live in a society that allows them to give and receive care. Continuing the analogy between justice ethics and care ethics, John Rawls considers the conditions for autonomy as basic goods, and Kantians consider being autonomous in one's decision making as the condition for being ethical. Care ethicists make an analogous argument: being loving or caring toward others is the condition for being moral. The conditions for promoting loving or caring relationships are basic goods. Thus, care ethics develops relationship as an essential ethical concept.

The claim that being loving or caring toward others is the basis for being moral is commonly seen as the main claim of care ethics. Both Carol Gilligan and Nel Noddings promote care as the primary moral virtue or moral code.[4] Arguments surrounding what exactly care entails as a moral response, virtue, or code are voluminous. The second aspect of care as ethical relationship, that the bases of promoting care relationships are basic social goods, has evoked less comment. However, two authors, Joan Tronto and Eva Feder Kittay, argue this point. In her book *Moral Boundaries,* Tronto argues that calling care ethics a development of women's morality is essentialist and allows care to be inappropriately trivialized as particular.[5] She refers to the arguments of Francis Hutcheson, Adam Smith, and David Hume to show that various authors have based their theories on moral sentiments. In addition, Tronto shows that traditional African American philosophy also focuses on care, cooperation, and interdependence. Like Foucault, Tronto argues that all moral theory is politically located and contextualized. Tronto argues that care work and care relationships are purposely relegated to the realm of the personal, the ethical, and the apolitical in order to keep women's needs out of the political realm. Tronto notes a discontinuity between women's traditional role as caretakers and feminism's goal of liberation. For Tronto, however, the road to liberation is through politicizing care and care work. Tronto proposes that care ethics can be more reflective about distributions of power because of its attention to the context of actions, the particularity of persons, and its valuation of sentiment.[6]

Eva Feder Kittay uses a Rawlsian framework to argue that care is a primary good. She adds a third principle of justice to Rawls's two to ensure the just social conditions for care work. Kittay shows the importance of considering dependency and care workers in public policy debates and develops what she calls the dependency critique of equality.[7] She argues that we should begin deliberations regarding a just society by considering the position of the least advantaged. If we construct principles of social justice by starting from the vantage point of the most dependent, then we will formulate social structures that allow for care and compassion, strong infrastructures to provide care and support care workers, and equal access to social services—all integral to a just society.

Arguing that a just society is one in which individuals can receive care and provide it without damaging their other claims to equal treatment seems directly in conflict with the telos of the Angel in the House. Instead of self-sacrifice and duplicity, Tronto and Kittay's telos is a politicized care worker who argues for a straightforward acknowledgment of the value and difficulty of care work. This telos is a far cry from the Angel in the House. Nevertheless, critics of care ethics abound. Critics have noted problems of racism, heterosexism, and anthropomorphism and have expressed concerns with paternalistic or maternalistic images that the word *care* invokes.[8] Tronto and Kittay address these critics, in part, by changing the focus of care from care as a virtue to the social and political systems that cast aspersions on care work. They strive to make the penalty of caring disappear, thus making the bases of care possible and making society more just.

THE ANGEL IN THE HOUSE AND ETHICAL TELOS

Working through the analogy between autonomy and ethical relationship helps to free care ethics from the Angel in the House. In order to formulate further a better vision of care ethics and to explore ethical relationship, it is important to think through the power of the fantasy of the Angel in the House. The Angel in the House is a social construction of femininity that informs ideals of the ethical woman. Consequently, it not only informs patriarchal views of women but, arguably, infiltrates feminist attempts to recuperate feminine values. I want to define some of the Angel's attributes, especially in terms of unstated racial and class assumptions.[9]

In *Black Feminist Thought*, Patricia Hill Collins argues that race, class, and gender discrimination require powerful ideologies to justify their continued existence. Controlling images used to describe and define women's lives are one instantiation of these ideologies. The actual social relations of power that define women's lives are quite distinct from these images. So, for example, when calling African American women "matriarchs," "mammies," or "welfare queens," the social realities of few well-paying jobs, poverty, racism, and sexism appear normal, natural, or ascribable to the moral deficiencies of African American women.[10]

According to Simone de Beauvoir, one of the tricks of oppression is to make oppression seem normal, natural, and part of everyday life.[11] Collins points out how controlling images help to naturalize black women's oppression. The telos of the Angel in the House naturalizes women's subordination in an analogous way. The controlling image of the Angel in the House is marked white and is a class-based phenomenon insofar as it is mainly middle-class women who are expected to act like refined ladies of leisure. Nancy Hewitt argues that the ideal of the lady of leisure, a variant of the Angel in the House, derives not so much from notions that all women deserve a life of refined leisure but, rather, from notions that white, middle-class women do.[12] As Adrienne Rich points out, this angelic fantasy of woman—the pure, nourishing mother—is part of a complex image of femininity, the other half of which is the diseased, corrupt prostitute. Recall Woolf's stress on the purity or chastity of the Angel in the House. Notice the assumed heterosexuality of the various sides of the image. Rich also notes that racism participates in the constitution of these roles, especially in the Antebellum South, where white women were constituted by patriarchal ideology as angels and African American women were constituted as prostitutes.[13] Paula Giddings argues that the basis for race ideology in the nineteenth century was this supposed sexual difference between the natural lasciviousness of African American women and the natural purity of white women.[14] A recent study shows that young Hispanic women in the United States are plagued with a similar ideal based on the Virgin Mary.[15] The fantasy of the Angel in the House is a racist, classist, heterosexist, Christianized ideal of femininity that is quite clearly sexist. Critics are correct in wanting to eradicate it.

Making the Angel in the House the telos of care ethics initiates power dynamics similar to those of the controlling image. While the telos of the Angel in the House assigns power to those who are marked by it, it also limits that power in particular ways and works to make cultural and social oppression, including racial hierarchy, appear natural. It controls women's actions by normalizing the expectation that women who are "Angels" will be sexually pure, self-sacrificing, and self-righteous in their belief of their own authority to judge others. As Marilyn Frye argues, part of the "whitely" attitude is the belief that one has the authority and responsibility to guide and judge others.[16] The telos of the Angel in the House perpetuates the myth that white, middle-class values supersede all others. These power dynamics both empower Angels and simultaneously limit what is viewed as acceptable action

and acceptable desire on their part. It also carries the entire social and political history of racism and classism discussed above.

Readers might note that the Angel in the House has gone from being a telos to being a controlling image in my account. This naturally leads to the
question of whether every telos is a controlling image. Following Foucault, I
would say that power works in diverse ways. The Angel in the House limits
women's actions (in various ways, based on race, for example) and empowers women's actions (again, in various ways). The same is true of any telos.
Some might think it better to envision an ethic without a telos. I am not sure
that it is either beneficial or possible. Ethics needs ideal images to inspire action. However, there are better and worse visions of ethical life and more or
less empowering and freeing ideals.

Feminist ethics needs a different telos than the Angel in the House—a new
way of envisioning the moral woman. Feminist ethics is troubled not only by
what its guiding ideals should be, and hence of what future it envisions, but
by how it can speak of women at all. This problem is the very next question
Woolf poses, after beating the Angel in the House to death with an ink pot: "In
other words, now that she had rid herself of falsehood, that young woman had
only to be herself. Ah, but what is 'herself'? I mean, what is a woman?"[17] Less
than twenty years later, Simone de Beauvoir poses the same question in her introduction to *The Second Sex*. Feminists have conflicting needs. We need both
to speak of women as a class in order to show that women have been oppressed as women and to reject the notion of our sameness and of idealized
stereotypes such as the Angel in the House. We need to speak of political goals
and solidarity without essentializing femininity. The foundation of feminism
lies in the belief that women do not have an inherent nature and that rights
should not be curtailed based on an assumption about women's natural role.
Recent feminist work emphasizes that women cannot speak in one voice
given racial and class divisions.[18] Yet feminists such as Uma Narayan argue that
universal human rights are necessary for insuring that women's needs not be
ignored by arguments for the sanctity of difference.[19] If feminist ethics needs a
telos to inspire action, it must be one that does not essentialize femininity, ho-
mogenize women, or ignore difference. It must be based on coalition, on
working together for political goals and human rights. A feminist ethic must
pose some ideal of women's excellence, of feminist excellence, or of the moral
goals of feminist action, or we must ask, Why speak of ethics at all?

IDEALS OF FEMALE AGENCY

Why do feminists want an ethic?[20] Becoming a feminist requires seeing the
world differently than one once did.[21] Central questions for any ethic, but especially for a feminist ethic, include, "What is the best life?" and "Who is the

moral agent?" Feminist ethics has the potential to provide a notion of empowered female agency. Ideas of empowered agency can be found in political and metaphysical feminist theories but are not always brought into feminist ethics. I am particularly interested in a notion of feminist ethical agency because the conviction that one can and does act justly motivates political action; those of us who are feminists need to know that we act justly when we act out our feminist political agendas in both our public and our intimate lives.

A telos for feminist ethics must inspire just action, both in building coalition and in responding to injustice. Claudia Card argues that care ethics cannot address situations of evil and that feminist ethics needs to be focused on preventing and redressing evils. For Card, part of this has to do with our "moral luck." We may have relationships with others that promote our autonomy and integrity, or we may have destructive relationships. Relying on relationships, then, seems a risky endeavor.[22] However, my claim is that feminist ethics needs and is developing an idea of moral relationship, which, like our ideas of moral autonomy, is an ideal. Actual relationships will often fall short of our ideal, just as actual enactments of our autonomy often do. Feminist ethics needs a telos that helps to determine when actual relationships fall short of the ideal. Feminist ethics needs a telos that allows for both relationship and autonomy, for both love and freedom.

Card notes that the past influences what we can be: "Pasts we inherit affect who we can become. As gendered beings in a society with a history of patriarchy, women and men inherit different pasts, and consequently different social expectations, lines of communication, opportunities, barriers. If these things influence character development, they make gender part of our moral luck."[23] Although Card is not addressing only the psychological conditions for ethical action, those too must be part of our past, part of what we imagine for our future. Ideal images of the moral woman play a role in our self-understandings. We currently seem stuck with the fantasy of the Angel in the House and that of the wickedly bad but sexually liberated woman. But these are simply two halves of a dichotomy, not images that can inspire new ideas.

Drucilla Cornell develops a feminist ethic in *Philosophy of the Limit,* which she furthers in her recent *At the Heart of Freedom: Feminism, Sex, and Equality.* Cornell argues that no one should be asked to give up freedom if it simply disturbs others or to give it up for the good of others. In order to pursue freedom, we need an ideal representative, a sense of self that can represent our ethical voice. In *Philosophy of the Limit,* Cornell names this ideal the *chiffonnier,* or rubbish collector, who picks through the refuse of philosophical systems to find useful strategies. For Cornell, the point of ethics is to aspire toward ethical relation. Using Adorno's and Derrida's criticisms of Hegel, Cornell shows that no philosophical system can save us from loss or the potential changes of the Other or give us absolute autonomy or protection from the Other. Cornell points out that we must recognize that in loving the Other we risk ourselves, but this risk is inevitable. We must aspire to a recognition of the Other's alterity that is both loving and just. Cornell discusses the ethical relation as having responsibility to the Other, reminiscent of Margaret Urban Walker's ethic of responsibility.[24] Cornell's ethic emphasizes compassion and alterity and is in sympathy with Nietzsche's suspicion of ethics that deny individual fulfillment.[25] Rather than a slave morality,[26] Cornell develops an ethic that is critical of systems of oppression, particularly legal oppression, and uses the power it has to change the terms of the ethical debate.

Unlike the Angel in the House, the rubbish collector does not recall a series of patriarchal fantasies of femininity. There is something quite accurate in viewing feminist philosophers as rubbish collectors, in the sense that we are always picking through the refuse of philosophical systems and ideas, trying to find what might be recyclable. But we are more like artists who find new ways of putting together the things we collect than like the nineteenth-century chiffonniers. Cornell weaves together the views of Derrida, Adorno, Beauvoir, and Irigaray with a complexity that is more like making a sculpture out of a hubcap, a wire hanger, and a variety of plastic bags than like simply recycling ideas. The "found art" of Cornell's ethic resides in her ability to take race, sex, and class into consideration in ways that none of her sources seems quite able to accomplish. So, although I feel some affinity with the telos of the rubbish collector, it does not completely encompass the telos that I think feminist ethics needs.

PURSUERS OF EROTIC JOY

In her most recent book, *At the Heart of Freedom,* Cornell develops the idea of the imaginary domain. The imaginary domain is "that psychic and moral space in which we, as sexed creatures who care deeply about matters of the heart, are allowed to evaluate and represent who we are."[27] This is the space of the fantasy of the ethical woman, the space in which we envision ourselves as both moral and free. This freedom empowers us to create a sense of self for ourselves and to imagine a world in which women would have sexual freedom: to be sexed, to have sex, and to love whomever we choose. The imaginary domain is the space for rethinking the telos of feminist ethics. Potentially, it is the space where each individual imagines her own ethical telos.

Rather than prescribing an ideal such as the chiffonier, Cornell argues that we need a more abstract idea of subjectivity to encompass the imaginary domain. A more abstract idea of who the moral subject is would allow a person to determine her own ideal self, subjectivity, and sexuality. Cornell writes that

> although we cannot be the fully authenticating source of our own values, in reality we should nonetheless be politically recognized as if we were. The abstract

ideal person is normatively recognized as the node of choice and source of value. *Abstraction—defining the person only through a normative outline—is the only way we can preserve freedom of the personality.* If the person were given "substance" by state-imposed meanings, say, of "normal" sexuality, then her freedom would be denied.[28]

The telos of Cornell's theory has evolved from the chiffonier to providing an open space, a placeholder, in which each individual develops her own model. I agree with Cornell that the best legal representation will not have a telos; the placeholder for the ideal self is empty. On the other hand, in my view Cornell suggests that the ethical telos is a person who can determine for herself how best to love. This ideal combines autonomy (determining for oneself) and relationship to the Other (how best to love). The ideal self is the one who can joyously and freely represent herself. This is a much less specific telos than the Angel in the House, which is a good thing, yet it is still a telos.

Cornell certainly is not writing an ethic of care. Her focus is on how we can love freely, and she searches for ways to make society just so that individuals can determine their own sexual being. She politicizes an ethic of love, as Tronto and Kittay politicize ethics of care. Just as Tronto and Kittay focus on the societal conditions that make care possible, Cornell focuses on the legal and social conditions that make free expression of sexuality possible. Cornell's emphasis is on freedom, but she argues for the freedom to express desire and form connection with others.

I turn here to the work of Simone de Beauvoir, in which we find neither Angel nor rubbish collector but, instead, creators of found art who pursue erotic joy. Beauvoir's telos shares some important characteristics with Cornell's ideal. Beauvoir presents a telos of female identity in her novels and in *The Second Sex* that, I believe, better suits the needs of feminist ethics. I am not suggesting that Beauvoir herself acted out the telos I describe below. Although Beauvoir's novels provide some examples of this telos, I will use *The Second Sex,* which provides the theoretical framework for Beauvoir's idea of the best life and which provides further for a telos of relationship and autonomy.

The configuration of Beauvoir's ethic is the topic of much contemporary scholarship. Karen Vintges shows that Beauvoir's project, throughout her philosophical texts, novels, and autobiographical writings, is to develop an ethical "art of living."[29] Vintges argues that Beauvoir's project is to provide a template for others on how to live a life of freedom by negotiating love, sex, and relationships in such a way that one can experience the joy of both union and freedom. Debra Bergoffen argues that Beauvoir develops an ethic of erotic generosity.[30] Margaret Simons shows that in Beauvoir's 1927 diary, before she had met Jean-Paul Sartre or begun her professional writing, Beauvoir was centrally interested in the problems of encounter with the Other, the limit of love, and the self-deception and bad faith that being overwhelmed by love could evoke. Simons argues that Beauvoir provides an alternative to Gilligan's "different voice" by viewing the problem of the Other from a radically different perspective.[31] These descriptions of Beauvoir's project show her emphatic engagement with the problem of the Other and the liberation that Beauvoir thought could be found through the celebration of fusion with another.

Early critics accused Beauvoir of adhering to a Cartesian mind/body dualism that would undermine some of the claims made above. However, recent scholarship, while acknowledging the problem with the framework of transcendence, understands Beauvoir as developing an embodied subjectivity. Unlike Sartre, Beauvoir does not adhere to an idea of absolute freedom or of radically free and independent subjectivity. Throughout her work, Beauvoir argues that humans are interdependent and that we need others to be free in order to take up our own freedom.[32] Human freedom is ambiguous. We are simultaneously free and unfree, subjects who act and who are acted on. In this way, Beauvoir accounts for agency and oppression. Beauvoir's account shares with Foucault's account the idea that power works in diverse ways. One is simultaneously empowered and disempowered by social forces and is simultaneously enforcer and recipient of the force of social power.

In *The Second Sex,* Beauvoir finds that sex is the one action that most exemplifies the ambiguity of the human situation and best helps us to understand that ambiguity, our sense of selves as both object and subject and as both animal and free. Beauvoir's view helps to form the groundwork for a feminist theory that encompasses both a liberatory independence and a recognition of the relationships in which we live.

Beauvoir writes that "the erotic experience is one that most poignantly discloses to human beings the ambiguity of their condition; in it they are aware of themselves as flesh and as spirit, as the other and as subject."[33] Sex, then, is the moment that most confounds mind/body dualism. It is the moment that one experiences oneself both as self and as object for the Other, while recognizing the Other both as object and as free human being. Patriarchal femininity is constituted in such a way as to encourage women to understand ourselves as flesh only, not as free, inspirited human beings. The erotic experience is the best site for comprehending the ambiguity of the human situation because if women can comprehend ourselves as simultaneously spirit and flesh in this experience, in which we are most encouraged to think of ourselves as flesh only, then women will be less apt to consider ourselves as inessential in other moments. If woman is One in her sexual liaisons, then her femininity surely cannot require her to be Other. For Beauvoir, the sense of self is closely tied to being able to act on desire; consequently, women's ability to think of self as One in sexual desire significantly enhances the overall sense of self as essential. In *The Second Sex,* descriptions of good sex require reciprocity. The woman feels herself to be essential, her lover recognizes her freedom, and "alterity no longer has a hostile implication."[34] Both partners acknowledge their own and each other's freedom and are "frankly desirous."[35]

Beauvoir also had the project of providing a critique of patriarchal ideology, especially ideas of heterosexual romantic love. In love, refusing to acknowledge one's own ambiguity or the ambiguity of the Other negates freedom, a claim Beauvoir developed early and worked throughout her life to show. *The Second Sex* shows that erotic love can provide a joyous experience of ambiguity or an exercise in the futility of given values. Other love relationships (such as parent–child relationships and friendships) can also provide experiences of ambiguity or futility. It is only in accepting the ambiguity of human existence, our status as free and not free, that we can see how our connection to others is necessary to our freedom. Our projects only have meaning when we can share them with another who can recognize their meaning. Relationship with others, however, also curtails freedom both in our erotic experiences, in which we are both subject and object for the other, and in our other lived experiences. Relationship, then, both creates meaning and curtails freedom. It is only from those moments of connection with others that we can understand ourselves as free, even while those moments simultaneously make us objects for the other. This is the ethical problem that Beauvoir shows us in *The Ethics of Ambiguity* and that is magnified in *The Second Sex*. Without relationship to others, life has no meaning, and yet those others have the power to treat us as objects. As Vintges argues, the challenge Beauvoir gave to herself and to her readers is to find some way to engage the other in freedom, not in a static role. This is only possible in mutual recognition of freedom, whereby both partners understand themselves and each other as ambiguous, as free, and as flesh.

Beauvoir further explores ethical relationships through her reflections on sexual engagement. While our everyday relationships may fail to live up to the ideals of reciprocity, engagement, and freedom that Beauvoir describes, the telos that her work suggests, the pursuer of erotic joy, is valuable for a feminist ethic that emphasizes both freedom and love.

A NEW TELOS

It is necessary to maintain the tension between freedom and relationship in order to exercise as much freedom as possible while still maintaining the relationships that give our freedom value. Some limit on freedom is necessary to ethical relationship. We may experience these limits as frustrating. However, we may experience these limits on our freedom not only as necessary to being in relationship with others but as exemplary of our choices—choices of particular relationships, choices to be ethical and create a life of loving and forgiving one another. The limit may make us understand and embrace the telos.

I propose that feminists embrace the telos of being pursuers of found art and erotic joy. As such, we deny both the purity and the duplicity of the Angel in the House. We can envision ourselves as craftswomen and artists, using the found art of philosophical systems to envision a moral agency we want to inhabit—a moral agency that allows us to create a valued and valuable world. We can also understand ourselves, as the works of Tronto and Kittay suggest, as politically engaged craftswomen who strive for social acknowledgment of the value and difficulty of care work. The telos encourages feminists in promoting the concept of ethical relationship as a necessary capacity of ethical agents and a basic social good. I think that this telos is abstract enough to satisfy Cornell's concerns. It adds the ideas of artistry and pursuit, through which I hope to encourage and generate feminist agency and action. Whereas the Angel in the House "never had a mind or a wish of her own," the creator of found art seeks to put old ideas together, adding her own sense of beauty or value to create new meaning. The pursuer of erotic joy seeks out her wishes, her desire for connection to the Other, and explores ethical relationship through those pursuits.

It could be argued that anytime one and only one ideal is chosen as the ethical ideal there must be some exclusion and a great deal of coercion. I do not mean to suggest that there needs to be only one ideal for all people or for all time. What I am trying to characterize is a telos that better fits the ethical systems feminists are writing about now. Perhaps the telos I suggest is one that awaits siblings. We need ideal images. Without them an ethical system is just a collection of codes and virtues—not the stuff that inspires action. In regard to the concern that any telos is a controlling image, it is important to point out that all ethical systems require some coercion, in the sense that ethics are practices that we encourage for others and ourselves in order to make ourselves ethical. All ethics participate in power. Not all power limits and oppresses; some liberates and empowers.

To define a moral agency that allows us to love and to be free—this is what feminist ethics is about. Freeing female subjectivity from the oppression that confuses love and subjection and that encourages self-sacrifice and duplicity has been the goal of feminist writers since Mary Wollstonecraft. The goal of a feminist ethics of care and love must be to find the erotic joy in loving friends, children, and lovers and to free it from subservience. This is a difficult task, for loving others always entails some check on our freedom. It is of utmost importance not to confuse the check that makes one who one is with the check that controls and dominates one. As Card points out, it may be women's bad moral luck to have been in the habit of confusing the two. Unfortunately, there is no rule book that can foretell which relationships are good and which are bad. Many are both good and bad. Some of those relationships will have to be abandoned. Others can be struggled with and remodeled. Ethics provides ideals of the best life. Ethics of love and care provide an ideal of ethical relationship. Our own relationships will often fall short of that ideal. What I think we need are lots of stories to give us lots of ideas about who we are and what we can be. We need new myths, new ideas of the telos of the ethical woman. Perhaps we can find some of these myths by imagining ourselves to be creators of found art and pursuers of erotic joy.

NOTES

An earlier version of this essay was given at the conference Feminist Ethics Revisited, in Clearwater Beach, Florida, on 1 October 1999. Special thanks go to Peggy DesAutels and Joanne Waugh for their thoughtful comments and suggestions for revisions. Some of the ideas for this essay are from my dissertation, *A Feminist Ethic of Freedom and Care,* written under the direction of Eva Feder Kittay, whose advice and suggestions were always inspiring. Ellen K. Keder and Jean Keller also commented on an earlier version of this essay. Thanks also go to Bruce Milem for comments and suggestions.

1. Virginia Woolf, "Professions for Women," in her *The Death of the Moth and Other Essays* (New York: Harcourt Brace Jovanovich, 1970 [1942]), 236–38.

2. Carol Gilligan explicitly addresses the criticism that *In a Different Voice* reasserts the Victorian Angel in the House in her essay "Getting Civilized," in *Who's Afraid of Feminism?* ed. Ann Oakley and Juliet Mitchell (New York: The New Press, 1997), 13–28.

3. Michel Foucault, "On the Genealogy of Ethics: An Overview of Work in Progress," in *Ethics: Essential Works of Foucault 1954–1984,* vol. 1, ed. Paul Rabinow, trans. Robert Hurley (New York: The New Press, 1997), 265. Foucault explains the four aspects of ethical relation to the self in "On the Genealogy of Ethics," 263–66, and also in "The Use of Pleasure," in *The History of Sexuality,* vol. 2, trans. Robert Hurley (New York: Random House, 1985 [1984]), 26–28.

4. Carol Gilligan, *In a Different Voice* (Cambridge: Harvard University Press, 1982); Nel Noddings, *Caring: A Feminine Approach to Ethics and Moral Education* (Berkeley: University of California Press, 1984).

5. Joan Tronto, *Moral Boundaries* (New York: Routledge, 1993).

6. Diemut Bubeck, in *Care, Gender and Justice* (Oxford: Clarendon Press, 1995), develops a class analysis of care work that furthers Tronto's view. Bubeck argues that social justice must be applied to the gendered division of labor, especially to the inordinate amount of care work done by women, for a fair distribution of society's benefits and burdens.

7. Eva Feder Kittay, *Love's Labor* (New York: Routledge, 1999). Other care ethicists have broadened the use of care as a moral principle. Fiona Robinson, in a recent book titled *Globalizing Care* (Boulder, Colo.: Westview Press, 1999), argues that care can and should be used in the global context of international relations.

8. These criticisms can be found in the very powerful articles in Mary Jeanne Larrabee's edited collection *An Ethic of Care* (New York: Routledge, 1993).

9. Care ethics has developed mostly in the United States and Canada. Most, if not all, of my analysis about race and class in this section is based on authors writing about North America.

10. Patricia Hill Collins, *Black Feminist Thought* (New York: Routledge, 1990), 67–68.

11. Simone de Beauvoir, *The Ethics of Ambiguity,* trans. Bernard Frechtman (Secaucus, N.J.: Citadel Press, 1948 [1947]), 83.

12. Nancy A. Hewitt, "Beyond the Search for Sisterhood: American Women's History in the 1980s," in *Unequal Sisters,* 2nd edition, ed. Vicki L. Ruiz and Ellen Carol DuBois (New York: Routledge, 1994).

13. Adrienne Rich, *Of Woman Born* (New York: W. W. Norton and Co., 1976), 34–35.

14. Paula Giddings, "The Last Taboo," in *Unequal Sisters,* 2nd edition, ed. Vicki L. Ruiz and Ellen Carol DuBois (New York: Routledge, 1994). Of course, there were some African American women who were considered to be pure. Collins refers to the controlling image of the mammy in this regard.

15. See Jill McLean Taylor, Carol Gilligan, and Amy M. Sullivan, *Between Voice and Silence: Women and Girls, Race and Relationship* (Cambridge: Harvard University Press, 1995).

16. Marilyn Frye, "White Woman Feminist," in her *Willful Virgin* (Freedom, Calif.: The Crossing Press, 1992), 147–69.

17. Woolf, "Professions for Women," 238.

18. See Hewitt, "Beyond the Search for Sisterhood," as well as Maria Lugones and Elizabeth V. Spelman, "Have We Got a Theory for You!" in *Women and Values,* ed. Marilyn Pearsall (Belmont, Calif.: Wadsworth, 1986).

19. Uma Narayan, *Dislocating Cultures: Identities, Traditions and Third World Feminism* (New York: Routledge, 1997).

20. Annette Baier, in "What Do Women Want in a Moral Theory?" in her *Moral Prejudices* (Cambridge: Harvard University Press, 1994), argues that what women want in moral theory is a discussion of love, which, according to Baier, must encompass an ethical notion of trust. Baier also shows that traditional moral theories that ignore child rearing and the reproduction of persons who will recognize obligations cannot be complete.

21. Sandra Lee Bartky makes the point in her influential article "Toward a Phenomenology of Feminist Consciousness," in her *Femininity and Domination* (New York: Routledge, 1990).

22. Claudia Card, *The Unnatural Lottery* (Philadelphia: Temple University Press, 1996).

23. Card, *The Unnatural Lottery,* 49.

24. Margaret Urban Walker, *Moral Understandings* (New York: Routledge, 1998).

25. Drucilla Cornell, *The Philosophy of the Limit* (New York: Routledge, 1992), especially 56–88.

26. I am thinking here both of Cynthia Willett's *Maternal Ethics and Other Slave Moralities* (New York: Routledge, 1995) and of Claudia Card's use of Nietzsche in *The Unnatural Lottery.*

27. Drucilla Cornell, *At the Heart of Freedom: Feminism, Sex and Equality* (Princeton, N.J.: Princeton University Press, 1998), x.

28. Cornell, *At the Heart of Freedom,* 38–39.

29. Karen Vintges, *Philosophy as Passion* (Bloomington: Indiana University Press, 1996 [1992]).

30. Debra B. Bergoffen, *The Philosophy of Simone de Beauvoir* (Albany: State University of New York Press, 1997).

31. Margaret A. Simons, *Beauvoir and The Second Sex: Feminism, Race, and the Origins of Existentialism* (Lanham, Md.: Rowman & Littlefield Publishers, Inc., 1999), 185–243, especially 232.

32. Eva Gothlin makes this point in her article "Simone de Beauvoir's Notions of Appeal, Desire, and Ambiguity and Their Relationship to Jean-Paul Sartre's Notions of Appeal and Desire," *Hypatia* 14, no. 4 (Fall 1999): 83–95. I also argue these points in "Care, Freedom, and Reciprocity in the Ethics of Simone de Beauvoir," *Philosophy Today* 42, nos. 3–4 (Fall 1998): 290–300.

33. Simone de Beauvoir, *The Second Sex,* trans. H. M. Parshley (New York: Random House, 1974 [1949]), 449.

34. Beauvoir, *The Second Sex,* 448.

35. Beauvoir, *The Second Sex,* 449.

9

Is Refusing to Forgive a Vice?

Nancy Potter

Jeffrie Murphy makes the claim that Fay Weldon, in railing against forgiveness in her novel *Female Friends,* is saying that women have been taught to forgive and accept when they should have been taught to resent and resist.[1] Murphy's remark prompts one to ask whether forgiveness is being treated like a universal principle when it should be treated as a virtue. One can forgive excessively and thus miss the moral mark. Virtues are context dependent; they concern feelings and actions that express themselves according to a mean between excess and deficiency. As Aristotle tells us, "We can be afraid, e.g., or be confident, or have appetites, or get angry, or feel pity, in general have pleasure or pain, both too much and too little, and in both ways not well; but [having these feelings] at the right times, about the right things, towards the right people, for the right end, and in the right way, is the intermediate and best condition."[2] In other words, virtues do not lend themselves to universal rules.

Considering forgiveness as a virtue has its problems too. It is plausible to believe that forgiveness is a virtue, but attitudes toward forgiveness may change when we examine how teachings on forgiveness play themselves out vis-à-vis power relations. When the parties most often called on to forgive are the oppressed, what looks like a virtue may turn out to be more of a vice. As Claudia Card suggests in "Gender and Moral Luck," moral character is socialized differently in the oppressed than in the oppressor.[3] Let us look at a novel in which the morally wronged person does not forgive her wrongdoer and consider whether her unforgiving attitude is not only reasonable but morally praiseworthy. In this case, would forgiveness constitute an excess?

While primarily a story of a young poor woman's experiences with escalating familial violence and devastating betrayal, Dorothy Allison's *Bastard Out of*

Carolina is also a novel of resistance. The main character, Bone, is born into a world in which hunger, desire, and powerlessness from class oppression intersect with gendered responses to material and psychic needs. Bone's identity is partly shaped by the attitudes and choices of those around her. But her character is also one of resistance—specifically, to the construction of females as forgiving of male violence and women who condone it.

The central theme of the novel is the development of Bone's character in a context of tyranny, betrayal, and deprivation. Bone's stepfather, Daddy Glenn, sexually violates her and brutally assaults her. While Mama tries to control the violence through various means, it becomes increasingly difficult to safeguard Bone. Mama is continually faced with a choice between protecting Bone and being loyal to Glenn. The developing dynamic reaches a crisis when Glenn's rage at his economic, social, and interpersonal impotence is expressed through the rape of Bone. Mama, who witnesses the scene, cannot leave Glenn and abandons Bone at the hospital. Although Bone comes to *understand* both Mama and Daddy Glenn, she forgives neither. In resisting the social and familial norms to forgive male violence against women and to forgive women who betray other women for the sake of their men, Bone exercises her agency even while she is ineffective in averting her own victimization.

WHAT FORGIVENESS IS AND WHY IT IS GOOD

What sort of response is called for when one has been subjected to moral wrongdoing? My framework for understanding forgiveness draws on the work of Jeffrie Murphy and Donald Shriver, who argue that forgiveness has an important place in our moral lives but that it is crucial that we disengage the concept from its religious overtones. According to Murphy, religious teachings on forgiveness do a disservice to the oppressed by treating forgiveness as a duty and by discouraging the relatively powerless from protesting wrongs and injustices done to them. The demand for forgiveness can become a silencing tool in the name of peaceable living. Many people are rightly suspicious of forgiveness either because they see it as a tool of oppression or because they are nonreligious and link the concept to reconciliation with a god in which they do not believe.

What is the content of this moral concept when separated from its religious connotations? For Murphy, forgiveness is one of a family of concepts in moral philosophy that concern the overcoming of negative feelings (such as resentment, hatred, or vengeance) directed toward another who has done one injury or harm. Jean Hampton suggests that resentment is not a single emotion but, rather, a mix of anger and fear.[4] In her view, resentment involves the feeling that one has been demeaned by another's wrongdoing and the fear that the conduct of the other has revealed one's low value. She writes, "People don't resent the injuries caused by earthquakes and tidal waves; they only resent injuries that have been deliberately inflicted by one who is able and required to respect—but does not—their value and rank."[5] She argues that resentment is not only a protest against the wrongs done to one but also a defense against the attack on one's self-esteem.[6] The fear component of resentment is that the wronged person deserved that treatment. Thus, Hampton defines resentment as "an emotion whose object is the defiant reaffirmation of one's rank and value in the face of treatment calling them into question in one's own mind."[7] Because resentment is a defensive position, Hampton reasons, it is an emotion that betrays weakness.[8]

Perhaps the equation of resentment with anger at having been wronged and with defensiveness and weakness helps to explain the prevalent social attitude that forgiveness is always morally preferable to resentment. But I doubt that Hampton's analysis of resentment applies as widely as she seems to think; I think that one can be resentful of a wrong done to one and yet be quite certain that having been wronged does not reflect one's actual value and rank. (One might be quite clear, for example, that any low value revealed lies in the conduct of the wrongdoer.) Fear that one has been exposed as less than valuable need not accompany resentment. And, although feeling angry without fear may still be defensive—for example, one may need to defend one's rights against another who violates them—it is not clear why such an orientation should count as a weakness. Hampton sees forgiveness as important partly because the emotions that call up the need for forgiveness are themselves taken to be undesirable. Given a more nuanced understanding of the emotions that may arise as a response to being wronged, our view of forgiveness as a universal duty may shift. I will offer below an alternative view of resentment, one that suggests that it plays an important positive role in motivating acts of resistance against subjugation.

Nevertheless, resentment can be an uncomfortable feeling—whether it is "naturally" so or because we have been taught that it is undesirable—and so forgiveness is often the preferred response to moral injury. Not only can forgiveness heal divisions; it also means we no longer have to endure that uncomfortable state. It is important to keep in mind, however, that forgiveness is distinct from other ways in which we respond to moral injury, for example, seeing it as justified, excusing it, or granting mercy to the wrongdoer.[9] To justify, to excuse, or to be merciful is not to forgive, for forgiveness applies to wrongs that it is initially proper to resent; if a person has done nothing wrong or was not responsible for what he or she did, there is nothing to resent (although there may be much about which to be sad). Resentment and forgiveness are directed toward *responsible* wrongdoing. To forgive is to say that what was done was morally wrong and that the wrongdoer is responsible for his or her conduct but that, given good moral grounds for overcoming resentment, one has overcome negative feelings toward the wrongdoer.[10]

The appeal to be forgiven is not a request to be handed over something but, rather, the expression of a desire that the wronged persons change their attitudes toward the wrongdoers.[11] What the wrongdoers wish, and what the wronged parties can grant in the expression of forgiveness, is an affirmation that the wrongdoers did indeed commit these acts but that they are more than the sum total of their wrong acts. To grant forgiveness is to say that the wrongdoers are forgivable—that they transcend their acts and their past and are not identical with them.

Beatty and Murphy seem primarily to focus on interpersonal and dyadic relationships, but Shriver argues that forgiveness has a powerful role to play in politics. For him, forgiveness "begins with memory suffused with moral judgment."[12] Someone remembers an alleged wrong, injury, or injustice and morally judges the wrongdoer. Moral judgment may lead to some sort of punishment or restitution, but forgiving the wrongdoer requires that one abandon vengeance. Like Murphy, Shriver holds that "forgiveness gets its real start under the double impetus of judgment and forbearance from revenge";[13] forbearance from revenge requires that one also feel empathy for the humanity of the wrongdoer and lays the groundwork for repairing the damage done in human communities. Empathy makes it possible for us to continue to live together as fellow human beings after harm has been done. This may lead to a renewal of human relationships; forgiveness "aggressively seeks to repair the fractures of enmity."[14] Shriver calls this new relation "reconciliation," which is the aim of forgiveness. In a political context, then, forgiveness "calls for a collective turning from the past that neither ignores past evil nor excuses it, that neither overlooks justice nor reduces justice to revenge, that insists on the humanity of enemies even in their commission of dehumanizing deeds, and that values the justice that restores political community above the justice that destroys it."[15]

Why think that being forgiving is a virtue and that being unforgiving is a vice? To be able to forgive is important to our moral, social, and political lives. Resentment diminishes the quality of our relationships and can fuel violence; overcoming resentment heals and restores. Gandhi suggests that the violence of injustice, oppression, and exploitation will never cease as long as we carry hatred in our hearts for those who have wronged us: "The real love is to love them that hate you, to love your neighbor even though you distrust him. I have sound reasons for distrusting the English official world. If my love is sincere, I must love the Englishman in spite of my distrust. Of what avail is my love if it be only so long as I trust my friend? Even thieves do that."[16]

Although holding onto hatred is often cast in spiritual terms as corruption of the soul, such an orientation to wrongdoers has significant cultural implications that bear examination. In *Rambo and the Dalai Lama,* Gordon Fellman contrasts the Western orientation of human relationships, which is fundamentally adversarial, with a more peaceable nonviolent paradigm of mutuality found in other parts of the world.[17] Adversarial relations construct moral subjects who respond to experiences of hurt and rage with a desire for revenge; revenge is "a ritual that assumes that hurting can be met properly not by understanding, compassion, empathy, mediation, or anything but hurting in return."[18] Fellman suggests that we replace this destructive energy with rituals of forgiveness. "A culture of recognizing feelings, of accepting responsibility for behavior, of learning to ask for forgiveness, to give it, to receive it, would displace that of hurt/anger/vow-to-vengeance/revenge."[19] Such a paradigm shift would require that individuals learn genuine ways of coping with the troublesome parts of themselves and of others and, in so doing, develop a character type that replaces the adversarial ideal.

Those like Shriver and Fellman, who point toward the politics of peace-keeping, suggest that having a disposition to hold onto resentments, embitterments, vengeance, and rage is part of the orientation that fuels wars, domestic violence, familial vendettas, and other acts of violence. Being forgiving, then, would seem to cultivate more peaceable relations—or at least it does not exacerbate violence.

But many people committed to forgiveness and nonviolence fail to conceptualize forgiveness as a virtue, with a mean, an excess, and a deficiency. Even for many secular writers, forgiveness is a universal duty. As someone committed to nonviolence, I am sympathetic with claims that holding onto resentment and enmity fuels violence; yet, because norms for forgiveness seem unduly to burden the oppressed, I am uneasy with the prospect of setting up a universal moral precept that good people are those who forgive their wrongdoers.

WHEN SHOULD WE FORGIVE OTHERS?

Murphy suggests five grounds for forgiveness when someone has willfully wronged another: (1) because the person repented or had a change of heart; (2) because the person meant well (her motives were good); (3) because the person has suffered enough; (4) because the person has undergone humiliation (e.g., through rituals of apology); or (5) for history's sake, on the basis of one's past relationship with the wrongdoer. But Murphy also argues that when one of those conditions is met, we are not *obligated* to forgive, especially in the case of deep and heinous wrongs. To seek restoration at all costs—even at the cost of one's self-respect—can hardly be a virtue: "A too ready tendency to forgive may be a sign that one lacks self-respect. . . . If I count morally as much as anyone else (as surely I do), a failure to resent moral injuries done to me is a failure to care about the moral value incarnate in my own moral personality."[20] Therefore, the background condition for forgiveness is that it must be compatible with self-respect, respect for others as moral agents, and respect for the moral community.[21]

Murphy's analysis of forgiveness leaves open the question of whether, once the wrongdoer is forgiven, the relationship with the wrongdoer is fully restored. Because forgiveness is the overcoming of resentment toward the other, but not necessarily the reconciling of relations, it appears that one can forgive a wrongdoer and yet not wish to be in a social or personal relationship with that person in the future. Shriver, on the other hand, suggests that the aim of forgiveness is to be able to live compatibly together again.

Beatty also views reconciliation as the end of forgiveness. For him, forgiveness makes sense when a relationship of concern exists or existed between parties. Forgiveness is preceded by feeling offended, and offense is directly related to the sorts of expectations of others that we hold; to be offended, we must have expected better treatment from the offender. Thus, Beatty offers another consideration that we can add to the grounds for forgiveness that Murphy suggests: "The precondition for forgiveness, then, is the existence of a positive relation which is disturbed and often brought to awareness by the offense itself."[22]

BONE AND NORMS OF FORGIVENESS

The world in which Bone grew up is one where females viewed males as overgrown, rambunctious boys. Bone tells us that, as far as the women were concerned, "men could do anything, and everything they did, no matter how violent or mistaken, was viewed with humor and understanding. . . . What men did was just what men did."[23] Uncle Earle's bitterness lent him an air of attractiveness (24). The men, too, participated in valorizing male aggression: the impression that Daddy Glenn might kill someone "earned him a little respect" from the men around him (38). Goodnaturedly, jokingly, the men would discuss Daddy Glenn's violent temper and potential for rape: "He gets crazy when he's angry," they laughed. "Use his dick if he can't reach you with his arms, and that'll cripple you fast enough" (61).

Bone also learns that women desperately need the love of a man and that other women understand that need.[24] Mama needs Daddy Glenn, Alma tells the others, "needs him like a starving woman needs meat between her teeth, and I an't gonna let nobody take this away from her. Come on, Maybelle, you know there an't no way to say what's gonna happen between a man and a woman. That an't our business anyway, that's theirs" (41). Bone's Granny, telling the story of her own grandmother, says affectionately, "Woman was just obsessed with that man, obsessed to the point of madness. Used to cry like a dog in the night when he was gone" (27). And when Mama learns of Uncle Wade's verbal abuse and the pain it causes Aunt Alma, Bone hears Mama reassure Alma that Wade is a loving man and that Alma loves him— and Alma agrees (272).

When Glenn rages and then apologizes, Mama—typically—says to him, "It's all right, honey. I understand" (69). Bone realizes that Mama thinks that being patient and loving to Daddy Glenn and "making him feel strong and important would fix everything in time" (233). It is the women's responsibility to mother the men. As Aunt Ruth explains why Daddy Glenn seems to hate Bone, she says, "There's a way he's just a little boy himself, wanting more of your mama than you, wanting to be her baby more than her husband. And that an't so rare, I'll tell you. . . . Men are just little boys climbing up on titty whenever they can. Your mama knows it as well as I do. We all do" (123).

Mama teaches these responsibilities and attitudes to Bone, including the idea that women, powerless in the face of violence, are nevertheless responsible to behave so as to control it. "Mama told me I should show him that I loved him" (62), Bone tells readers. And after a severe beating behind a locked door, Bone is held and rocked in Mama's arms, but Mama asks, "Oh, girl. Oh, honey. Baby, what did you do? What did you do?" (107).

Afterward, Mama listens to Daddy Glenn's excuses and then comforts him. But Bone begins to question Mama's picture of the world: "What had I done?" Bone returns the question. "What was she asking? I wanted her to love me enough to leave him, to pack us up and take us away from him, to kill him if need be" (107). But Mama continues to coddle Daddy Glenn. Later, when it is clear that Glenn's frustration at his family's mistreatment of him threatens to escalate his rage, Mama warns Bone, "Let's be careful for a while, Bone. Be real careful, Baby" (207).

Bone internalizes this sense of responsibility: "I would stand rigid, ashamed but unable to pull away, afraid of making him angry, afraid of what he might tell Mama, and at the same time, afraid of hurting his feelings" (108). Through both Glenn's overt harms and Mama's alliance with him, Bone comes to see herself as evil:

> When Daddy Glenn beat me there was always a reason, and Mama would stand right outside the bathroom door. Afterward she would cry and wash my face and tell me not to be so stubborn, not to make him mad. . . . Sometimes when I looked up into his red features and blazing eyes, I knew that it was nothing I had done that made him beat me. It was just me, the fact of my life, who I was in his eyes and mine. I was evil. Of course I was. I admitted it to myself. (110)

When Glenn again assaults Bone, and Mama has to face public humiliation as Earle and Beau beat up Glenn in retaliation, Bone again assumes responsibility: "It was my fault, everything. . . . I kept trying to figure out how I could have prevented it all from happening . . . gone to Mama and made sure she knew that I had deserved that beating" (249).

Although Bone internalizes certain cultural and familial beliefs and values (for example, awareness of class inferiority, desire for economic stability and discouragement at its unattainability, and dependency on the hierarchy of racialism to bolster the status of "poor white trash"), that internalization is not complete: she becomes increasingly confused and then skeptical, questioning females' responsibility. *Why* is men's violent and intimidating conduct excusable when they don't get what they want? *Why* does Mama suggest that Bone is responsible to control Daddy Glenn's violence? And why is it *Bone's* responsibility to protect Mama from hurt?

This confusion over responsibilities extends to the mother–daughter relationship. Early on, Bone understands that she has the task of "being happy for Mama" so Mama can heal (49). Because of Bone's intense passion for Mama, and because she understands that Mama needs Daddy Glenn, Bone wants to protect Mama from the knowledge of the abuse: "More terrified of hurting her than of anything that might happen to me, I would work as hard as he did to make sure she never knew." But this role reversal burdens Bone with mothering responsibilities that she is not capable of handling and, at the same time, deprives her of the protection she so badly needs herself: "It was as if I was her mother now, holding her safe, and she was my child, happy to lean on my strong, straight back" (118). Mama's sense of responsibility to her daughter having been gradually eroded, Bone's vulnerability to Glenn's repeated assaults culminates in rape and abandonment.

IS REFUSING TO FORGIVE A DEFICIENCY IN THIS CASE?

The moral wrongdoing for which Glenn is accountable is the long-term trauma Bone suffers because of physical and sexual assault. The moral wrongdoing for which Mama is responsible is the betrayal and abandonment of Bone, the neglect of her duties as a mother to protect her child from harm. Still, one of the central themes in *Bastard Out of Carolina* is the socialization process by and through which male violence is tolerated or condoned; women are placed in a moral landscape in which they should and do forgive men's violence and in which a woman's love for her man is often so (understandably, naturally) overpowering that she cannot help but value her relationship with him above all else and protect it at all cost.

In spite of this moral landscape, more is happening with Bone internally than just the absorption of cultural and familial attitudes toward violence and gender: Bone comes to see both Mama and Glenn as culpable. As Bone grows up, she absorbs the meaning of being a poor female: "This body, like my aunts' bodies, was born to be worked to death, used up, and thrown away. . . . I was part of the trash down in the mud-stained cabins, fighting with the darkies and stealing ungratefully from our betters, stupid, coarse, born to shame and death" (206). Bone's desire for release from shame— shame of want, shame of invasion—becomes a desire for power: "It was hunger I felt then, raw and terrible, a shaking deep down inside me, as if my rage had used up everything I had ever eaten . . . that dizzy desperate hunger edged with hatred and an aching lust to hurt somebody back. It was a hunger in the back of the throat, not the belly, an echoing emptiness that ached for the release of screaming" (98). Bone longed to be half again as dangerous as the males in her culture (100), to have powerful fists like Daddy Glenn's (109), and thus found herself identifying with masculinity, revenge, and antisocial conduct (217).

So Bone understands Glenn's shame; she too has experienced the hunger of poverty, the desperation of want, the humiliation of inferiority (207). But understanding is not the same as forgiving. "Hateful man," Bone whispers. "I don't care if his daddy does treat him bad. I don't care why he's so mean. He's hateful" (209). And after tormenting herself with blame for having revealed her bruises to Mama and setting in motion the retaliatory beating of Daddy Glenn, Bone releases herself from responsibility for Glenn's actions: "No, it did not matter whether I had screamed or not. It had all been the way he wanted it. It had nothing to do with me or anything I had done. It was an animal thing, just him using me" (253).

But exonerating herself with respect to Mama is a different matter. As Bone increasingly realizes that Mama loves Daddy Glenn more than her—or at least is willing to sacrifice Bone to protect her relationship with Daddy Glenn—Bone is compelled to confront her disillusionment with and resentment of her mother. Before Glenn became part of their lives, Mama had been a source of intimacy and safety. "I would have cut off my head before I let them cut my hair and lose the unspeakable pleasure of being drawn up onto Mama's lap every evening," Bone says (30). But as Mama becomes increasingly torn between her love for Glenn and her responsibility to her daughter, she becomes more and more unfeeling toward Bone (252). Likewise, Mama goes from being a source of truth (18) to being someone who lacks perception. Bone speculates that she has more clarity of vision than her Mama does (277, 306). And when Mama consoles Daddy Glenn after having witnessed the rape scene, leaving Bone in the car, Bone says, "Rage burned in my belly and came up my throat. I'd said I could never hate her, but I hated her now for the way she held him, the way she stood there crying over him. Could she love me and still hold him like that?" (291).

It is Aunt Raylene who inadvertently plays a central role in shifting Bone's moral framework about her mother. Raylene presents, perhaps, the most significant, if subtle, pressure on Bone because Raylene herself defies norms for femininity and Bone has come to trust her. Raylene tells the story of the woman she had loved. Raylene says she had made her lover choose between her baby and Raylene and that Raylene's lover had chosen her baby. Raylene's point is that no woman should be put in that position, and she presses upon Bone her conviction that Mama still loves Bone and will never forgive herself for having abandoned her. After offering an excuse—Mama was put in an impossible situation, these are mitigating circumstances—Raylene goes on to offer grounds for Bone to overcome her resentment and thus forgive Mama—for the sake of history and the love between them, because Mama would suffer terribly the consequences of her wrongdoing, and so on.

But the idea festers in Bone's mind. She lies still in bed, thinking about the woman Raylene had loved, "the woman who had loved her child more" (302). Bone considers again the possibility that Mama's actions are excusable. And she concludes that they were not. And it was Raylene who gave her the answer: Mama could have chosen otherwise. Another woman had done so. Bone, then, is left with the choice of overcoming her resentment toward Mama or withholding forgiveness. And, although Raylene is probably right to suggest that grounds for forgiveness can be met, Bone rejects that line of reasoning: given the nature of the wrongdoing, those conditions are not sufficient. For all her love and understanding, Bone could not spare her Mama at the end: "I wanted to tell her lies, tell her that I had never doubted her, that nothing could make any difference to my love for her, but I couldn't. I had lost my mama. She was a stranger to me" (306); "My mama had abandoned me, and that was the only thing that mattered. . . . How do you forgive somebody when you cannot even speak her name?" (302).

In examining forgiveness as a virtue with respect to Bone and the harms done to her, I will begin with a discussion of Daddy Glenn. If acknowledging one's wrongdoing is important to reconciliation, as both Shriver and Murphy suggest, then Bone does not have a *reason* to reconcile with Daddy Glenn. Daddy Glenn gives little indication of being genuinely sorry for the numerous injuries he inflicted on Bone. Nor does he seem to have suffered as a result of his wrongdoing. Furthermore, if we consider Beatty's claim that the existence of a positive relationship is a precondition of forgiveness, then Bone has another reason not to forgive Glenn, for their relationship was, from the start, infused with conflict, jealousy, and suspicion.

But Bone's response to Daddy Glenn is more complicated than that. Looking at her response from Shriver's framework, we see that her moral judgment of Daddy Glenn does not preclude her ability to empathize with him, but neither does it negate her fantasies of revenge. Even if the wrongdoer, Daddy Glenn, does not give her a reason to forgive him, does Bone have other moral reasons to overcome her feelings of vengeance and resentment?

The opportunity to forgive arises when one becomes aware that a wrong or injustice has been done. Feelings of anger and resentment and a desire for revenge signal the unjust situation or event. As Marilyn Frye explains, one has these feelings when one sees oneself as wronged—when someone has hindered one in a way that one takes to be unjust or unfair.[25] Thus, anger and resentment are cognitively linked to perceived injustices or wrongs. And Aristotle argues that not to feel anger when one or someone who matters to one has been insulted is a deficiency of character. In other words, feelings of anger and resentment are both morally appropriate and epistemologically significant with respect to wrongs and injustices. The question the wronged party faces is what ought to—or can be—done about that wrong or injustice? Deciding when to forgive, then, often involves considerations of what one can do to best serve justice. And justice may require that the wrongdoer be punished—for example, through the legal system. As Shriver says, forbearance of vengeance does not require that one give up *all* versions of punishment.[26] But when it is clear that the wrongdoer is not going to be punished, as it is in Bone's case, then the relation between injustice and just deserts is not served. Feelings of vengeance, then, function as an important reminder that an injustice yet remains to be addressed.

Nonetheless, there is a risk involved in holding onto such feelings, as Shriver reminds us, because these feelings fuel new enmity: "Who are more ferocious in battle than the morally empowered? Who is more tempted to make sure that the enemy pays for its crimes many times over?"[27] Yet there is a danger, too, in letting go of feelings of vengeance and resentment; to do so runs the risk that the injustice will fade from memory, eliding the moral judgment and moving the wronged toward acquiescence to a wrongful action or condition. Bone seems to be *finding the mean* by not suppressing feelings of vengeance toward Daddy Glenn. She is, as Murphy puts it, taking herself seriously as a self-respecting member of the moral community by doing what she can to stake a claim in the realm of justice.

What about her unforgiving attitude toward her mother? There is legitimate concern that such a position feeds a cultural climate of mother blaming. Paula Caplan argues that our culture is fixated on blaming mothers for a myriad of issues that are better understood as the effects of socialization on a historically oppressed class of individuals.[28] Daughters, then, learn to blame, rather than understand and forgive, their mothers. In my view, however, it is not so much that Bone blames her mother as it is that she refuses to overcome her resentment. That is, she exhibits empathy with her mother's situation while still holding her mother accountable.[29] That this accountability is both psychologically and morally significant is suggested by a brief look at Alice Miller's work.

Miller argues that for someone who has been morally wronged to heal therapeutically, that person must be able to know truths about his or her feelings. Miller disagrees with therapists who view being unforgiving as hampering one's healing process. She argues that such an approach by therapists constitutes "pedagogic manipulation—one, moreover, whose purpose was to serve only traditional morality but not the interest of the patient."[30] Traditional morality, as I have suggested, urges the wronged subjugated person to forgive more powerful, abusive, or oppressive wrongdoers. In pressing traditional morality about the universal value of forgiveness, Miller argues, therapists obscure the very process the patient is undertaking, for to advocate forgiving one's parents is to imply that the patient must repress feelings of anger, betrayal, and hurt, which may make a superficial reconciliation possible—but at great cost to the wronged person.

In interesting ways, the views of Martin Luther King on the moral attitudes necessary for black people's success in the civil rights movement both complement and complicate an understanding of the moral status of being unforgiving. Like Shriver and Miller, King argues that those who are in positions of relative powerlessness and are resentful of injustices and wrongs done to them must come to understand the sources of their bitterness before any sort of healing can take place. Furthermore, King, like Miller, worries that repressed emotions do more harm than good: "The Negro has many pent-up resentments and latent frustrations, and he must release them. So let him march; let him make prayer pilgrimages to the city hall; let him go on freedom rides—and try to understand why he must do so. If his repressed emotions are not released in nonviolent ways, they will seek expression through violence; this is not a threat but a fact of history."[31] Still, King does not seem to take the view that remaining unforgiving toward one's wrongdoers would ever be morally permissible, let alone appropriate. Abhorring forces of bitterness and hatred, King advocates that black people demonstrate good will and a refusal to seek revenge: "Many white men fear retaliation. The job of the Negro is to show them that they have nothing to fear, that the Negro understands and forgives and is ready to forget the past."[32]

Although Miller and King agree that repression of resentment has worse psychological consequences for a person than the acknowledgment and understanding of it, they seem to disagree on the moral evaluation of resentment. King would not, I believe, approve of Bone's unforgiving stance toward either her father or her mother because King views forgiveness as an obligation we owe one another; meanwhile, Miller—in repudiating traditional morality—champions the wronged party who withholds forgiveness. Murphy, too, would likely accept the interpretation that Bone does not have grounds to forgive either Mama or Daddy Glenn.

I am inclined to think that Mama's betrayal and abandonment of Bone repeatedly in Bone's life and especially at the end of the novel, after Mama has witnessed Daddy Glenn's rape of Bone, are unforgivable. In other words, I am suggesting that Mama's conduct does not fall in what Card calls a "gray zone."[33] If we consider forgiveness a virtue, being unforgiving in this case does not constitute a moral deficiency.

Mama's betrayal of Bone is unforgivable—but, I would add, things are only unforgivable *as they stand*. Bone's feelings of resentment and anguish toward Mama have a different history from her feelings toward Daddy Glenn; Bone's body memories of Mama signify a deeply held passion and longing that has not yet been extinguished. As both Shriver and Beatty argue, forgiveness enables people in conflict with one another to be able to live together again, and Beatty seems to imply that an earlier positive relationship between an injured party and a wrongdoer is a strong impetus to forgive. Given Bone's character and her long-held love for Mama, it is likely that Bone will suffer from her own unforgiving stance, grieving her loss of Mama's love and aching for reconciliation. *Bastard Out of Carolina* is a work of fiction, of course, but we might ask how Bone will continue to live with such conflicting feelings. Perhaps Bone needs to hold onto her resentment of Mama; in this way Bone can see clearly that the devastation wrought on their relationship is not her fault but, rather, Mama's responsibility. Perhaps, also, although it is appropriate not to forgive her now, it may cease to be appropriate not to forgive as the years go by. As Aristotle suggests, part of finding the mean with respect to anger is knowing when it is time to let go of it: we show an excess of anger if we hold grudges too long. What is the moral and temporal balance between being unforgiving and honoring past positive relationships?

One indicator might lie in the distinction between resentment and vengeance. If being unforgiving means holding onto resentment, it is one thing, and if being unforgiving means holding onto desire for vengeance, it is another. Vengeful feelings are likely to be more volatile, clearer in focus, stronger in energy, and perhaps more driven toward expression. If this view of vengeful feelings is right, then it suggests that there is more to worry about over time with respect to unforgiving attitudes that involve vengeance. It is significant, then, that Bone's negative feelings toward her mother are of a different degree than those toward Daddy Glenn: she feels vengeful toward her abuser and resentment toward her complicit mother. This differentiation in being unforgiving strikes me as appropriate—Bone has found the mean with respect to each person and each of their wrongs. But whether this mean *continues* to be the best response toward Mama remains open to the future—a future in which Mama could still turn out to be "the woman who had loved her child more" (302).

CONCLUSION

There are no necessary and sufficient conditions with respect to the mean for the virtues. But let me draw on Aristotle's advice in finding the mean. Every virtue has two contraries (the excess and the deficiency), and for nearly all virtues, one of the contraries is more opposing than the other. The more contrary extreme is the worse one. And Aristotle tells us that, when we are uncertain about where the mean lies, we ought to avoid the worse extreme. In the case of forgiveness, I believe that the more opposing contrary is being unforgiving. So if we are to err, we ought to err on the side of excess; that is, it is better to be too forgiving than to be deficient in forgiving.

Second, Aristotle suggests that each of us needs to know what we have a tendency to do and then, when uncertain about the mean, we should compensate by aiming in the other direction. If one has a disposition to be overly forgiving, one would want to aim more toward being less forgiving or forgiving less hastily. But allow me, on this point, to take liberties with Aristotle's advice: not only do we need to know what we individually are inclined toward, but we need to know how structural power relations have socialized us to view virtues and vices differently for different groups of people. In other words, we need to apply Aristotle's advice about compensating for individual tendencies to insights about socialized tendencies that, in the oppressed, prompt an excess of forgiveness in response to injustices and call being unforgiving a deficiency in character.

What would happen if, like Bone, women were less forgiving of those we love when they deeply and profoundly betray us? Pressure to forgive moral wrongdoings (fathers who rape, mothers who abandon) does not necessarily lead to forgiveness, but it can lead to guilt about one's feelings of resentment that, in turn, confuses accountability in one who has internalized self-blame for others' wrongful acts. Perhaps Bone can serve as a reminder to readers that accountability for certain harms is one of the more easily obscured and mystified aspects of our moral lives. Just retaining clarity on who is accountable for what requires that one stand against forces that obscure our moral understanding; it is itself an act of resistance.

NOTES

1. Jeffrie Murphy, "Forgiveness and Resentment," *Midwest Studies in Philosophy* 8 (1982): 503–16.
2. Aristotle, *Nicomachean Ethics,* trans. W. D. Ross, in *The Basic Works of Aristotle,* ed. Richard McKeon (New York: Random House, 1941), 1106b20.
3. Claudia Card, "Gender and Moral Luck," in *Identity, Character, Morality: Essays in Moral Psychology,* ed. Owen Flanagan and Amelie Rorty (Cambridge: MIT Press, 1990). Card does not use the language of virtue, however.
4. Jean Hampton and Jeffrie Murphy, *Forgiveness and Mercy* (Cambridge: Cambridge University Press, 1988).
5. Hampton and Murphy, *Forgiveness and Mercy,* 54.
6. Hampton and Murphy, *Forgiveness and Mercy,* 56.
7. Hampton and Murphy, *Forgiveness and Mercy,* 59–60.
8. Hampton and Murphy, *Forgiveness and Mercy,* 148.
9. Murphy writes,

To *justify* is to say that an action is prima facie wrong; but given other morally relevant factors (e.g. the need to save a life), the action was—all morally relevant factors considered—the right thing to do.

To *excuse* is to say that an action is morally wrong; but given certain factors about the agent (e.g. insanity), it would be unfair to hold the wrongdoer responsible or blame him for the wrong action.

To be *merciful* is to treat a person less harshly than given norms or standards dictate. When Portia advises Shylock to show mercy, she is asking that he accept a payment less harsh than the one which, given the terms of his bargain, he has a right to demand. To pardon someone is not simply to change the way one feels about her, but to let her avoid what may well be her just deserts. (Murphy, *Forgiveness and Resentment*, 506)

10. I am assuming, but will not argue for, a cognitive theory of emotions.

11. Joseph Beatty, "Forgiveness," *American Philosophical Quarterly* 7, no. 3 (1970): 246–52.

12. Donald W. Shriver Jr., *An Ethic for Enemies: Forgiveness in Politics* (New York: Oxford University Press, 1995), 7.

13. Shriver, *An Ethic for Enemies,* 8.

14. Shriver, *An Ethic for Enemies,* 8.

15. Shriver, *An Ethic for Enemies,* 9.

16. Mohandas Gandhi, *Gandhi on Non-Violence* (New York: New Directions Publishing Co., 1965), 58.

17. Gordon Fellman, *Rambo and the Dalai Lama: The Compulsion to Win and Its Threat to Human Survival* (New York: State University of New York Press, 1998).

18. Fellman, *Rambo and the Dalai Lama,* 173.

19. Fellman, *Rambo and the Dalai Lama,* 173.

20. Murphy, "Forgiveness and Resentment," 505.

21. Murphy, "Forgiveness and Resentment," 508.

22. Beatty, "Forgiveness," 247.

23. Dorothy Allison, *Bastard Out of Carolina* (New York: Plume, 1993), 23. Hereafter, page citations appear in the text.

24. The women also acknowledge that Daddy Glenn desperately needs Mama, but his need is disapproved of whereas Mama's need is endorsed: "Yeah, Glenn loves Anney. He loves her like a gambler loves a fast racehorse or a desperate man loves whiskey. That kind of love eats a man up. I don't trust that boy, don't want our Anney marrying him" (41).

25. Marilyn Frye, "A Note on Anger," in her *The Politics of Reality: Essays in Feminist Theory* (Freedom, Calif.: Crossing Press, 1983), 85.

26. Shriver, *An Ethic for Enemies,* 8.

27. Shriver, *An Ethic for Enemies,* 8.

28. Paula Caplan, *Don't Blame Mother: Mending the Mother–Daughter Relationship* (New York: Harper and Row, 1990).

29. My sense is that there is a difference in contemporary society between blaming someone and holding someone accountable, but the development of this idea is beyond the scope of this chapter. In brief, though, I think that the contemporary concept of blame is but a truncated version of the ancient Greek notion of blameworthiness and that our version of blame short-circuits the important step of giving and taking an accounting of one another's conduct. *Blame,* nowadays, is a pejorative term, but appropriately so, because when we blame someone we are skipping the dialogical process that all parties need to be engaged in of trying to understand how and

why moral wrongs have come to be done and, even, whether or not a prima facie moral wrong should be assessed as one.

30. Alice Miller, *Banished Knowledge: Facing Childhood Injuries,* trans. Leila Vennewitz (New York: Anchor Books/Doubleday, 1990), 153.

31. Martin Luther King Jr., "Letter from Birmingham Jail," in his *Why We Can't Wait* (New York: Harper and Row, 1964).

32. Martin Luther King Jr., *Stride toward Freedom* (New York: Harper and Brothers, 1958), 215.

33. This term is from Claudia Card's keynote address at the Feminist Ethics Revisited Conference in 1999.

IV

THINKING RIGHT, FEELING GOOD

10

Gender and Moral Reasoning Revisited: Reengaging Feminist Psychology

Phyllis Rooney

I should like to take up two topics that were very much a part of feminist philosophical discussions in ethics in the early to mid-1980s yet have been somewhat in the background in the past decade or so. The first is the question of moral *reasoning* and, especially, how feminist work can contribute to enhanced notions of moral reasoning. The second (related) topic is the role of feminist work in psychology and how it might continue to interact productively with feminist work undertaken more directly under the rubric of philosophy.

Carol Gilligan's work on moral development has provided the by now well-known catalyst for a significant conversation between feminist psychologists and philosophers (among others) about the role of gender in moral reasoning.[1] The familiar articulation of this work proposed differences between the female-inflected "care voice" or "care reasoning" and the male-inflected "justice reasoning" in moral deliberations. Although further studies have raised questions about the significance of the gender correlation with the two voices, many feminist ethicists have proceeded to effectively use the care/justice dichotomy as a useful tool with which to engage questions about the "maleness" of much traditional moral theorizing. This has motivated significant reflection on aspects of moral life that were not granted sufficient attention in traditional philosophical theories. The following are among the areas and topics that have benefited from this feminist attention: conceptions of selfhood and agency, autonomy, moral perception, partiality and impartiality, responsibility, friendship, and relationships of dependency.

Relatively absent, however, from this list of topics directly attended to by feminists is moral *reasoning*. I do not want to suggest that this topic is quite separate from these others. On the contrary, as part of my discussion will show, feminist ethics contributes to an understanding of moral reasoning, especially by helping to show that moral reasoning cannot be adequately theorized independently of a more sophisticated understanding of moral reasoners. This enhanced understanding takes into account moral agents' situatedness with respect to various kinds of relationships; the forms of agency, autonomy, and community granted them in their social and cultural settings; and the political contexts they inhabit that enable or inhibit various forms of moral perception and moral deliberation. Yet I think that we also need to foreground a more direct feminist revaluation of moral reasoning for two reasons. First, some aspects of traditional theorizing about moral reasoning and gender still need to be quite directly challenged by feminists, and second, more recent work on *gender* in feminist psychology (on gender and cognition specifically) suggests interesting new ways to think about gender and moral reasoning and lays the groundwork for developing enhanced general models of moral reasoning.

The meaning and deployment of *gender* as an analytical category has been quite contentious in feminist theory. And, certainly, questions about the extent and significance of gender in connection with the two moral voices have contributed to that debate. It is useful to recall some of the specific concerns that have arisen concerning this proposed gender correlation. First, subsequent empirical studies cast doubt on the existence and extent of the gender correlation with the two moral voices; second, it was noted that even if some kind of gender correlation emerged from a particular study (in a particular social context), there were serious problems with generalizing to other social and cultural contexts; third, even if some kind of gender correlation emerged in a particular context, the complex role of gender stereotypes and expectations (on the part of subjects, data collectors, theoretical interpreters, and commentators) rendered such a correlation less than transparent; and, finally, even if women in certain contexts were more likely to speak in a "different" care voice, this was not something that could be readily affirmed by feminists (as, say, a different yet equally valuable voice) because it could well bespeak the voice of the oppressed—and feminist endorsement could then amount to a kind of normalization of that oppression.[2] All of this, at the very least, provoked further reflection on the theoretical understandings of gender used in various social and psychological studies and, for feminist interests in particular, drew attention to the ways in which such understandings might reveal or conceal the workings of gender as they are situated within and constituted by structures of inequality and power. I will explore some of these significant *situational* aspects of gender, as suggested by work in feminist psychology in particular. By pressing this line of exploration with the reason and gender issue, we can also begin to shed new light on important *situational* aspects of moral reasoning. First, though, some backtracking is necessary to foreground specific problems with older ways of thinking about reason and gender and to clear the way for new ways of thinking about gender and about reasoning.

Despite problems with gender correlation, feminist philosophers have effectively used the care/justice dichotomy as a useful tool with which to review various aspects of traditional moral theorizing, especially those that had acquired gender associations. For example, critical reflection on particular aspects of the "justice" ideal in moral reasoning have helped to bring into sharper relief some concerns with the traditional predominance of *moral rationalism*. In placing reason at the heart of morality, moral rationalism gives prominence to the systematization of moral rules or principles with relatively high degrees of generality and abstraction, typically assuming attendant modes or qualities of moral agency and selfhood that stress autonomy, consistency, and control.[3] The gender issue here involves, in part, the traditional association of these modes or qualities with maleness. That issue, as I want to develop it here, is *not* the question about whether in fact males are more likely to exhibit these approaches and qualities. (Too often this particular question has functioned as a red herring, deflecting attention from other important questions. In addition, empirical studies on gender and moral development have shown how complicated and intractable this question can be.) The concern, instead, is that these modes and qualities have regularly *been associated with* maleness in their theoretical and imaginative elucidation: as a special case of philosophical accounts of reason more generally, these qualities have often been valued through an explicit or implicit contrast with different (and often devalued) modes or qualities cast as female or "feminine."[4]

Because of the traditional significance of reason in moral deliberation, philosophers regularly claimed or assumed that women's weaker reasoning capacities excluded them from the ideals of moral rationality to which men could aspire (though women were, on occasion, assigned their own special moral understandings and virtues). Arthur Schopenhauer's views are not atypical in this regard:

> The weakness of [women's] reasoning faculty also explains why it is that women show more sympathy for the unfortunate than men do . . . and why it is that they are inferior to men in point of justice, and less honorable and conscientious. For it is just because their reasoning power is weak that present circumstances have such a hold over them, and those concrete things which lie directly before their eyes exercise a power which is seldom counteracted to any extent by abstract principles of thought, by fixed rules of conduct, firm resolutions . . . or regard of what is absent and remote.[5]

Claims about women's "different" moral voice must, I think, continue to be assessed against the backdrop of this historical legacy, which (among other things) constructed women's difference in terms of their supposed weaker reasoning capacity.

It would be inaccurate to say that this assumption about women's inferior rationality has been an explicit (or perhaps even implicit) element in the articulation of the different moral voices—by Gilligan or her commentators. Yet I contend that in the feminist literature there has been *an insufficient reading against the grain* of this traditional supposition. This is so despite the fact that Gilligan, in a later work, uses the term *care reasoning* to describe the "different" moral perspective and despite her clear admonitions against reading the care perspective as anything less than an equally valuable one.[6] The problem, as I see it, has been as much in the descriptions of the different voices that her interpreters expanded on as it has been in Gilligan's own wording—though, as I will indicate with some textual examples below, Gilligan contributed somewhat to this problem. In short, the problem is that we are the inheritors of a historical legacy that made the association between maleness and rationality (or, more accurately, a particular conception of rationality) so automatic that we need to take specific steps to counteract it, especially when we set out to read and hear different voices while being mindful of the workings of gender.

Marilyn Friedman quite accurately recapitulates a familiar articulation of the different moral voices when she writes,

> The standard, more typically "male," moral voice . . . derives moral judgments about particular cases from *abstract, universalized moral rules and principles* that are substantively concerned with justice and rights. . . . By contrast, the different, more characteristically "female," moral voice that Gilligan heard in her studies *eschews abstract rules and principles*. This moral voice derives moral judgments from the contextual detail of situations grasped as specific and unique. . . . [T]he motivating vision of this ethics is "that everyone will be responded to and included, that no one will be left alone or hurt."[7]

As my emphasis in this quote indicates, I want to draw attention to this hearing/reading of the male voice in terms of the application of abstract moral principles and of the female voice in terms of the absence of such an application. The difference could quite plausibly be expressed in terms of the application of different kinds of universal principles (as, indeed, some have argued). One could well argue, I think, that the "motivating vision" of the care ethic that is mentioned at the end of the above passage is a universal principle, perhaps even an abstract one. The meaning of the term *abstract* is not as transparent as is often assumed in these discussions. Abstraction is, in fact, something of a relative and situated notion—as when we abstract from *some* of the *specifics* or *saliencies* of a given *situation* and not others. Abstracting from a (multifaceted) moral situation with respect to particular kinds of relationships and responsibilities among individuals in it, and not with respect to specific juridical rights of those individuals as autonomous agents, is one way of abstracting from the situation; another way involves abstracting with respect to the latter and not the former (and these, clearly, need not be the only ways of abstracting). It is, unfortunately, the traditional association between conceptions and ideals of maleness and of rationality (typically fleshed in terms of principles, autonomy, universality, and abstraction) that seems to automatically lend voice to certain ways of reading gender differences in these contexts and not alternative ways that, I am suggesting, are also quite plausible.

In some cases, commentators' descriptions of the different voices have gone beyond what Gilligan actually says; indeed, her work lends itself to multiple readings and interpretations, and she does note in her introduction that she was setting out to "focus a problem of interpretation rather than to represent a generalization about either sex."[8] However, at the cost of going over well-traveled ground again, I want to draw attention to a few places where Gilligan expands on her respondents' words in a way that is somewhat problematic. In one chapter she draws substantial generalizations about the justice and care voices from two specific eleven-year-old respondents, Jake and Amy. Why these two? They highlight specific contours of difference that Gilligan wants to elucidate in her distinction between the care and justice voices. But it is not entirely clear whether these two are quite typical of male and female respondents, respectively, in which case one might attempt to make some generalizations about gender from them. More problematically, Gilligan characterizes some of the differences between them in a way that, for my purposes in this chapter, is not distanced enough from some gender stereotypes about reasoning.

Gilligan notes that, when presented with some moral dilemmas, Jake used such wording as "the only thing that is totally logical," "sort of like a math problem with humans," and "there can only be right and wrong in judgment."[9] From this Gilligan summarizes thus: "[Jake] relies on the conventions of logic to deduce the solution of this dilemma. . . . Failing to see the dilemma as a self-contained problem in moral logic, [Amy] does not discern the internal structure of its resolution."[10] In these contexts Gilligan seems to latch onto words like *logical* in Jake's response and draws conclusions that, in my view, go beyond what is warranted. Presumably Jake was using *logical* in the regular colloquial sense as something like "clear," "organized," "precise"—there is no reason to think that, given his age, he was at all familiar with the conventions of deductive logic that Gilligan attributes to him. (It is not at all evident that, in fact, the conventions of deductive logic readily apply to the way Jake was going about his deliberations.)

In another example, Gilligan notes that when asked how responsibility to oneself and responsibility to others should be distributed in cases of conflict, Jake answered, "You go about one-fourth to the others and three-fourths to yourself."[11] Gilligan summarizes here as follows: "Jake constructs the dilemma as a mathematical equation, deriving a formula that guides the solution: one-fourth to others, three-fourths to yourself."[12] The more precise mathematical language here (with "mathematical equation" and "formula") is something that, again, is Gilligan's addition. Furthermore, she alters Jake's comment—he had said *"about* one-fourth"—adding a degree of precision that presumably justifies the use of the mathematical terms *equation* and *formula*. One could well imagine alternative follow-ups to these statements by the somewhat laconic Jake. For example, if he were asked "Why do you say *'about* one-fourth . . . '?" he might well give an answer like, "Well, it would depend on whether these others were my buddies, or my parents, or people I didn't care about"—in short, an "Amy-type" answer! The point of being somewhat picky about wording here is to highlight my resistance to readings of differences that I think draw too readily on traditional gender-inflected stereotypes about reasoning. In this case, we are also getting too close to traditional assumptions about "natural" male superiority in mathematics and logic, which (in part because of that supposed superiority) were typically taken as paradigms of reason—to the point, in fact, that many philosophers have thought that moral reasoning should conform to modes of mathematical and logical reasoning. My concern here also ties in with the concern about the selection of the seemingly hyperlogical and hypermathematical Jake as Gilligan's prime representative of the justice voice in this particular context.

While, as I stress earlier, Gilligan's work lends itself to multiple interpretations (including, as I will discuss below, multiple gender-sensitive ones), and while some of the familiar generalizations about gender associated with the care and justice voices are in part due to commentators' additions, my point here has been to note some ways in which Gilligan herself fails to discourage possible gender-stereotypical expansions. Friedman has commented that, despite subsequent empirical studies that cast doubt on the significance or even existence of a gender difference in moral voices, that difference has taken hold in various ways. She speculates that this is because of the way the difference picks out the fact that morality is "gendered" and that the genders are "moralized": in most middle-class Western industrial contexts, she contends, "women and men are associated with different moral norms and values at the level of stereotypes, symbols, and myths that contribute to the social construction of gender."[13] In other words, the "difference" at least corresponds closely to norms and expectations of female and male moral behavior—whether or not it corresponds to actual behavior. In addition, as feminist work in psychology and sociology has been showing, it is not easy to perceive, read, or hear outside such gender norms, expectations, and symbols in significantly gender-regimented societies.[14] This is not to say, however, that conscious willful attempts to read against the grain of certain kinds of gender stereotypes is impossible—indeed, such readings form the basis of much feminist perception and theorizing.

I have so far been arguing for a particular corrective for one aspect of the familiar rendering of the care/justice difference—one that specifically draws attention to traditional assumptions about gender and moral reasoning. But now various questions can arise: How are we to proceed from here? Do we deny or overlook possible gender differences? Might we still usefully cull something about gender and moral reasoning from these empirical studies, something that does not draw (however subtly) on old presuppositions about women's weaker reasoning capacity? As mentioned earlier, one approach that Gilligan and others have adopted involves talking about a different yet equally valuable (perhaps, to some, more valuable) "care reasoning." But my argument so far also speaks against the ready adoption of this alternative, for it implies that justice reasoning and care reasoning are two relatively distinct, internally coherent forms or modes of moral reasoning. To my mind, this distinction is problematic in that it draws on questionable assumptions about gender: for example, as noted earlier, gender-marked differentiation too easily prompts the supposition that one mode of reasoning uses abstract principles and the other does not. More generally, the problem is that these two forms of moral reasoning are granted a kind of coherent uniformity and identity that rest significantly on the stability of certain kinds of gender assumptions and symbols, linked to presumptions about gender dimorphism that have come under critical scrutiny in feminist theory.

On the other hand, one cannot assume that gender never makes a difference in moral deliberations. As I discuss below, empirical studies continue to provoke interesting reflection on gender in relation to moral reasoning. What I promote is a more direct critical examination of the meanings and interpretations of *gender* that are used throughout this discussion. I proceed to explore a particular form of analysis that has emerged more recently in feminist work in psychology, and I examine some implications of this type of analysis for our thinking about moral reasoning.

Psychological research on sex/gender differences in the past two decades has engendered much debate about the meaning and significance of *gender*. From this somewhat broader critical perspective, some take Gilligan's approach as representative of a body of work that assesses gender and gender differences in terms of relatively stable "inner" intrapsychic traits or dispositions, which might be thought of as the result of *distal* factors of nature or nurture or some combination of both. "Distal" has here the sense of long-term causation and development along the lines of biology or socialization and other "distant" factors with long-range effects. This approach to gender is contrasted with an understanding of gender as a significant site of social regulation, as *situationally* reinforced and maintained in an *ongoing proximal* way by gender norms, practices, and expectations, linked in some cases to power differentials. This focus on different theoretical approaches to gender has emerged, in part, out of feminist psychologists' drive to open up space in psychology for reflection on the political commitments involved in different research programs. Martha Mednick describes a specific limitation of the individual, intrapsychic approach to sex differences in terms of this larger political focus: "An intrapsychic emphasis places the burden of change *entirely* on the person and does not lead scientific inquiry to an examination of cultural, socioeconomic, structural, or contemporaneous situational factors that may affect behavior."[15]

This shift to a more situational view of gender has been significantly encouraged by reflection on the many empirical studies on gender and various cognitive and behavioral capacities (including moral capacities and deliberations) that, taken together, have yielded quite mixed results concerning the existence and extent of sex differences. One prominent theorist in this field, Rhoda Unger, has remarked that these numerous studies began to yield gender differences that had a "now you see them, now you don't" quality![16] What is additionally noteworthy is that these appearances and disappearances were often the result of modifications of the experimental *situations*. Among such modifications are the following: changing the types of instructions given with specific tasks (this seems to draw differentially on gender expectations), changing the experimenter to one of a different sex, changing tasks from public to private contexts or vice versa (people seem to conform more to gender roles and gender stereotypes in public settings), and changing the sex or status composition of groups in cases in which group behavior and interaction were involved.[17] Modifications like this latter one, in particular, have also helped to locate sex/gender as one parameter of social/status differentiation that can interact with (or, in some cases, be eclipsed by) other differences that are socially salient in specific contexts— these might relate to race, class, employer/employee status differentials, or something else. Clearly, these results amplify the concern, mentioned earlier, about generalizing gender findings—about moral reasoning and so forth— from particular social and cultural contexts to others.

Findings about the ways in which gender-inflected traits and differences are situationally sensitive prompt a move toward incorporating an understanding of gender as significantly *dynamic* and *interactive*. "Sex-related phenomena," in the words of one theorist summarizing this research, involve a "process . . . molded by situational pressures and ultimately understandable only in the context of social interaction."[18] Gender differences are often more apparent in gender-schematic situations and around gender-schematic people—that is, people who draw (more than others) on gender as an organizational tool in their perceptions and thinking about themselves and others. This view of gender directs our attention "outward" to the ongoing practices, mechanisms, and institutions of gendering in gender-schematic social contexts, instead of simply "inward" to biological and psychological mechanisms in the development of relatively *stable* "inner" traits. It would be a mistake to take these two approaches to gender as simply antagonistic or mutually exclusive: what is perhaps most pertinent is the critical perspective on gender that the debate about these approaches has engendered in feminist psychology, particularly in the way that the debate brings attention to the (often implicit) social and political commitments involved in different methodological programs adopted for the scientific study of sex and gender.[19]

It is instructive for my purposes here to note a particular study that was designed to address this "stable versus situational" question with respect to gender and moral reasoning. Nancy Clopton and Gwendolyn Sorell took up the concern expressed by some psychologists that "Gilligan's theory may derive from a bias that exaggerates differences in disposition between women and men and overlooks differences in social structure, such as power differentials, that press for different behavior in the two sexes."[20] In assessing "how situational characteristics affect moral reasoning orientation," they restricted their study to female and male parents of both handicapped and nonhandicapped children, and moral dilemmas were restricted to real life parenting situations—some that the parents elicited from their own experience. No significant gender differences were found in what the researchers call "moral reasoning orientation scores" (including "care scores") when the dilemmas were restricted in this way. They also mention other studies using standardized hypothetical dilemmas that found no gender differences and others still that did find some gender differences when respondents could elicit descriptions of dilemmas from their own life experiences (that is, without the kind of restrictions that Clopton and Sorell developed in their own study). They find that their study supports the general conclusion that, where they occur, "[gender] differences in moral reasoning orientation result from differences in current life situations rather than from stable gender characteristics."[21] Though Gilligan is often cast on the "stable intrapsychic traits" side of this gender debate, it is noteworthy that in a later article she recognizes something of a situational effect with moral perspectives when she notes studies that revealed that many of the subjects could spontaneously "switch" moral orientations following an interviewer's cue about whether there were other ways to approach the moral problem.[22]

Clopton and Sorell's study also suggests that insofar as *care* and *justice* are terms that apply to something, they apply, not insignificantly, to different kinds of moral situations in the kinds of responses they evoke. Following Gilligan's suggested method for the investigation of moral orientation, Clopton and Sorell found that the real life parenting dilemmas that their respondents rated high on scales of importance, difficulty, and personal relevance elicited somewhat higher "care scores" from both female and male parents.

All of this calls for greater critical attention to the factors with which perceived differences, including gender differences, are correlated. Clopton and Sorell's study, in particular, draws attention to the significance of situational variables like parent/nonparent and parent of handicapped child/parent of nonhandicapped child in assessing differences with respect to moral response. In some settings, it seems, these kinds of situational differences can be the primary variables of differentiation that are relevant. Gender might then factor in secondarily, for example, in contexts in which more women than men are primary parents or caretakers of dependent or vulnerable others. Such an emphasis is less about overlooking gender than it is about examining what situational factors motivate the functioning of gender in specific ways. This study also indicates that when we investigate situational effect, especially as it pertains to gender, we find it not just in the immediate situations locating specific moral dilemmas but also in life "situations" more broadly. When women and men reason differently, it may be "for reasons having to do with the differences in men's and women's daily lives."[23]

This shift to a more situational view of gender in gender and cognition studies also prompts a shift toward a more situational view of cognition. Specific situations may convey different roles and norms for participants, and these can factor into different reasoning strategies for those involved. It is important, however, not to confuse this emerging notion of situated reasoning with contextual reasoning. Care reasoners have often been described as contextual reasoners, requesting more details about specifics of people and relationships and framing their deliberations in terms of qualifications that depend on these and other particulars of moral situations. In effect, principles reasoning has often been contrasted with contextual reasoning. The emerging picture of situated reasoning that I am drawing here cuts across both. The point is that all moral reasoning is situated in one way or another and that gender, as a salient attribute of social location in certain contexts, may construct that situatedness differently.

What this means is that justice or principles reasoning can also be read as a specific form of situated reasoning. I argue earlier against a too-hasty reading of particular aspects of the justice voice in terms of generality, principles, and abstraction—sometimes embellished with mathematical and logical vocabulary. If it turns out that in certain contexts males are indeed using rules referring to "rights" and "principles" more than females are, we might ask, What are the possible markers of the situatedness of these "justice" reasoners that constrain them to reason in this way? For example, some feminist theorists have argued that the reported tendency of "care" reasoners to hesitate, to ask for more contextual details, and to be more tenuous in offering definite solutions could well indicate a diminished sense of self and agency linked to oppression. But there is a corresponding reading of the justice reasoner who responds more quickly, with more conviction, with clear-cut rules guiding a solution. In assuming their role as the "manly" sex, males are often expected to at least appear to be in control and have definite solutions. Asking for more information, or having too many qualifying "it depends on . . ."

remarks in their responses, may give the impression of a hesitancy or sensitivity that could brand them "sissies" in cultural contexts that clearly exclude such behavior from "proper masculinity." Where this is so, we, as moral theorists, will surely want to hesitate before constructing a moral ideal out of this kind of response.

It is important to note that, insofar as I am reading this particular aspect of the justice voice in relation to gender, it is a sense of gender as constructed and situated within a specific set of social norms and expectations. Males are also gendered in quite specific ways (often in correlation with, or as complementary to, specific ways of female gendering), and when gender differences seem to surface they need to be read against social and cultural backdrops that situate both genders. It is, unfortunately, the legacy of traditional views of gender in moral theory (and philosophy more generally) that males are still often seen as the "neutral" gender and females are seen as the "gendered" gender. Thus, for example, it has become quite natural to read the female "difference" in terms of contextual details, concrete situations, emotional involvements within specific relationships, and so on, and the male "difference" as not situated with respect to these ever present particulars of living. Thus, it becomes very easy to hear male responses in terms of rules or principles marked by neutrality, abstraction, and generality—as if these latter terms were self-explanatory. As I argue earlier with the notion of abstraction, by loosening the hold of some historical senses of "neutral" masculinity associated with these terms we can begin to render them more contextually meaningful and situated. For example, we can begin to reason better about different kinds of principles that different situations suggest or evoke, about when and how principles are appropriate and applicable, and about when and how we might generalize or abstract from some specifics of situations and not others. In effect, alternative readings and understandings of gender encourage new understandings of moral terms that have been too long constrained by particular gender inflections.

There are, clearly, some broader implications of my discussion, beyond those that pertain to specific arguments about gender and moral reasoning. Though a fuller account of them goes beyond the scope of this essay, it is important to note some of them. One of the main points made by those who view gender as situational is that gender interacts with and, to a certain extent, is constructed by multiple axes of social differentiation (linked often, though not always, to power and status) and that these various axes combine to shape the salience of gender in specific contexts. Thus, this work is giving insight into the significant situational effect on reasoners generally—that is, it cannot be bracketed off as "just" relating to gender. Because of this, it is work that any moral theorist ("feminist" or otherwise) who proposes a more active role for a naturalized moral epistemology in moral theorizing needs to take into account.

Much of this work grants a more active role to moral situations than is regularly assumed by ethicists. Some of the specific studies I have mentioned suggest that moral situations and moral practices create, evoke, and nourish moral capacities—in a way that may be difficult to accomplish without them. This applies to situations of parenting no less than to situations of ruling or lawmaking. Situations, thoughtfully encountered, can bring morality to people: it is not simply that people bring morality (in the form of "inner" capacities and virtues, consistent sets of moral principles, and so on) to situations. But this speaks also to the question of the moral damage that occurs in social and cultural contexts wherein roles and expectations—related to gender or something else—dictate that only some people can experience certain kinds of situations or that they can only adopt certain kinds of positions in those situations.[24]

The view of moral situations emerging here (along with the kinds of moral reasoning the situations evoke and exemplify) seems like such a far cry from the depiction of moral situations elicited by the kinds of hypothetical moral dilemmas we so often encounter in moral theory. One of the problems with these dilemmas is that they preselect for somewhat limited forms of moral rationality: indeed, this is often their main purpose—to exhibit the workings of different systems of moral rules (utilitarian versus contractarian systems, for instance). The point is not simply that these rarely capture the complexity and reality of most "real life" moral situations (though that is a worthy point to make) but also that they carry with them models of cognition and reasoning that may rarely (or at best minimally) apply to *moral* situations—as differentiated, say, from mathematical or logical situations. Fabricated dilemmas that negate any possible situational factors other than the relatively generic individual with specific reasoning capacities facing a somewhat rigidly framed puzzle with a limited range of possible solutions suggest that no other factors are relevant or ought to be relevant for a good moral reasoner. One of the benefits of real situational effect (whether in reality or perhaps imaginatively embellished in literature and good storytelling) is that humans can draw on a whole range of imaginative and affective capacities that, with moral practice and the development of moral integrity, enhance rather than diminish the range of human reasoning capacities. Only a historical legacy that has regularly pitted reason against these other human capacities (which were regularly set aside as "feminine"), and has sought to deny the fact that all reasoning is engaged in specific contexts and practices, could have come up with the very limited models of moral reasoning that we still see so often in moral theory. In continuing to read against the grain of limited gender assumptions and symbols that still have not quite gone away (even in some feminist projects), we can point the way not simply to different forms of moral reasoning but to better ones.

NOTES

A significant part of the work on this essay was undertaken while I was supported by a fellowship from the American Council of Learned Societies in 1998–99. I also benefited from presentations of earlier drafts of this chapter at the Feminist Ethics Revisited Conference, sponsored by the Philosophy Department and the Ethics Center at the University of South Florida in fall 1999, and at the annual philosophy conference hosted by the Royal Irish Academy in Dublin in spring 2000. I had valuable discussions about some of the topics in this chapter with David Bricker and Todd Weber. I also thank Peggy DesAutels and Joanne Waugh for their thoughtful suggestions on an earlier draft.

1. Carol Gilligan, *In a Different Voice: Psychological Theory and Women's Development* (Cambridge: Harvard University Press, 1982).

2. For helpful collections of essays on many of these methodological and other concerns that received significant attention in response to Gilligan's work, see *Social Research* 50, no. 3 (Autumn 1983); and Eva Feder Kittay and Diana T. Meyers, eds., *Women and Moral Theory* (Totowa, N.J.: Rowman and Littlefield, 1987). Marilyn Friedman provides a very clear account of many of these concerns—along with important references—in part 2 of her book *What Are Friends For? Feminist Perspectives on Personal Relationships and Moral Theory* (Ithaca, N.Y.: Cornell University Press, 1993).

3. It should be noted, however, as many feminist ethicists have argued, that Hume's and Aristotle's views cannot be readily assessed in terms of the forms of moral rationalism that predominated elsewhere in the history of moral theory. For a helpful discussion of the specific forms of moral rationality refined in what she calls the "theoretical-juridical model," which has shaped much twentieth-century moral theorizing, see Margaret Urban Walker, *Moral Understandings: A Feminist Study in Ethics* (New York: Routledge, 1998), especially chapter 2. This model of what Walker calls "codifying a compact core of unsituated, purely moral knowledge" places significant emphasis on particular forms of intellectualism, rationalism, and individualism. Walker draws in part on feminist work to argue for replacing this view of ethics with "an expressive-collaborative one that focuses on understandings of responsibility" (*Moral Understandings,* 14).

4. I have developed parts of this larger argument in more detail in "Gendered Reason: Sex Metaphor and Conceptions of Reason," *Hypatia* 6, no. 2 (1991); and in "Rationality and the Politics of Gender Difference," *Metaphilosophy* 26, nos. 1–2 (1995).

5. Arthur Schopenhauer, "On Women," in *Philosophy of Woman,* ed. Mary Briody Mahowald (Indianapolis: Hackett, 1994), 138.

6. Carol Gilligan, "Moral Orientation and Moral Development," in *Women and Moral Theory,* ed. Eva Feder Kittay and Diana T. Meyers (Totowa, N.J.: Rowman & Littlefield, 1987), 22, 28, 31.

7. Friedman, *What Are Friends For?* 92, emphasis added.

8. Gilligan, *In a Different Voice,* 2.

9. Gilligan, *In a Different Voice,* 26–27.

10. Gilligan, *In a Different Voice,* 29.

11. Gilligan, *In a Different Voice,* 35.

12. Gilligan, *In a Different Voice*, 37.

13. Friedman, *What Are Friends For?* 122.

14. For a careful account of the way in which *gender schemas* structure observation, cognition, and behavior, see Virginia Valian, *Why So Slow? The Advancement of Women* (Cambridge: MIT Press, 1998). Valian also highlights the significant social and political ramifications of this for women in various professional/work situations.

15. Martha T. Mednick, "On the Politics of Psychological Constructs: Stop the Bandwagon, I Want to Get Off," *American Psychologist* 44, no. 8 (1989): 1120.

16. Rhoda Unger, "Imperfect Reflections of Reality: Psychology Constructs Gender," in *Making a Difference: Psychology and the Construction of Gender,* ed. Rachel T. Hare-Mustin and Jeanne Marecek (New Haven, Conn.: Yale University Press, 1990), 107.

17. In addition to works mentioned above, see Kay Deaux, "From Individual Differences to Social Categories: Analysis of a Decade's Research on Gender," *American Psychologist* 39, no. 2 (1984).

18. Deaux, "From Individual Differences to Social Categories," 115. Unger, in "Imperfect Reflections of Reality," notes that there is some disagreement among feminist psychologists about the precise use of the terms *sex* and *gender* in these discussions, and some use *sex/gender*. She herself defines *gender* as "a scheme for the social categorization of individuals" ("Imperfect Reflections of Reality," 109).

19. Kay Deaux and Brenda Major have given a quite detailed model of "gender-related behavior" that might be used in social and psychological research designed to further study "the degree to which gender-related behavior is variable, proximally caused, and context dependent," yet it is also a model that they present as a "supplement to existent models of sex differences" ("Putting Gender into Context: An Interactive Model of Gender-Related Behavior," *Psychological Review* 94, no. 3 [1987]: 869–89). For a good view of this debate about "the science and politics of comparing women and men," see the March 1995 issue of *American Psychologist,* which was primarily devoted to this topic. I have explored various aspects of these different methodological approaches to the study of gender and cognition in "Methodological Issues in the Construction of Gender as a Meaningful Variable in Scientific Studies of Cognition," in *Proceedings of the 1994 Biennial Meeting of the Philosophy of Science Association,* vol. 2, ed. D. Hull, M. Forbes, and R. M. Burian (East Lansing, Mich.: Philosophy of Science Association, 1995).

20. Nancy A. Clopton and Gwendolyn T. Sorell, "Gender Differences in Moral Reasoning: Stable or Situational?" *Psychology of Women Quarterly* 17 (1993): 86.

21. Clopton and Sorell, "Gender Differences in Moral Reasoning," 85.

22. Gilligan, "Moral Orientation and Moral Development," 27. However, it is not unproblematic, I think, that she characterizes the switch as a gestalt-type switch between the two gender-marked care and justice perspectives. For a useful discussion of this gestalt metaphor and of the relevance of cognitive scientific work on gestalt perception, see Peggy DesAutels, "Gestalt Shifts in Moral Perception," in *Mind and Morals,* ed. Larry May, Marilyn Friedman, and Andy Clark (Cambridge: MIT Press, 1996).

23. Clopton and Sorrell, "Gender Differences in Moral Reasoning," 99–100.

24. Claudia Card effectively addresses the question about the "moral damage that a rosy view of women and care may disguise" in "Gender and Moral Luck," in *Identity, Character, and Morality,* ed. Owen Flanagan and Amélie Oksenberg Rorty (Cambridge: MIT Press, 1990).

11

Constructing Feelings: Jane Austen and Naomi Scheman on the Moral Role of Emotions

James Lindemann Nelson

On returning from her journey à deux with Mr. Willoughby to see the house he hopes to inherit upon his aunt's death, Marianne, in Jane Austen's novel *Sense and Sensibility,* meets her sister's incredulity that she should do so ill-judged a thing with the claim that she had "never spent a pleasanter morning in her life":

> "I'm afraid," replied Elinor, "that the pleasantness of an employment does not always evince its propriety."
>
> "On the contrary, nothing can be a stronger proof of it, Elinor; for if there had been any real impropriety in what I did, I should have been sensible of it at the time, for we always know when we are doing wrong, and with such a conviction, I could have had no pleasure."[1]

It is not implausible, I think, to see as a central theme of Austen's novel the refutation of Marianne's view—that feelings as such reliably indicate where propriety lies. Marianne cultivates her feelings, trusts them implicitly, and gives herself to them entirely. As a result, she is repeatedly and profoundly mistaken in her judgments of character, continually loses sight of the reasonable claims of those around her to her respect, uses them routinely as mere means to her ends, and comes close to dying for unrequited love. Elinor, in contrast, struggles successfully throughout the novel to keep her own strong and sympathetic feelings under the discipline of her judgment. She is able to weigh probabilities carefully and entertain likely possibilities against the contrary inclinations of her emotions; she retains a lively sense of what is owing even to those whose conduct she finds distasteful; and she maintains sufficient control over her own deep sorrows and the attendant temptations to envy and resentment so as to preserve her dignity and her effectiveness as a sister, a daughter, and a friend.

Nor is it likely accidental that Marianne's particular form of engagement with her feelings is so plainly depicted as installed and supported by her local society and by the temper of her culture. Her mother, Mrs. Dashwood, is identically disposed, and even a sensible man like Colonel Brandon finds Marianne's vivid and quick feelings very alluring. Her imagination is dominated by preromantic pastoral poets (Cowper is cited in particular), and her enthusiasm for the prevailing picturesque aesthetic is often remarked on and comes in for considerable teasing. In exactingly connecting Marianne's emotional propensities to her rearing, to a specific set of literary works, and to a thickly mediated connection to nature, Austen indicates that her novel's focus is not merely on the development of one young woman's character but, in fact, on a set of socially created and renewed resources contributing to the construction of feelings, the intelligibility of the world, and the direction of action.

As a narrative that probes the authority of sentiment, both as the primary medium of a human life and as tempered by judgment, *Sense and Sensibility* illustrates the aptness of themes common in feminist thought concerning the social character of emotion. At the same time, the novel seems to assign to emotion the same epistemically problematic role as has the mainstream tradition, against which feminists working in moral psychology and epistemology have often inveighed.[2] Marianne's feelings are epistemically and morally distorting, as indeed are those of other characters whose emotions are not carefully governed by reason. What extricates Marianne from her thralldom to sensibility is nothing but empirical evidence of the most vivid kind that her passions have been a source of false beliefs, vain hopes, and bad actions.

In this chapter, I have two aims. The first, and more fully realized, is to excavate and contrast Austen's understanding of what emotions are with what I regard as a highly sophisticated feminist analysis of emotions, that of Naomi Scheman. My second aim is to rough out—and I use the phrase advisedly—some of the different implications of Austen's and Scheman's views for matters relevant to moral epistemology. I will be trying to show that Scheman's use of literary examples to bolster the plausibility of her comparatively radical social ontology of emotions is open to Austenian counterexamples, as well as to forms of redescription that save the phenomena but do not rely on Scheman's view that emotions are, as it were, socially constructed "all the way down." On the other hand, I portray Scheman's view of the emotions as proceeding from a better balanced view of their potential contributions to moral perception and deliberation than the fears about emotions menacing moral judgment that seem dominant in *Sense and Sensibility*. At the same time, however, I am concerned that Scheman's metaphysical views have implications that run counter to her own moral epistemic ambitions.

EMOTION'S ONTOLOGY

In her important essay, "Feeling Our Way toward Moral Objectivity,"[3] Naomi Scheman continues to develop themes she has explored earlier, particularly in her much discussed "Individualism and the Objects of Psychology" and "Anger and the Politics of Naming."[4] She argues that emotions are not properly regarded as states of individuals at all; their elements lack the kinds of causal relationships that would allow them to persist as complex entities independent of a social context. Rather, emotions exist only against the backdrop of certain explanatory frameworks. At the same time, she denies the more mainstream philosophical (and apparently Austenian) view that emotions have a particular tendency to threaten the achievement of moral knowledge. Scheman holds, rather, that "the social constructedness of emotions and the ineliminable role of emotions in moral judgment work together to provide the possibility of moral objectivity."[5] This is an intriguing alliance of views: if one believes in both the possibility of objective moral knowledge and the contribution of emotions to its attainment, it would seem more promising to emphasize the cognitive character of emotions and their ability to convey accurate representations of certain states of affairs, as indeed some feminists, conspicuously Richmond Campbell, have.[6] Scheman's view, however, entails that emotions are not identifiable in terms of their causal effectiveness outside of particular forms of social practices and explanations. Construing emotions as altogether the creatures of particular social arrangements—the vast majority of which, from a feminist point of view, must surely be viewed with suspicion—makes it more difficult to understand how emotions can claim authority as reliable contributors to an objective critique of social realities.

Emotions, as Scheman sees them, are complex entities in much the same way as constellations are. The elements that make up an emotion borrow their coherence from their employment in "irreducibly social, contextual explanatory schemes,"[7] even as some selection of stars becomes a constellation only given a background of stories told about the night sky by various cultures on a particular planet; *sans* a background scheme, all we have is a jumble.

The intended contrast is with the way in which galaxies constitute a complex entity; Scheman takes the stars in a galaxy to be related "causally and spatially" in such a way as to constitute an entity independent of social context. As complex entities with respect to a social system, emotions do not qualify as states of an individual; an emotion (unlike, to use an example of Scheman's, a disease) is not something one could experience outside a set of social understandings that relate kinds of behavior, thoughts, feelings, sensations, and so forth to each other in an individuated, heuristically coherent package. This view makes it hard to see how emotions could have a cognitive, representational character to them, except as mediated by more fundamental beliefs, as when we might say that a pattern of stars represents a great bear—but only because some of us *take* it to do so.

Scheman's view resides in a neighborhood in the philosophy of mind known as "externalism" or "anti-individualism." Broadly speaking, the leading idea in anti-individualist approaches is that the individuation conditions of mental phenomena—paradigmatically, thoughts and beliefs—include features of the world outside of the mind. A familiar source of support for this approach in mainstream discussions comes from "Twin Earth" thought experiments: Tyler Burge asks us, for example, to consider someone who believes that *arthritis* properly denotes a rheumatoid ailment of the thigh as well as of the joints. This belief is false. But we can imagine a world consisting of just the same set of persons and events as the real world, except that there *arthritis* is used to denote thigh pain as well as joint pain. Burge thinks, not implausibly, that the person in the twin world has a different thought from that of the person in the real world—despite the fact that there is nothing distinguishable in what is manifest to either of their consciousnesses and that all their physical states are, ex hypothesi, the same. What differentiates these thoughts, then, is something in the social context of each speaker.[8]

Scheman's arguments have a more ambitious aim. Rather than confine her externalist analysis to mental contents such as thoughts, she extends it to what are often thought of as mental facilities or powers—namely, having an emotion. Her arguments also have a different tenor. Rather than speculate about our intuitive responses to philosophical hypotheticals, she draws attention to features of ordinary life that illustrate the gratuitous assumptions that drive rival views. When Scheman does use hypotheticals, her favored strategy is to explore examples drawn from literature; the argument of "Feeling Our Way toward Moral Objectivity" is largely composed of such examples, and it is those on which I will concentrate.

Given Scheman's employment of literary examples to motivate her anti-individualist position, what strikes me as so interesting about *Sense and Sensibility* as I read it is that it embodies a distinct conception of the relationship of the emotions to both social context and moral knowledge. For Austen, emotions are socially shaped in their intensity, direction, and significance. But her reader is not forced to identify emotions solely via their role in social explanations; as I will try to show, a very natural interpretation of Austen's text identifies emotions, in effect, by reference to the causal powers they have in their own right—prominently, the power to represent the world in certain fashions.

"Feeling Our Way toward Moral Objectivity" relies most heavily on two broadly literary examples: Shakespeare's Sonnet 116 ("Love is not love that alters when it alteration finds") and a scene from the film *Torch Song Trilogy*. In her discussion of the sonnet, Scheman construes its famous opening line as what Wittgenstein might have called a grammatical remark about love, one that marks its place in how we use this idea to understand ourselves and others (she quotes from *Zettel*: "Love is not a feeling. Love is put to the test, pain not").[9] If a person's feelings fail the test of constancy, we are urged to withdraw from them the honorific label "love" but *not* because some element in the person's feelings we believed to be present turned out to be lacking. Rather, we should deny that the concept was ever rightly applied because of our moral understanding of what love entails: "What is at stake is less what 'it' is than what we are, what we care about, value and honor."[10] Love, then, is not to be identified with any internal "it," with any state, process, or phenomenon a person experiences or undergoes at a given moment in time. If we change our minds about whether someone loved another, we need not be saying we were mistaken in our notion about what the person felt at the time.

In Austen, though, we see another picture. Early in the novel, readers encounter Marianne's endorsement of love's absolutely constancy. "Does your sister make no distinction in her objections against a second attachment? or is it equally criminal in every body?" asks Colonel Brandon, in a not-entirely-disinterested way. Elinor replies, "I only know that I never yet heard her admit any instance of a second attachment's being pardonable."[11] Marianne's conviction that "love alters not" is so complete that she will not allow that anyone who has truly loved one person could ever possibly come to love another. But this is treated as another of her charming and absurd excesses. She does come ultimately to accept Colonel Brandon as her husband; it might be claimed that she never really loved Willoughby at all, in keeping with Scheman's point that there is a retroactive character to the ways in which we understand the proper assignment of emotions. Yet, from a reader's point of view, a retrospective annulment of the attribution of this emotion here seems mistaken. Austen does not portray Marianne as simply "swayed by the intensity of passing feeling," as Scheman at one point describes what might pretend to the status of love,[12] or as being merely infatuated. Marianne's fervent hope that at some point in their courtship Willoughby had truly loved her and her continuing concern with his character both help constitute a pattern of behavior that at least exceeds the interpretive resources of what we typically think of as infatuation and seems to have reasonable claim to be regarded as love—a love that alters when all the beliefs about the object with which it was joined are shown to be false.

Thus far, however, this reading of Austen seems compatible with the spirit, if not quite the letter, of Scheman's account. A choice to see Marianne's emotion in one way rather than another, as love rather than infatuation, despite its changeableness, might reflect the judgment that interpreting the matter so preserves the best overall fit with the role love plays in our explanatory schemes—"Love alters not" would turn out, then, to be an inapt description of the grammar of the language game we play with love, Shakespeare to the contrary notwithstanding. But admitting the inaptness of the description does not entail seeing love as what Hume might call an "independent existence," malleable by social practices but not created by them. It remains possible to see love as altogether a social construct—although, *pace* Shakespeare, Marianne, and Scheman, the way we play the language game of love is not quite so romantic as they think.

Yet there are deeper worries occasioned by Scheman's general analysis of the emotions. Scheman writes as if emotions were composed, roughly speaking, of two elements: feelings in the sense of sensations, which may be states of individuals but which are not really even essential to having an emotion (being angry, say, is compatible with many different kinds of feelings, surely), and what are broadly sets of behaviors, as interpreted by certain social, contextual explanatory schemes. These behaviors and feelings are loosely unified with reference to the ways in which we try to make sense of ourselves and others—explanatory schemes that are themselves composed in part of normative aspirations. But both Austen's text and more explicitly philosophical considerations provide reason to think that emotions play the role they do in social explanations in part because of distinctive and causally effective traits of their own. For example, emotions are often thought to possess more or less distinctive kinds of conative force, broad inclinations toward general categories of action. Further, the conative forces associated with particular emotions may be structured by representations of the world that those emotions convey. I think that it is plausible to see emotions as having such conative/representational force and that this dimension of their character is not much discussed in Scheman's analysis. Nor is it likely to be well modeled by her approach.

A view of emotions that emphasizes their representational power is nicely expressed in Cheshire Calhoun's essay "Cognitive Emotions?" Calhoun argues that emotions cannot be plausibly regarded simply as beliefs of a certain kind—for example, fear, in her account, cannot be regarded as either incorporating or entailing a belief that one is in a dangerous situation. Calhoun notes, among other reasons she offers, that the emotions we experience may conflict with beliefs we avow. I can, for example, fear spiders while believing them harmless. However, neither are emotions rightly understood simply as clusters of sensations. Calhoun attributes a nondoxastic but still cognitive character to emotions, largely on the grounds that "there is something defective about beliefs accompanied by inappropriate emotions."[13] Imagine someone, for example, who fears flying while believing flying to be a very safe form of transportation, in part because of that person's own abundant and uniformly uneventful experience. Calhoun is willing to credit both the person's fear and the person's belief—neither should be denied or explained away—but claims that the fear, as it were, "degrades" the belief, a conclusion that seems to require that emotions have some cognitive element.[14]

The account that Calhoun develops to accommodate this kind of interaction between discordant beliefs and feelings requires that our cognitive lives consist of more than merely sets of beliefs we are willing to own, share, or defend. There are also what she refers to as "dark" cognitive sets, unarticulated but influential interpretive frameworks that incline us to respond to evidence in certain ways. Calhoun identifies emotions with such sets, frameworks, or patterns of attention; for Calhoun, "to have an emotion is, in part, for the world to seem to be a certain way."[15]

With respect to their depictive abilities, Calhoun's understanding of emotions seems at least roughly consistent with views recently expressed by Richmond Campbell. Consider his analysis of fear as "a representation of immanent danger":

> The idea is not that one judges there to be immanent danger and consequently feels fear, or that one judges the feeling to be about immanent danger. Rather, the feeling itself represents danger. A reason for treating fear this way is that we take the feeling itself to be irrational when no evidence of danger exists. It is as if the representation embodied in the fear is not justified when no evidence supports it. Furthermore, our intuition in this case cannot be explained away as simply a case of mistakenly calling the fear irrational when it is one's judgment that, properly speaking, lacks rationality; for one may feel fear when one judges oneself to be in no danger.[16]

Calhoun would presumably say that such a person's judgment does lack a full measure of some epistemic virtue it should have, if not precisely rationality. But both of these understandings rely on the idea of emotions as representations. In a "Calhoun-Campbell"-type analysis, then, emotions seem identifiable not solely by their roles in social explanations but by their inherent power to bring it about that the world appears to us in certain ways; considered as representational states, emotions appear to be more like galaxies than constellations after all.

I will later discuss whether Scheman's anti-individualist analysis might accommodate a representational view of the emotions, but first I want to claim that Austen's text makes plainer sense construed in the light of this kind of account. In loving Willoughby, Marianne had represented him to herself under the aspect of a sort of highly particularized, highly elevated, and multidimensional worthiness, which influences her desire to have a lasting and intimate relationship with him; that was how the world—or at least that portion of it that contained and involved Willoughby—seemed to Marianne to be. After he is revealed as a cad, a practiced deceiver of women, part of Marianne's pain seems a kind of cognitive dissonance. Her judgment reveals him to be unworthy, but her lingering affection represents him in a very different light. What Marianne yearns for is a creditable account of Willoughby's actions that makes him seem less coldheartedly heinous: "If I could be satisfied on one point, if I could be allowed to think that he was not *always* acting a part, not *always* deceiving me;—but above all, if I could be assured he was *never* so very wicked as my fears have sometimes fancied him."[17] When Elinor provides her with evidence to this effect, she is able to construct a unified representation of the man that reconciles the demands of discursive reason and representational emotions.

What juxtaposing Sonnet 116 with *Sense and Sensibility* indicates, then, is not a merely incidental disagreement between Scheman and Austen about how to analyze a particular emotion. Austen is perfectly plain about the way in which a certain set of understandings of emotion and its role in life has been socially installed in Marianne. But, as if anticipating Calhoun and Campbell, Austen portrays Marianne's feelings in terms that suggest their representational functions and their ability to incite action, as well the forms in which her sensibility has been socially sculpted. At the end of the day, this may turn out to be a philosophical mistake, but there does not seem to be anything patently confused about it, nothing demonstrable simply by adverting to the kinds of examples Scheman employs. While emotions can clearly be cultivated, shaped, deflected, and distorted by "social, contextual explanatory schemes," as Austen amply shows, it does not follow from their social pliability that the identity and properties of emotions are altogether determined by those schemes; indeed, emotions may be so ubiquitously useful an explanatory device just because they are, in the end, more like galaxies than like constellations. How we make sense of action simply must take account of them.[18]

The point thus far is not that Austen has "refuted" Scheman's analysis of the emotions—perhaps anti-individualist views can cope with the intentional structure of emotions and the cognitive and conative forces they seem to possess; perhaps conative/representational analyses of emotions are fated for a bad end. The point is, rather, that one can accord a very important role to society in influencing how we understand and use our emotions, without portraying them as existing *only* with reference to those understandings and usages, and that the instances of poetry and drama Scheman offers in support of her thesis are susceptible to other interpretations.

The *Torch Song Trilogy* reference, I believe, lends itself to reinterpretation as well. Scheman provides a very compelling reading of an interchange between Arnold, who is saying the prayer for the dead for his recently murdered lover, Alan, and Arnold's mother, who is performing the same office for her husband. Arnold's mother angrily asks him what he is doing, and Alan answers that he is doing just the same as she is. This infuriates her; she hurls back at him the reply that she is saying Kaddish whereas he is blaspheming his religion.

Arnold's mother plainly lives her life drawing on different sets of explanatory schemes than those of her son. Accordingly, Scheman understands

Arnold's mother as refusing to allow that her son is "feeling grief, as she is feeling grief, and . . . felt for Alan love, as she felt love for her husband."[19] These words are open to different understandings. It would seem that, to support Scheman's analysis most decisively, we should see Arnold's mother as witnessing Arnold engaged in a "meaningless jumble"; what would be most dramatic as an illustration of Scheman's view would be a portrayal of a mother who is wondering whether her son has *anything that could be called an emotion at all.* Call this the strong interpretation.

An interpretation that less decisively supports Scheman's view would see Arnold's mother as denying that Arnold is feeling what she is feeling, where "what she is feeling" is understood as something that might be called "conjugal grief." I mean by this phrase the kind of pattern of emotions and attendant social responses appropriate to the loss of a husband or a wife. Call this the weak interpretation.

How Scheman wants us to understand this interchange between mother and son is important, for one implication of her view is that there is a certain parity, at least in principle, between the standing of the two parties as they understand Arnold. Arnold perceives the patterns differently from how his mother does, he weighs differently the similarities and differences, in the context of his and her lives, and ends up seeing the same patterns of love and grief.[20] This suggests that he is engaged in some behavior with respect to whose meaning he is situated (epistemically, if not politically) just as his mother is situated. His behavior gets whatever sense it has (or lacks) according to how it is placed against a backdrop of different sets of paradigms and disanalogies, which provide various explanations of his feelings, sensations, occurrent thoughts, and behavior.

The plausibility of this parity varies, I believe, as these different understandings of "the same" pass in review. In an extended discussion of the same graveyard scene in a later article, Scheman claims that, while the liberal political momentum of *Torch Song Trilogy* as a whole may be to incline the audience to see Arnold's interpretation of his feelings as the correct one ("If you cut her, does not a drag queen bleed?"), political developments subsequent to the film call the correctness of such a reading into question.[21] From the perspective of a politically alert, oppositional queer consciousness, the supposed analogies between straights and gays that would underpin univocal ascriptions of conjugal grief to gay people who lose their partners are contestable, and the political—and hence social—character of the emotions is revealed by the contestation. (Sometimes, Scheman says, we may have good reasons to show that "the whole apparatus is an apparatus, and that it's one we do not have to accept."[22])

It seems to me that the strong interpretation of "the same feeling" is dubious; it is surely not forced on us by the action of the play, and the notion that whether or not Arnold is experiencing an emotion is hostage to what emerges from a three-cornered confrontation among his mother, himself, and a certain variant of queer praxis neglects, among other things, the asymmetry between first and third person psychological ascriptions. There is no textual reason to construe Arnold experiencing his grief as a solution to any puzzle presented by his behavior—it is not a matter of weighing this similarity against that dissonance. Rather, he is suffering a deeply tragic loss, and while what touches off suffering, how it is directed, and how it is expressed are surely not innocent of cultural situations, there seems nothing inferential or interpretive about his experience of suffering. Even if it were granted that Arnold's mother does not know that her son is grieving, we might have to say the same about Arnold, though for quite different reasons. Arnold's mother may indeed be blocked from recognizing Arnold's grief, perhaps, as Scheman thinks, by her utilization of a different interpretive scheme or simply because her homophobia prevents her from a basic sensitivity to part of what is transpiring in her immediate environment. But about Arnold himself, we may wish to say what Wittgenstein said of the first person experience of pain: "It can't be said of me at all (except perhaps as a joke) that I *know* I am in pain. What is it supposed to mean—except perhaps that I *am* in pain."[23]

Anti-individualists in the philosophy of mind debate whether their view deprives people of the special relationship that they are typically taken to have to their "own" mental phenomena; if the identity conditions for such phenomena include things that occur "outside" me, the worry goes, then I would not be able to "grasp" those phenomena in any epistemically distinctive way. But one does not need to believe in the incorrigibility of privileged access to regard Arnold's relation to his own feelings as having an authority that his mother's lacks or to think that this authority is awarded as the result of ethical and political deliberations that go to the tensions between Judaism and homosexuality or between liberalism and queer theory. It is indeed sometimes the case that we have to conjecture about, and even learn from others, how best to make sense of our feelings; there may be powerful obscuring forces at hand. Yet this is not true of our emotional experiences as such. Nor does it seem clearly the case that Arnold's mother's inability to comprehend his feelings as real emotions is better explained with reference to the nature of emotion, as opposed to the nature of her own emotions and judgments.

Again, the contrast with Austen's story may be instructive. Whatever the social powers are that have shaped Marianne into a woman who elevates considerations of feeling over all else, they have not had the same effect on her sister. Elinor has a different relationship to that social and contextual explanatory scheme. Early in the story, she seems to regard Marianne and her mother with a kind of amused tolerance—she does not "fully and wholeheartedly occupy" their "interpretive perspective."[24] However, in rejecting that interpretive perspective, Elinor does not regard their feelings in an ironic, mocking sense, a sense that for us would require scare quotes. Even when the sentimental perspective has been shown as bankrupt and dangerous, Elinor does not see her sister's emotional life as a congeries of ill-fitted, uninterpretable elements but, rather, continues to accept it in its own terms. This suggests that, despite their schematic differences, Elinor sees Marianne's feelings for what they are. She recognizes that Marianne did love—not "love"—Willoughby deeply and that her sister suffers greatly, both as a result of his inconstancy and because of her conviction that he lacks moral substance. Marianne was mistaken, not about the character of her own feelings but about the character of her lover.

The weak interpretation is the most plausible way of understanding Arnold's feelings as in some way up for grabs: what I have here called "conjugal grief" does seem internally linked to a series of social practices that assign a special status to the bereaved survivor, social practices concerning what is understood by marriage. What Arnold's mother may resent is her son laying claim to the position made available by those practices; what queer theory may object to is the endorsement of the authority of marriage and marriage-like relationships implicit in the way in which Arnold mourns. These objections arguably have their respective points, and even the resentment may be understandable. But showing that conjugal grief may have a strongly socially constructed, politically negotiable character is not to show that the same analysis holds for simply having an emotion at all—or for love or grief as such. The attempt to get Arnold to understand his grief for Alan in a different way might be liberating; an effort to get Arnold to deny that he grieved at all would be brainwashing.

My argument thus far has relied on showing that literary examples featuring the play of emotions are as amenable, or more amenable, to an analysis that attributes to emotion causal—in particular, representational—powers, as they are to Scheman's view. The argument, however, has assumed that attributing such powers to the emotions makes them more like galaxies than like constellations, causally powerful particulars characterizing individuals rather than variable, interpretative social structures. Recently, Scheman has tried to show that an anti-individualist understanding of mental phenomena, including emotions, can handily accommodate the role such phenomena play in causal explanations.

In "Feminism in Philosophy of Mind: Against Physicalism," Scheman tries to defuse the persistent belief that a proper understanding of mental phenomena must require either a physicalist or a dualist theory of the relationship between "mind" and "body." She directs our attention to concert performances: "There is nothing going on in addition to the physical movements of the bodies of the members of the orchestra, but there is no way of appealing just to physics to specify which of those movements are parts of the complex event that is the performance and which are not. What

is and is not part of the event has to do with what sort of thing a performance is, what norms and expectations determine what its parts are."[25] The
analogy, of course, is to mental phenomena, including emotions. They, like
performances, do not consist in anything ontologically over and above the
distribution and redistribution of microphysical states, but they cannot be
identified solely within the proprietary vocabulary of physics.

Scheman points out that the performance can figure into causal explanations in two different ways. If, for example, a crack in the ceiling appears
contemporaneously with the performance, the crack may have been caused
by "physical events more or less loosely associated with the performance"
but not by the performance per se. On the other hand, a riot may break out
during a performance (as happened at the Parisian premier of Stravinsky's *Le
Sacre du Printemps*), and in such an instance the performance itself may be
the cause of the disturbance. *Le Sacre du Printemps* incited rioting qua performance because it interacted with the beliefs, desires, expectations, and
emotions of people attending it; this suggests that the arguments Scheman
deploys against individualism leave open the possibility that at least some
mental phenomena have causal powers in their own right. If the causal powers are not lodged there, where, one might wonder, do they come from?

I understand Scheman's answer as follows: there are rough correlations
between emotions and other mental phenomena, which are best understood
in an anti-individualist style, and physiological states that are themselves
causally powerful particulars. To use an example from "Feminism in Philosophy of Mind," we speak of "getting angry" as a possible cause of elevations
in blood pressure. However, the causal story here runs through certain kinds
of physiological tensions that are typically, but not always, associated with
being angry. To speak more precisely, what causes the blood pressure to rise
is the tension.[26] One might, of course, wonder, "What causes the tension,
then?" but, given the contingency of the connection between anger and tension, it seems possible to see tension as one among many otherwise discon-
nected physiological and behavioral states that get swept up, as it were, in
some attributions of anger and not in others.

But this line of thought seems to lead in the direction of saying that the
fundamental causal explanation of why people rioted after hearing *Le Sacre
du Printemps*—why their blood pressure soared, why their adrenaline
pumped, why they ran where they ran, yelled what they yelled, and
smashed what they smashed—would ultimately be at the level of physiological tensions, spasms, and twinges, somehow roughly correlated with the au-
ditors' beliefs, values, and emotions. Presumably, the multitude could have
instantiated just the same pattern of beliefs, values, and emotions without
such correlations, and in such a case, although everyone involved would
have thought and felt just as they did on the actual occasion, there would
have been no riot. If this is indeed the consequence of seeing the individua-

tion conditions of mental phenomena as exclusively social, it is not clear that emotions do have a role to play in causal explanations.

But if emotions have a representational/conative structure, there is a more straightforward way of understanding their role in causal explanation. If we accept, say, that anger necessarily involves not tensions or pangs (which may or may not occur) but the shaping of our experience of the world in a certain wide-ranging but not completely open-ended set of ways, and that such shaping carries along with it certain inclinations toward behavior, then the first person dimension of anger would seem to have identifying content in its own right. Social practices might affect anger in many ways—trigger it, shape it, control what counts as acceptable expression of it, associate it and the forms of its expression in different ways according to gender or class—but not by providing it with the conditions that are essential to its having its identity at all.

EMOTION, OBJECTIVITY, AND MORAL JUDGMENT

Does sorting out competing accounts of the ontology of the emotions matter for the project of understanding how emotions contribute to moral judgment? Does Austen's view of emotions make it clearer why she seems more suspicious of "sensibility" than of "sense," and does Scheman's view show how emotions can serve us as we feel our way toward moral objectivity? My view is that the ontological discussion does matter for moral epistemology, though not, perhaps, in just the ways that Austen and Scheman think.

For the Austen of *Sense and Sensibility*, emotion is allied with fanciful and perilous departures from the careful, measured, impartial assessments of persons and circumstances that lead to sound moral judgment. Like Marianne, Elinor is aware of both the attractions and the weaknesses of those around her, but her assessments are always balanced with due attention to the respect owed to people in virtue of their social roles and their particular relationships. Her own feelings are very keen, but they are never allowed to overcome her judgment—the sort of thing that feelings are, apparently, rather apt to do. If Elinor's wisdom relies at all on her emotions, their role would seem to be that of a kind of generalized benevolence.

Scheman does a very effective job in criticizing this sort of view. As she points out, the mainstream idea has been that we can most reliably attain objective knowledge by practicing an "epistemology of parsimony"—one that strives to identify and discount in advance classes of error-inducing influences. Emotions, as they are represented both in *Sense and Sensibility* and in the tradition more generally, figure largely among such influences. Scheman sees parsimony as a perverse strategy. The goal of objectivity is best attained through an "epistemology of largesse," in which beliefs are justified to the extent to which they meet the widest possible range of actual criticism and are maintained in social settings that encourage further possible criticism.

Emotions are welcome—indeed, positively courted—in this epistemology. Emotions make salient what is significant in the tasks of moral perception as seen by a variety of quite standard moral theories—in deontological and utilitarian accounts as well as in Aristotle's. Emotions also constitute some important part of morality's subject matter—what it is that we care about. Further, emotions trace out the fault lines among competing social explanatory schemes. This is particularly true of what Alison Jaggar has called "outlaw emotions"—that is, "emotions, according to the hegemonic view of the situation, one is not supposed to feel."[27] When one feels an outlaw emotion, one is confronted both with evidence that competing schemes are present and with an indication as to which scheme is subordinate. For example, women are supposed to feel flattered by, not angry at, catcalls; sexist, racist, or homophobic jokes are not supposed to elicit resentment when they are told in certain social settings. Because emotions are functions of explanatory strategies, outlaw emotions indicate the existence of strategies that have a subordinate status. Objectivity requires that their status be unsubordinated, that those who draw on them have the chance to participate in a democratic fashion in the process of challenge and response that leads to stably sharable beliefs and the emotions appropriate thereto. Taking outlaw emotions seriously can often reveal obscured, morally significant features of a situation. In particular, they can help us see and appreciate the evils enfolded into the standing social conditions.

The role of outlaw emotions is central to Scheman's conception of the moral epistemological role of the emotions, and I think she is precisely right about their importance. But, as she observes, the understandings that serve as the conditions for outlaw emotions do not deserve to prevail simply because they give rise to such feelings. How will one assess outlaw emotions and the systems of social explanation from which they proceed?

Consider Marianne's pleasure in driving unchaperoned with Willoughby to his aunt's estate and her subsequent indignation at Elinor's remonstrances as outlaw emotions. Are these emotions from which we can learn? On the one hand, they surely reveal restrictions on women that are morally indefensible. On the other hand, her feelings are part of a system of emotional practices that the readers—and eventually, the character—come to see as dangerous, in that they leave those who engage in them prone to serious errors of several different kinds. It is hard to imagine that Marianne's outlaw emotions would fare very well in the process of democratic dialectic leading to stable, sharable, morally objective knowledge. At the end of the (long) day, Marianne would be equipped with a much different set of beliefs and embedded in a much different social context, offering her a much different set of resources for interpreting her feelings, thoughts, and actions.

This much, I think, is uncontroversial. What is unclear, though, is how in Scheman's account emotions would play any direct role in determining whether a given selection of saliencies deserves the attention it garners in forming social explanations, understandings, and practices; whether what we do care about is what we ought to care about; and whether our outlaw emotions should be freed or further banished. Much of the central work of moral deliberation and justification is done at the level of the explanatory schemes against which emotions are alleged to have their being. For Scheman, the attainment of moral objectivity is a matter of holding a set of "stably sharable beliefs" that have survived real confrontation with the widest possible set of alternatives and continue to seek out further confrontation. Although emotional differences might alert us to an explanatory scheme we might otherwise overlook, emotions would seem to have no direct role in adjudicating the claims of contending possibilities. Outlaw emotions would reveal the complexities in the social and contextual explanatory systems that, in Scheman's view, give emotions their reality. But that point raises the worry that emotions can correctly contribute to judgment only if they proceed from a system of explanation and assessment that is itself morally defensible. Unless emotions enter in some especially significant way into the identification of defensible systems, their moral epistemic contributions seem at best derivative. We would have to have good, nonemotion-based reasons for thinking that we were on the right track morally before we could confidently utilize our emotional resources to ethical ends.

If one's understanding of the individual contribution to the nature of emotions is a bit more robust—if, as in my reading of Austen, their representational and conative characters play a role in their individuation apart from their location in schemes of social explanations—then they can serve more directly as data for the ongoing effort to achieve the kind of stable and sharable agreement that, for Scheman, constitutes moral objectivity. That a pattern of social life consistently causes women to feel shame, say, is itself a *pro tanto* reason against that pattern, not merely an occasion for noting a certain relationship among contending explanatory schemes. One need not think that the attribution of moral significance to the feeling has to wait on a determination that the system that assigns such feelings their outlaw status is dubious on other grounds.

For Austen, the case is rather different, and indeed, feminists might take her work as a warning that, unless we regard emotions as not just socially shaped but as socially constructed from the bottom up, we play into the hands of mainstream moral epistemology and its relentless debunking of the emotions.[28] Emotions may in some ways be like perceptions, in that they convey representations, but, according to Austen, emotions—or at least those particularly on display in *Sense and Sensibility*—are like inherently unreliable perceptions, ready to steer us wrong at every turn. But there seems to be no compelling reason to follow Austen in this particular view. In conveying a picture to us about each other, ourselves, and the world we share, emotions can get it right as well as wrong. It is not, for example, in principle immoral for women to choose to take an unchaperoned drive; perhaps Marianne knew something Elinor did not, after all.

NOTES

I am grateful to Allen Dunn for comments on an early version of this essay, to the participants in the Feminist Ethics Revisited Conference for discussion of the presented version (most especially to Naomi Scheman), to Hilde Lindemann Nelson for her attention to later drafts, and to Joanne Waugh and Peggy DesAutels for their thoughtful editing of the final copy.
   1. Jane Austen, *Sense and Sensibility* (Oxford: Oxford University Press, 1978), 68.
   2. There is a fine discussion in Margaret Olivia Little, "Seeing and Caring: The Role of Affect in Feminist Moral Epistemology," *Hypatia* 10, no. 3 (1995): 117–37.
   3. Naomi Scheman, "Feeling Our Way toward Moral Objectivity," in *Mind and Morals: Essays on Cognitive Science and Ethics,* ed. Larry May, Marilyn Friedman, and Andy Clark (Cambridge: MIT Press, 1996), 221–36.
   4. Both are included in Naomi Scheman, *Engenderings: Constructions of Knowledge, Authority and Privilege* (New York: Routledge, 1993).
   5. Scheman, "Feeling Our Way toward Moral Objectivity," 234.
   6. Richmond Campbell, *Illusions of Paradox: A Feminist Epistemology Naturalized* (Lanham, Md.: Rowman & Littlefield, 1998), 72.
   7. Scheman, "Feeling Our Way toward Moral Objectivity," 222.
   8. Tyler Burge, "Individualism and the Mental," *Midwest Studies in Philosophy* 4 (1979): 73–122.
   9. Scheman, "Feeling Our Way toward Moral Objectivity," 224.
   10. Scheman, "Feeling Our Way toward Moral Objectivity," 224.
   11. Austen, *Sense and Sensibility,* 56.
   12. Scheman, "Feeling Our Way toward Moral Objectivity," 224.
   13. Cheshire Calhoun, "Cognitive Emotions?" in *What Is an Emotion?,* ed. Cheshire Calhoun and Robert Solomon (Oxford: Oxford University Press, 1984), 339.
   14. In Calhoun's analysis, degraded beliefs are those that are held "intellectually" in conditions that ought to allow them to be held "evidentially"—that is, emotions can bring us to treat as merely the result of inference beliefs that we should regard as arising from our own experience. I am less confident in Calhoun's analysis of degraded belief than I am in her overall conclusions—that emotions can conflict with belief and that this is best understood by attributing to emotions a cognitive, representational character. My suspicion about her particular story about degraded beliefs stems from the possibility of having a well-founded intellectual belief that runs afoul of one's feelings. A belief that air travel is enormously safe, for example, need not be founded on one's own experience but, perhaps, on a rich series of implicit and explicit inferences from the testimony of others.
   15. Calhoun, "Cognitive Emotions?" 339.

16. Campbell, *Illusions of Paradox*, 72.

17. Austen, *Sense and Sensibility*, 344.

18. Scheman does distinguish constellations from emotions on the point of their indispensability; constellations she would be quite prepared to jettison, while emotions depend on enormously deep and powerful explanatory schemes ("Feeling Our Way toward Moral Objectivity," 222). But whatever it is that Scheman would say accounts for the depth and power of schemes that employ the concept of the emotions, it is not the truth of the following claim: there are items that have the power to make the world take on certain aspects that exist independently of the schemes but whose existence the schemes allow.

19. Scheman, "Feeling Our Way toward Moral Objectivity," 225.

20. Scheman, "Feeling Our Way toward Moral Objectivity," 225.

21. See Naomi Scheman, "Forms of Life: Mapping the Rough Ground," in *The Cambridge Companion to Wittgenstein,* ed. Hans Sluga and David G. Stern (Cambridge: Cambridge University Press, 1996), 383–410.

22. Scheman, "Forms of Life," 399.

23. Ludwig Wittgenstein, *Philosophical Investigations,* 3rd edition, trans. G. E. M. Anscombe (New York: Macmillan, 1958), section 246. I do not mean by citing Wittgenstein in this connection to obscure differences between pain and grief, or to deny that some people sometimes may not clearly understand their own emotions—or perhaps even their own sensations—or that marginalized people may encounter special difficulties in achieving such self-understandings. The point, rather, is that there are ways of acknowledging the first person–third person asymmetry that do not involve epistemic incorrigibility.

24. Scheman, "Feeling Our Way toward Moral Objectivity," 223.

25. Naomi Scheman, "Feminism in Philosophy of Mind: Against Physicalism," in *The Cambridge Companion to Feminism in Philosophy*, ed. Miranda Fricker and Jennifer Hornsby (Cambridge: Cambridge University Press, 2000), 49–67.

26. Scheman, "Feminism in Philosophy of Mind," 61.

27. Scheman, "Feeling Our Way toward Moral Objectivity," 229.

28. I must admit that Cheshire Calhoun seems to be in agreement with Austen on this point. "Cognitive Emotions?" stresses how emotions can make our beliefs defective; there is no discussion of how, in altering how the world seems to us, it might make our beliefs better. Campbell is much more of Scheman's mind, being optimistic about the epistemic utility of emotions.

V

TAKING RESPONSIBILITY

12

Does Managing Professionals Affect Professional Ethics? Competence, Autonomy, and Care

Joan C. Tronto

> We are here to consider facts. And the facts . . . seem to prove that the professions have a certain undeniable effect upon the professors. They make the people who practice them possessive, jealous of any infringement of their rights, and highly combative if anyone dares dispute them. Are we not right then in thinking that if we enter the same professions we shall acquire the same qualities? And do not such qualities lead to war? In another century or so if we practice the professions in the same way, shall we not be just as possessive, just as jealous, just as pugnacious, just as positive as to the verdict of God, Nature, Law and Property as these gentlemen are now?
>
> —Virginia Woolf, *Three Guineas*[1]

> Professionals present a crucial problem for management because of the close association between professionalism and autonomy. . . . If (to put it rather crudely) professionalism involves acting on autonomous judgement, and management involves getting other people to do what one wants, then there is a potential conflict.
>
> —Stephen Harrison and Christopher Pollitt, *Controlling Health Professionals*[2]

Virginia Woolf's disdain for the arrogance of professionals does presage the way in which professionals have received their comeuppance in recent years. The nature of professional life is changing: increasingly, managers survey and control the activities of professionals. Yet to see this discussion solely in terms of the loss of professional autonomy or the gain of managerial control is to miss some dimensions of the problem and more appealing solutions. This chapter considers the ethical dimensions of this development

from the standpoint of a feminist ethic of care and argues for a different way
to understand the conflict between managers and professionals by rethinking the relationship of competence, autonomy, and care.

In the past, one of the key elements of professional life was professional
autonomy. Professions were largely self-governing and self-regulating. Professionals themselves devised the standards for admittance to the profession;
for rules of conduct, codes of professional ethics, standards of care; and for
disciplining members of the profession. Professionals have made the claim
that, given the complex and technical nature of professional activity, they are
the only actors capable of regulating their profession and other professionals in it. On the other hand, critics of the professions have argued that professionals make such arguments primarily to retain their own control and
power and that the professions themselves make people arrogant and controlling.

At present, professionals find their work and their control of their professions increasingly surveyed by managers. In the health field, for example,
managers have come to play an increasingly central role in various forms of
health care systems, from the privatized U.S. system of "managed care" to the
National Health Service in the United Kingdom. The justification for inserting
managers into the work of professionals is to control costs; the more disturbing question that underpins these changes is the question of the nature
of professional life itself and the question of the role of such managers.

To what extent is the special moral status of "professions" a matter for *feminist* ethics? An important lesson of feminist ethics has been to argue for the
importance of context in making ethical judgments. Feminists have argued
that scholars and actors should rely less on principles as a way to resolve
moral or ethical disputes and should pay more attention to the meanings assigned to principles in reflexive moral practices.[3] In light of this concern for
context, it might be useful to rethink this question about the special status of
professions and professional ethics from a feminist perspective. Is there
something about the managerial rebuttal of the claim that professions should
devise and monitor their own ethical standards that is particularly troublesome from a feminist point of view?

If we put on our gender lenses, we will see the conflict between professionals and managers in a different light. Celia Davies has noted how thoroughly the account of the autonomous professional is a model that draws on
heroic conceptions of masculinity. The relevant actor is the isolated individual whose training and expertise prepare him to face the crises that are likely
to arise in the practice of the profession. He has been armed with the skills
and temperament that he needs to succeed in the world. We might further
note that there is a strange gender dynamic in the way that we often understand the conflict between managers and professionals.[4] As Kathy Ferguson
has argued, nonprofessional workers in bureaucracies are often conceived

as feminine, as exhibiting the qualities of women.[5] The conflict between professional and manager thus becomes, in an exaggerated but perhaps illuminating way, the conflict between the autonomous male who is trying to follow his own course and the feminine manager who uses subtle and indirect means of controlling and containing his spirit and will. Portrayed this way, the conflict between professional and manager is a never-ending battle, a struggle for power and control.

Might there be another way of resolving this situation? I believe that there is, but it requires us to take another look at professionals' claims to autonomy based on expertise. I shall argue, in the first section of this chapter, that competence needs to be understood as a key point of professional ethics and its meaning needs to be enlarged for all professionals. Making competence more centrally a part of professional ethics has two consequences, and these form the basis of the subsequent sections of this chapter. The first consequence is that it explains why management of professionals is ethically dubious. The second consequence, however, is that competence also requires that professional life change. Professions need to become more democratic, less elitist, and more relational.

COMPETENCE IN PROFESSIONAL PRACTICE

Drawing on the feminist ethic of care, a widely used feminist approach to ethics, let us consider the nature of professional ethics. In arguing for a broad understanding of the place of care in human life, it is useful to start from the definition of *care* devised by Berenice Fisher and myself: care is "*a species activity that includes everything that we do to maintain, continue, and repair our 'world' so that we can live in it as well as possible.* That world includes our bodies, our selves, and our environment, all of which we seek to interweave in a complex, life-sustaining web."[6] We also delineate component phases in the process of caring that provide us with the basis for an analysis of care. There are four component phases: caring about, that is, becoming aware of and paying attention to the need for caring; caring for, that is, assuming responsibility for some caring; caregiving, that is, the actual material meeting of the caring need; and care receiving, that is, the response of the thing, the person, the group, and so on that received the caregiving.

I have subsequently argued that each of these phases of care also has a kind of moral question attached to it, none of which matches the standard ethical questions of obligation, duty, or rights.[7] Caring about requires attentiveness. Caring for requires responsibility. Care receiving requires moral responsiveness. Caregiving requires competence.

If these dimensions of care do require these moral qualities, then what does it mean, from the standpoint of the feminist ethic of care, to say that professionals are required ethically to be "competent"?[8] This claim is part of the care ethic's assertion that it is important to think about the moral nature of doing everyday work well rather than poorly. Another part of this concern is to stress (as have such theorists of care as Patricia Benner)[9] that competence is not simply an agglomeration of technical knowledge and accomplishments but, rather, must be understood as something more complex. But what more complex thing is it? In trying to answer this question, I have realized that "competence" is not the only virtue of caregiving and that all of the moral dimensions of care that I have identified are part of caregiving. Thus, professionals, as well as other caregivers, will not be able to separate attentiveness, responsibility, and responsiveness from competence.

DEFINING COMPETENCE

What does it mean to be "competent" as a professional? *ANA Standards for Nursing Professional Development: Continuing Education and Staff Development* describes competence as the "demonstration of knowledge and skills in meeting professional role expectations."[10] On the first level, competence obviously requires the capacity necessary to fulfill assigned tasks. Several scholars of nursing, in particular, have looked more closely at competence and have determined, though, that there is something more "holistic" about it than simply knowing the requisite knowledge and skills.[11] It requires as well the capability to perform in the real and ever changing world, to be both confident and cautious about changing conditions.[12] What such a notion means in practice varies with the context in which it is being discussed.

On the most basic level, many professions recognize that competence is a part of their legal "standard of care."[13] Increasingly, professions such as nursing turn to "competency-based education" as a way to ensure that professionals complete their training with not simply the necessary knowledge but a capacity to apply their knowledge in various settings.[14] What constitutes this "reasonable standard of care" is determined by the practices of the profession at any given time and makes the notion of continuing professional education and development essential for professionals.[15] This notion of competence presumes that it is largely a matter of knowing and applying technical expertise.

John Raven and his colleagues in Glasgow conceive of competence broadly to be about "understandings and patterns of motivation needed in modern society. It is about the roles, abilities, attitudes and dispositions required by managers, employees, politicians, public servants and citizens." He presumes that competencies are "self-motivated, value-laden qualities" and provides a partial list of thirty-six components of competence, including such elements as a tendency to clarify values and attitudes, a willingness and ability to learn without instruction, self-confidence, tolerance of cognitive complexity, a willingness to utilize new ideas and innovation to achieve the goal, critical thinking, persistence, trustworthiness, an ability to exercise self-control, and an ability to work with others to achieve a goal. Although Raven's competent person bears a striking resemblance to a good Boy or Girl Scout, his emphasis on cognitive, affective, and technical skills takes the points already made by the more narrowly professional thinkers about competence and places them on a broad social level.[16]

Competence can therefore have a technical meaning that is narrowly focused or broad. Nevertheless, feminist theorists of care have argued for a still broader meaning for competence.

BEYOND TECHNICAL COMPETENCE TO "THE EXTRA"

The legal requirement that professionals provide "a reasonable standard of care" refers to the more minimal and technical understanding of competence. When Berenice Fisher interviewed people about what constitutes care, respondents were often reduced to using language implying that someone who really cares provides something "extra."[17] What is it that people are perceiving when they say that someone has provided this "extra"? To answer this question, we need to look more closely at the actual practices of care.

Perhaps the "extra" refers to a usually unarticulated problem faced by recipients of care and professional services: there is a basic problem of power inequality in any relationship that requires professional competence. Professions generally provide the kind of care that Kari Waerness has called "necessary care."[18] Unlike the category she labels "personal service," in which the care work could be done by the self or by another (hiring someone to clean one's house or to cook one's meals, for example, is personal service), "necessary care" grows out of a need on the part of the care receiver that can only be met by the expertise or accomplishment of the caregiver. Because the caregiver here is not only the provider for the service but also the person with the knowledge about what constitutes "good" or "competent" care in this setting, the professional has a great deal of discretion to provide or not to provide *genuinely* competent care. Clients of lawyers, doctors, engineers, public relations experts, accountants, and so forth are much less able to assess the adequacy of the care that they receive. This puts an additional burden on the professional, not only to provide care but to include reassessing the effect of care on the client as a part of the competent provision of care.[19] Within mainstream professional ethics, this problem is recognized as a special kind of obligation. Because the relationship between the professional and the client is a relationship between a stronger and a weaker party (this is not my language but, rather, the standard language for this relationship), the relationship is understood to be a case of a *fiduciary* duty: a responsibility to assist the weaker party and to fulfill the trust with which the fiduciary has been entrusted.[20]

From the standpoint of the ethic of care framework that I have invoked here, we would think of such care differently. This "extra," then, that constitutes good care is the ability of a caregiver or professional to go beyond the technical "reasonable standard of care."[21] Caring well requires looking at any caring process both in terms of the individual act of care necessary at a given moment and in terms of the entire caring process. Caring well also requires the use of multiple perspectives to make certain that care is not being distorted by relations of power and imposed or ignored needs. Caring well will develop as a professional's experience and sensitivity improve over time. Fisher and I argue that meeting caring needs often leads to the creation of new caring needs. The caring professional thus is one who is attentive to such needs, who weighs the responsiveness of clients and objects of care, and who sees what responsibilities are not being met and adjusts the nature of care accordingly.

What I have argued, then, is that while "competence" may be the virtue particularly relevant to caregivers, given the nature of the relationship between professional and client, competence in professional settings requires that the professional invoke and apply a wider range of moral virtues than simply exercising "a reasonable standard of care." Focusing too narrowly on the requirements of "competence" may result in missing the larger opportunity to care well. Knowing when and how to broaden one's vision, without losing sight of the task ahead and without losing a sense of how to keep the task at hand as the central priority, seems also to be a part of genuine professional competence. To put the point in the language that I use in *Moral Boundaries,* professionally competent caregiving requires that one be attentive, responsible, and responsive at the same time that one is technically competent.

COMPETENCE AND MANAGEMENT

As is clear from this account of competence, it is difficult to specify ahead of time what a particular incident or case of caring will entail. The most important point to notice about competence is that it requires professionals to engage in *complicated and complex* processes. It draws on the professional's tacit as well as explicit knowledge and on experience as well as technique.

Managers, who have been advised about technical knowledge and technique, cannot guess correctly about the requirements for professional activity. From the perspective of care, this lack is a result not of the incompetence of managers but of the fact that that they are necessarily asking the wrong kinds of questions. Questions of efficiency (in completing and dividing tasks) as well as questions of motivating workers interfere, by their nature, with the holistic process of care that genuine competence requires. To put the point baldly, the task of the manager is to manage away the "extra" that we have seen marks a key element of the moral performance of a professional's work. Thus, although it is possible to understand the dispute between managers and professionals as a dispute over the ability of professionals to control their time or as a dispute over competing accounts of the science of organization,[22] I have argued here that a more accurate way to describe this dispute is to see it as a dispute about the capacity of professionals to act ethically.[23]

So far, I have argued that the dispute between professionals and managers is a real dispute. Nevertheless, it is wrong to presume that managerial control is the solution to the problem of the broad autonomy of professionals. From the standpoint of the feminist ethic of care, this solution is problematic because management necessarily impinges on the competence of professionals. To so argue is not, however, to deny that there is a problem if professionals are only self-regulating. In the next section of this chapter, I explore some of those problems and some solutions to them that arise if we consider the practices of the professions themselves and how professions situate themselves in society.

COMPETENCE AND AUTONOMY:
IMPROVING PROFESSIONS WITHOUT MANAGERS

Autonomous Professional Individuals versus Autonomous Professional Practices

Professionals have to exercise their judgment, draw on their knowledge, and use their skills in a variety of settings. One idealized assumption that theorists of professional ethics often make is that the relationship between professional and client is dyadic: that there are two, and only two, parties. In truth, professionals almost always rely on the work of other professionals in accomplishing their own tasks. Furthermore, care and service always happen in a context that is usually more complex than one that simply comprises the interactions of the client and the professional. Thus, it becomes vital to understand the role of conflicting demands and interests in care or service settings and to recognize the central roles of *power* and *distance.*

Power and distance are clearly elements of professional lives. The notion that professionals are set apart from the public by their knowledge grants them power at the same time that it makes them more distant. Professions have often used these dimensions of their status to try to avoid the control of managers. Adding managers to the mix, however, does not diminish the distance of professionals. It adds another level of actors in the middle. Nor does it simplify the complex dimensions of power at work in professional relationships; it adds another set of possible disputants in determining where and how power ought to be exercised. These dimensions of professional life are present, a potential problem, and not resolved by the addition of managers.

The clearest way to talk about this dimension of care is to draw on a recent study that explored the working relationships of pilots, consulting surgeons in operating rooms, and staffs in intensive care units. Examining attitudes toward stress, hierarchy, teamwork, and error, Robert Helmreich and his colleagues discovered that pilots were more willing to admit, even in abstract terms, that stress could adversely affect their performance.[24] They were less committed to hierarchy in their workplaces and, as a result, were more committed to teamwork. This greater willingness to see others as their equals and to acknowledge their own potential vulnerability led to a different sort of work culture. The pilots' willingness to work more closely with other members of their crews and to discuss errors and problems led them to be more effective. In their limited study of intensive care units and operating rooms, this Texas research team discovered much higher levels of hierarchy among the high-status professionals (i.e., surgeons and doctors), as well as an unwillingness to admit the possibility of error. Doctors perceived in the ICU that they were highly communicative, whereas the nurses perceived them as not very communicative. While the authors establish no relationship between these particular professionals and the level of medical errors, they do observe that medical error is probably the eighth most common cause of death in the United States.

This finding is remarkable in suggesting several limits of our current accounts of competence that arise out of power differentials and social distance. I take the following lessons from this study:

1. Hierarchy and power differentials are likely to interfere with, rather than contribute to, the exercise of competence.[25]
2. Competence needs to be understood not as an attribute of an individual but as an attribute of the relevant professional "team," whether that is an individual, a working group, a faculty, and so on. Competent individuals still need the support of others to accomplish their ends.
3. Recognition of the possibility of failure or error increases the likelihood of solving problems and avoiding errors. Ironically, then, being more vulnerable makes a group stronger.
4. Improving competence is not only about the competence of individuals; it is also about fostering team training in which individuals are taught how to cope in a nonpunitive manner with errors.[26]

Moral competence requires more than individual virtue, then. Professionals have to organize their work so that they can become accountable and vulnerable to the competent judgment and expertise of other professionals, both within and outside their own professions. This point is much easier to say than to put into practice. Nevertheless, it is as crucial as the first steps of determining and inculcating caring competence in individual professionals. Inducing moral rectitude in individuals without recognizing the social settings in which they practice their professions has two deleterious effects. Not only does it prevent the individual morally sensitive professional from acting in a way that best accords with moral requirements, it also breeds contempt for the institutional setting and allows individuals to excuse themselves from responsibility for them.

Professional autonomy cannot, then, be understood in a caricatured way as providing the individual professional with unrestrained conditions for self-expression. Further, not only do professionals have to work with others in their own profession, but increasingly, the tasks of complex societies require many sorts of professionals to cooperate with one another. The result is that professional autonomy also requires professionals to assume responsibility for the ways in which their professions are organized.

PROFESSIONAL COMPETENCE AND AUTONOMY IN SOCIAL PERSPECTIVE

So far we have examined competence as an element of the ethical concerns both for individual professionals and for a team of professionals. There is a long-standing dispute in the field of professional ethics around the question of whether professional ethics requires a different set of ethics for professionals than for people in general and whether there are different ethical standards for particular professions.[27] One way to understand the argument that I have just made is to see the issue of moral responsibility among professionals as not so very different from that among other people in a good society. Although their technical forms of expertise may differ, professionals, I have argued are, in other ways, like others who give care.

But I now want to push the following question a bit further. In what ways are professions set apart from the rest of the society? What does it mean to be a professional? Returning to Virginia Woolf for some inspiration, I shall argue that, given the increasingly precarious place of the professions in the changing world order, professions now face a fateful choice in thinking about their status in society.

Recall Woolf's concern that if women become professionals, they will become as jealous, as self-sure, and as narrow-minded as male professionals. Her portrait is a quite unflattering account of elite groups working to maintain their distance from others in the society.

Scholars kindly disposed toward the professions describe them in this way: professions are based on general and systematic knowledge, professions have an orientation to community interest, professions are self-monitoring through internalized codes of ethics, and professions emphasize rewards that symbolize accomplishments in work and are sought as ends in themselves.[28] Such an account is meant to distinguish being in a profession from another way of being in the world. Consider the auto mechanic, for example. No matter how talented, the person who repairs a machine is not seen as having systematic and general knowledge or as orienting him- or herself toward the community good or stressing the accomplishment of the work rather than the monetary reward of the work. Although professions have a high degree of prestige, professionals are seen as different from those who are simply interested in making money because professionals have a "calling."

Of course, such an account of the professions ignores the reality that one of the reasons for the professions to set themselves off as special is precisely to enhance their social and economic status. In the words of Jack Haas and William Shaffir, professionalization is a process whereby the

> chosen . . . convince society, through what is actually the enactment of a moral drama of the myth of their specialness, of their legitimacy to profess and to claim an honorific status. . . . The basis of professional dominance centers upon a process by which they mystify their competence. Thus they obscure the basis of their authority, providing the ideological justification for unequal status, closure of access, manipulation of knowledge and control over definitions of the situation.[29]

By this account, a central task of the professions is what Haas and Shaffir call "reputational control."[30] Such control depends on the donning of what Robert Edgerton called, in the 1970s, a "cloak of competence."[31] If professionals have an interest in policing their perceptions of their own sense of competence and in keeping any incompetence within the ranks outside of public view, then it is easy to see why they also want to control the meaning of "professional ethics," claiming that only they are able to understand the ethical imperatives of their activities.

We see, then, that both praiseworthy and depreciative accounts of professions emphasize similar aspects of these institutions. Professions claim to be special because of their function (based on a special knowledge), their selflessness, and their relative lack of interest in pecuniary rewards. They wish to control their own world and are jealous to protect this separate world.

Here we might ask about the cost of maintaining such boundaries, but I want to make the predicament more dire before trying to solve it. The view that professions are aimed at the improvement of the object of their concern, the denial of overt power while manipulating the outcomes of events, even, in Woolf's account, their concern for "sartorial splendor"[32]—all of these are characteristics that we usually associate in our culture not with masculinity but with femininity. Any tears in the "cloak of competence" may perhaps reveal that all professionals are not entirely competent and trustworthy. Furthermore, it may reveal that, at bottom, their work is not like the work associated with virile men but, rather, like the work associated with women: they care.

Celia Davies has argued that professions are organized along a masculinist model because they share the attributes of heroic masculinity built into complex bureaucratic organizations. She draws especially on the work of Max Weber to demonstrate this point. Here I am making a parallel argument about the masculinist nature of professions, but I ascribe to the professions a different motivation than Davies does.[33] Rather than seeing the masculine organization of professions as simply a "default value" of following the path of thinking along masculinist ways, I am arguing that professions are different from other forms of bureaucratic organization in having still more at stake in maintaining their masculinized "cloak of competence." One way to accomplish this task is to insist on the strongest of the masculine virtues as one of the qualities of professions: autonomy. An important way to understand the codes of ethics that emerged for the professions in the past half century is to see them as a way to assert their autonomy. Even with regard to moral practices, professions claim to be special and need to be treated differently. What would happen, though, if instead of seeing the professions as strong and forceful bodies in control of themselves and their futures, we see them as relatively fragile and trying desperately to protect themselves from the charge that they are just like the more feminine helping professions?[34]

Feminist scholars stress that to take care seriously also requires that we alter our most fundamental account of human nature.[35] People are not only rational, autonomous, and competent. They are also always vulnerable and dependent.

We have painted a predicament, then, whereby the professions, in order to assert their autonomy, centrality, and, I have suggested, in one way their masculinity, must maintain a distance from all others in the society. In doing so, however, they must assert claims for their specialness that become increasingly dysfunctional in the modern world and seem to invite control by managers.

What can be done about this circumstance? I will point to two possible directions, but before doing so, let me return briefly to Virginia Woolf's view of the solution. Woolf offered two solutions to her anxiety that if women joined the professions they would end up being the same as the pompous male advocates of "God, Country, Nature, and Property." She attached two conditions to the guinea that she sent to the women's society to help women advance in the professions:

> You shall have it . . . on condition that you help all properly qualified people, of whatever sex, class or color, to enter your profession; and further on condition

that in the practice of your profession you refuse to be separated from poverty, chastity, derision and freedom from unreal loyalties. . . . By poverty is meant enough money to live upon. That is, you must earn enough to be independent of any other human being and to buy that modicum of health, leisure, knowledge and so on that is needed for the full development of body and mind. But no more. Not a penny more.

By chastity is meant that when you have made enough to live on by your profession you must refuse to sell your brain for the sake of money. That is you must cease to practice your profession, or practice it for the sake of research and experiment; or, if you are an artist, for the sake of the art; or give the knowledge acquired professionally to those who need it for nothing. . . .

By derision, a bad word, but once again the English language is much in need of new words, is meant that you must refuse all methods of advertising merit, and hold that ridicule, obscurity and censure are preferable, for psychological reasons, to fame and praise. . . .

By freedom from unreal loyalties is meant that you must rid yourself of pride of nationality in the first place; also of religious pride, college pride, school pride, family pride, sex pride and those unreal loyalties that spring from them. Directly the seducers come with their seductions to bribe you into captivity, tear up the parchments; refuse to fill up the forms.[36]

Woolf's first demand, that professions become open to all who qualify, has become increasingly met. What Woolf did not recognize, and what we are slow to recognize as well, is that this change is not just a surface change in who sits in the chairs of professionals but, in fact, it subtly begins to change the status of the professions themselves. The demands to police the borders of the professions thus become even more imperative. One way to try to achieve this distance is to assert that professions have a role that is outside of the normal sphere of ongoing political, economic, and social battles. Eugin Isin has asserted that professionals now constitute a "new class" that veils its political role:

The new class and its factions dominate the public sphere. These ideologies allow the new class to obfuscate its own directives and interests by adopting a language of conflict in which it does not figure. The ideology of the professional ideal purports that it serves the people, the public, the disaffected, the helpless, the marginal, the powerful, the discriminated against, and so on, but not itself. While much of contemporary politics is about the struggle between the factions of the new class (between public sector and private sector professionals and between local and global professionals) for wealth, status, and power, on the surface it appears that it is between the working class and the bourgeoisie.[37]

Professions are thus trying to maintain a sense of their importance in the face of social changes that belie their claims to uniqueness. As the professions become more diverse, their "cloak of competence" frays as members of the public now see before them not a "doctor" but a *woman* doctor or a doctor *with an accent*—that is, a professional who is not marked with the trappings of high social status but, rather, a professional marked with previously devalued qualities. With an increasingly broad commitment to "flat hierarchies" in society, the special status of professions comes into question. Professions try to set themselves apart in order to enhance their economic and social status. Increasingly, though, wealth flows not to professionals, who increasingly have less control over their own work lives, but to entrepreneurs and others who are able to take advantage of the luck of the market. Most professions have also begun to worry about declining levels of public trust: as Haas and Shaffir note, a profession can only continue to claim special status if that claim is viewed as legitimate.

Here, then, are the fateful choice and the two possibilities that present themselves. On the one hand, professions can attempt to shore up their borders and assert more forcefully their special competence and need to control the world around them through such means as professional ethics. They can declare "managers" as their enemies and proceed to try to stave off attacks on their autonomy.[38] On the other hand, professions can follow Woolf's suggestion and change the nature of their claim for special status.

The first scenario requires a reassertion of the uniqueness of the professions. To accomplish such a vision requires a new insistence on the uniqueness of the profession's claims to competence, a continued assertion of the profession's autonomy. If professions follow this path, they will try to make professional ethics still more professionalized and assert their unwillingness to cooperate with managers more forcefully. We can imagine longer and more elaborate codes of professional conduct, more complex mechanisms for evaluating professionals, and a greater reluctance to allow outsiders and the general public to have any role in the shaping of professional life.

A second scenario is that professions will realize that they have a fateful and critical role to play: that as they become deprofessionalized by economic and other forces more powerful than they, simply reasserting their old ways of claiming competence and privilege no longer works. In this scenario, they will embrace the arguments that I have made, that the usual distinctions used to mark the professions do not distinguish their activities of caring from those of others engaged in care work. Contrary to Isin's dyspeptic critique, they will decide that they *are* interested in advocating for their own status, recognizing their status not as something special but as something that is a part of everyone's condition.

This second scenario is, in some ways, an updating of the second condition insisted on by Virginia Woolf. Her hope that women entering the professions would transform the professions may still come true.

CONCLUSION

In this essay, I have argued that to apply the feminist ethic of care to professional ethics requires a rethinking of questions of "competence" on three levels. Individual professionals need to understand that their competence is embedded in a more complex set of concerns, teams of professionals need to understand their competence in more cooperative terms, and professions themselves will do best to understand their competence not as a cloak in which they can make special demands on society but, rather, as the basis for providing their services to society in a caring way. On all three levels, I have suggested that the change demanded requires professionals to see their own work in a broader context, to admit their capacity for error, and to accept the nature of their vulnerability.

I began with the dispute between professionals and managers, and at first I defended professionals against the incursions of managers. I then suggested some ways in which professions need to reform themselves. In the end, though, I have really called for a fateful change in attitude and orientation. If, instead of using their considerable power to obscure how they operate as a new class, professionals should try to articulate a view of society in which, because all are cared for, none need be especially vulnerable, then professionals would no longer need to be set apart in the ways that they now are. Instead, they could join the movement to reorient society so that all are well cared for, well able to care, and able to pursue fully human lives.

NOTES

1. Virginia Woolf, *Three Guineas* (New York: Harcourt, Brace, 1938), 66.
2. Stephen Harrison and Christopher Pollitt, *Controlling Health Professionals: The Future of Work and Organization in the National Health Service* (Buckingham: Open University Press, 1984), 1–2.
3. See, for example, Margaret Urban Walker, *Moral Understandings: A Feminist Study in Ethics* (New York: Routledge, 1998).
4. See Celia Davies, *Gender and the Professional Predicament in Nursing* (Buckingham: Open University Press, 1995).
5. Kathy E. Ferguson, *The Feminist Case against Bureaucracy* (Philadelphia: Temple University Press, 1984).
6. Berenice Fisher and Joan C. Tronto, "Toward a Feminist Theory of Caring," in *Circles of Care: Work and Identity in Women's Lives,* ed. Emily Abel and Margaret Nelson (Albany: State University of New York Press, 1990), 40.
7. Joan C. Tronto, *Moral Boundaries: A Political Argument for an Ethic of Care* (New York: Routledge, 1993).
8. For an illuminating application of this approach, see Marina Pantazidou and Indira Nair, "Ethic of Care: Guiding Principles for Engineering Teaching and Practice," *Journal of Engineering Education* (April 1999): 205–12.
9. Patricia Benner, *From Novice to Expert: Excellence and Power in Clinical Nursing Practice* (Menlo Park, Calif.: Addison-Wesley, 1984).

10. Quoted in Terasa Astarita, Gayle Materna, and Cynthia Blevins, *Competency in Home Care* (Gaithersburg, Md.: Aspen, 1998), 4.

11. Astarita, Materna, and Blevins, *Competency in Home Care*.

12. Benner, *From Novice to Expert*.

13. In the section entitled "Ethics" in their introductory chapter, Astarita, Materna, and Blevins observe that "competency is a professional and paraprofessional standard of care for health care providers" (*Competency in Home Care*, 16). In construction, the legal standard to which architects and engineers are held is the "reasonable standard of care," which requires "that degree of care and skill and that judgment which is common to the profession" (Bell, quoted in Jacob Feld and Kenneth L. Carper, *Construction Failure,* 2nd edition [New York: John Wiley, 1997], 455).

14. Astarita, Materna, and Blevins, *Competency in Home Care*.

15. Astarita, Materna, and Blevins, *Competency in Home Care*; see also Marina Pantazidou, "Soil Mechanics and Competence," <http://caae.phi.cmu.edu/edm/soil>, accessed April 2000.

16. John Raven, *Competence in Modern Society: Its Identification, Development and Release* (London: H. K. Lewis, 1984), 2, 8, 188–99.

17. Berenice Fisher, "Alice in the Human Services," in *Circles of Care: Work and Identity in Women's Lives,* ed. Emily Abel and Margaret Nelson (Albany: State University of New York Press, 1990).

18. Kari Waerness, "Informal and Formal Care in Old Age: What Is Wrong with the New Ideology in Scandinavia Today?" in *Gender and Caring: Work and Welfare in Britain and Scandinavia,* ed. Claire Ungerson (London: Harvester, Wheatsheaf, 1990), 110–32.

19. To assess the nature of the client's reaction to care is also no simple matter. Sometimes clients are incapable of providing any response; and sometimes their responses are likely to be mixed with anger, regret, or other effects of the care that may or may not reflect their own best account of what has happened.

20. On the nature of fiduciary responsibilities, see, among others, Edward D. Pellegrino, Robert M. Veatch, and John P. Langen, eds., *Ethics, Trust and the Professions: Philosophical and Cultural Aspects* (Washington, D.C.: Georgetown University Press, 1991); Joan Callahan, ed., *Ethical Issues in Professional Life* (New York: Oxford, 1988); and Pantazidou, "Soil Mechanics and Competence."

21. For one account of the reasonable standard of care, see Feld and Carper, *Construction Failure*.

22. See Olusela Oni, *Who Should Run the Health Service? Realignment and Reconstruction* (Oxford: Radcliffe Medical Press, 1997).

23. Deborah Stone describes this moral dilemma for care workers similarly in "Care and Trembling," *The American Prospect,* no. 43 (March–April 1999): 61–64.

24. J. B. Sexton, E. J. Thomas, and R. L. Helmreich, "Error, Stress, and Teamwork in Medicine and Aviation: Cross Sectional Surveys," *British Medical Journal* 320, no. 7237 (18 March 2000): 745–49.

25. A colleague of mine once quipped, "We always say that democracy isn't the same as brain surgery, but maybe brain surgery needs to be more democratic."

26. Sexton, Thomas, and Helmreich write,

Airlines initiated a new approach to training and assessing pilot skills by moving away from training the individual pilot to training the entire crew, recognizing that safety and good performance was not just a function of the captain but of the captain using all available resources. The aviation approach is to deal with errors non-punitively and proactively, and this approach defines behavioral strategies taught in crew resource management training . . . as error countermeasures that are used to avoid error whenever possible, to trap errors when they do occur, and to mitigate the consequences of error before they escalate into undesirable states. ("Error, Stress, and Teamwork in Medicine and Aviation," 745–46)

27. See, for example, William F. May, "Professional Virtue and Self-Regulation," in *Ethical Issues in Professional Life,* ed. Joan Callahan (New York: Oxford University Press, 1988), 408–11.

28. Barber, quoted in Pellegrino, Veatch, and Langen, *Ethics, Trust and the Professions,* 23–24; see also Joan Callahan, ed., *Ethical Issues in Professional Life* (New York: Oxford University Press, 1988).

29. Jack Haas and William Shaffir, *Becoming Doctors: The Adoption of a Cloak of Competence* (Greenwich, Conn.: JAI Press, 1987), 4.

30. Haas and Shaffir, *Becoming Doctors,* 82.

31. Robert B. Edgerton, *The Cloak of Competence,* 2nd edition (Berkeley: University of California Press, 1993).

32. They distinguished themselves by, among other things, dress: "It not only covers nakedness, gratifies vanity, and creates pleasure for the eye, but it serves to advertise the social, professional, or intellectual standing of the wearer" (Woolf, *Three Guineas,* 20). Woolf observes that such "sartorial splendors" are for men only; "a woman who advertised her motherhood by a tuft of horsehair on the left shoulder would scarcely, you will agree, be a venerable object" (*Three Guineas,* 20–21).
Anthropologists who write about modern professions often describe the attempt to provide the profession with a similar "cloak of competence." Yet, as Woolf asked, it is important to note which kinds of professions are marked by dress and which are not. The markings of professional attire may change, but they indicate an important demarcation. Is the recent change in dress codes among lawyers meant to compete with dot-com businesses, or is it meant to change impressions of the profession?

33. Davies, *Gender and the Professional Predicament in Nursing.*

34. Consider Ilene J. Philipson's claim in *On the Shoulders of Women: The Feminization of Psychotherapy* (New York: Guilford Press, 1993) that psychoanalysis has been feminized. Other feminists have made still broader claims. Donna Haraway, in "A Manifesto for Cyborgs," predicts that all work is being feminized in our culture:

[In] the homework economy . . . [w]ork is being redefined as both literally female and feminized, whether performed by men or women. To be feminized means to be made extremely vulnerable; able to be disassembled, reassembled, exploited as a reserve labor force; seen less as workers than as servers; subjected to time arrangements on and off the paid job that make a mockery of a limited work day; leading to an existence that always borders on being obscene, out of place, and reducible to sex. ("A Manifesto for Cyborgs," in *Feminism/Postmodernism,* ed. Linda Nicholson [New York: Routledge, 1990], 208)

35. See Selma L. Sevenhuijsen, *Citizenship and the Ethics of Care* (London: Routledge, 1998); and Eva F. Kittay, *Love's Labor* (New York: Routledge, 1999).

36. Woolf, *Three Guineas,* 80.

37. Eugin F. Isin, "Who Is the New Citizen? Towards a Genealogy," *Citizenship Studies* 1, no. 1 (February 1997): 130.

38. See, for example, Oni, *Who Should Run the Health Service?*

13

Political Care and Humanitarian Response

Natalie Brender

[Charity] is a matter in which the immediate effect on the persons directly concerned, and the ultimate consequence to the general good, are apt to be at complete war with one another: while the education given to women—an education of the sentiments rather than of the understanding—and the habit inculcated by their whole life, of looking to immediate effects on persons, and not to remote effects on classes of persons—make them both unable to see, and unwilling to admit, the ultimate evil tendency of any form of charity or philanthropy which commends itself to their sympathetic feelings. . . . [T]his waste of resources and of benevolent feelings in doing harm instead of good, is immensely swelled by women's contributions, and stimulated by their influence. Not that this is a mistake likely to be made by women, where they have actually the practical management of schemes of benevolence. . . . But women who only give their money, and are not brought face to face with the effects it produces, how can they be expected to foresee them?[1]

In his 1896 essay "The Subjection of Women," John Stuart Mill advances an argument for women's social and political equality by considering how the public sphere has been influenced by feminine sensibilities. He claims that women's contribution has consisted in "softening influences of individual delicacy and generosity" that are evident both in the premodern ethos of chivalry and in the propagation of pacifism and philanthropy in Victorian Britain. While these tendencies are intrinsically admirable, Mill argues that "in the particular applications" women's influence gives a direction to these tendencies that is "at least as often mischievous as useful."[2] Lacking appropriate education and practical experience, women go awry in their philanthropic efforts because their sympathy is not directed by a reflective understanding of social problems. What particularly concerns Mill is that women's impulsive and unreflective generosity, together with their own situation of social dependence, produces modes of charity that foster dependence rather than self-sufficiency in recipients. These considerations, he contends, militate in favor of granting women better education, social standing, and practical experience in order that their sympathies can influence the public sphere more constructively.

In the past decade's debates over care ethics, certain lines of critique have echoed Mill's argument about the sources of deficiencies in women's ethical sensibilities. In contrast to initial formulations of care ethics that unequivocally celebrated the practical ethos arising out of women's experience, later critics have articulated versions of the Millian claim that healthy ethical sensibilities cannot arise out of the restrictions and norms that have characterized much of "women's experience." Reacting against the unnuanced valorization of extant feminine sensibilities, philosophers such as Claudia Card and Sandra Bartky have noted the ethical harms that existing social structures in Western culture have done to women's characters.[3] As Bartky and Card show, even intimate relationships that embody purported attributes of care such as selflessness, responsiveness, and particularity can be profoundly unhealthy. Such critiques update the point made in previous centuries by Mill as well as by Mary Wollstonecraft and Virginia Woolf:[4] gendered subjectivities formed under conditions of gender oppression *cannot* be ethically sound.

While these critiques have usefully surveyed the pitfalls of "feminine" care in intimate relationships, the theorization of care has more recently turned to the sphere of impersonal relationships among strangers in civil and global society. Some philosophers believe that insofar as care is an intrinsically "motivation and desire"–inflected encounter between persons, it cannot address questions of an individual's conduct toward strangers whom he or she cannot encounter particularistically and hence cannot care for. When relations among strangers are in question, such commentators conclude, care ethics must be supplemented by a discourse of justice.[5] On the other hand, proponents of a nonparochial care ethics argue that care can and does inform engagement beyond the intimate sphere. Such a view is expressed in Marilyn Friedman's claim that foreign aid and famine relief are forms of care "designed to relieve suffering and attend to human needs."[6] Similarly, Virginia Held asserts that

> the commitment to justice needed for agreement *in actual conditions* on even minimal requirements of justice is as likely to demand relational feelings as a rational recognition of abstract principles. Human beings can and do care, and are capable of caring far more than at present, about the sufferings of children quite distant from them, about the prospects for future generations, and about the

well-being of the globe. The liberal tradition's mutually disinterested rational in-
dividualists would seem unlikely to care enough to take the actions needed to
achieve moral decency at a global level.[7]

Believing that care does indeed motivate practices such as foreign aid and
famine relief, advocates of a comprehensive, politically relevant care ethics
hold that the pressing practical question is how a disposition toward care (or
what Held terms "relational feelings") can be fostered within justice-fixated
Western societies.

Amid this recent extension of ethics to the political sphere it is notable that
none of the critical debate has yet addressed the Millian concern that Card
and Bartky have turned on care in the context of intimate relations. In its
most general form, the worry is that feminine ethical sensibilities formed under conditions of gender oppression cannot produce wholly sound relationships in *any* social sphere. Does this claim hold true for impersonal as well
as intimate relations? According to Mill, when women of mid-nineteenth-
century Britain turned their attention to public concerns, their narrowly sentimental education and limited worldly experience led their practical judgment to focus on immediate particularities to the exclusion of abstract and
causally remote considerations. These factors make women "both unable to
see, and unwilling to admit, the ultimate evil tendency of any form of charity or philanthropy which commends itself to their sympathetic feelings."[8] In
contemporary Western societies, the causal factors Mill identifies have significantly changed; yet these changes have been relatively recent and may
coexist with a substantial carryover of sensibilities from previous modes of
"femininity." Consequently, it is worth considering ways in which the one-
sidedness that Mill diagnoses in "feminine" public philanthropy of his own
day might subtly inflect the contemporary theory and practice of care in the
public sphere.

THE CRITIQUE OF HUMANITARIAN RELIEF

To begin exploring these topics, it will be useful to focus on a particular context in which caring for the suffering of distant strangers typically becomes a
pressing issue for inhabitants of prosperous Western countries. An incite-
ment to care actively about strangers' suffering often takes the form of a humanitarian crisis that is both visually dramatic and accessible to mass media
coverage. Suddenly there is a blitz of heart-wrenching images on newspaper
covers and television screens: typically, images of hollow-eyed, emaciated
children lying listlessly on the hot ground of some Third World country.
Filled with shock and compassion, sympathetic Westerners send off checks
to the relief agencies that promise to save these children from certain death.

There is every reason to take such responses as sincere expressions of compassion; but before they are valorized under the rubric of care, their effects must be further examined. Recent critiques of humanitarianism suggest that in certain cases such compassionate donations are terribly counterproductive and not the ethically worthy acts they seem to be. For theoretical and practical reasons, it is crucial to understand why some cases of compassionate giving to suffering strangers might not be instances of successful political care.

Following the perceived failures of relief efforts on several continents after the end of the Cold War, the past decade has seen a wave of popular, academic, and professional critiques of humanitarian relief.[9] In an examination of this trend, an article in *The New York Times* observes that humanitarian aid has done much good but has also produced much evil: "sustaining a war economy, legitimizing outlaw authorities, creating refugee movements and encouraging parties to play one agency against another."[10] In a scathing op-ed piece in *Newsweek* magazine, former famine relief worker Michael Maren focuses on the way in which the consciences of Western donors are manipulated—and ultimately misdirected, as he argues—by mass media images of distant suffering. Media imagery typically conveys a beguilingly simple message:

> Skeletal, starving Africans are back in the news, this time from Sudan. If you are moved—and you'd have to be heartless not to be—operators are standing by to take your check or credit-card number. If you have any doubts that your contribution will really help, the charities will assure you that food will reach these victims quickly and save their lives, at least until the next famine. It's that simple. Defeating hunger means getting food to this emaciated man, to his family, to his children.[11]

Contrary to this simplistic picture suggested by the charities' ads, Maren argues that neither the causes of famine nor its remedies are as straightforward as the media message purports. In the case of Sudan, people are starving not because of cruel fate, poor weather, or underdevelopment but because of the *political* reality that "starvation is a weapon in Sudan's 15-year-old civil war."[12] The warring Sudanese government and rebels are jointly responsible for creating—often deliberately so—the conditions of famine in the southern regions of the country. These parties complicit in the crisis actually include international relief agencies themselves, which cooperate with and aid the Sudanese government in order to get food to the starving. Here, as in many other cases of politically generated suffering, Maren notes, the co-opting of relief provisions by militias on both sides results in a large proportion of resources being diverted away from the intended civilian recipients. Hence the donations of conscience-struck Westerners backfire in a terrible irony: "Food goes into the bellies of the militias and is sold to purchase weapons and ammunition. . . . So the primary beneficiaries of charity are the people who caused the problem to begin with."[13] Although these facts are suppressed in the charities' fund-raising appeals, Maren reports that they are well known to relief workers themselves: "After spending their days delivering food and supplies, they often sit and lament how saving one group of children can mean arming other children. Yet how is it possible to stand by when there is even a small chance that food can save the wide-eyed, swollen-bellied children they see every day? Aid workers never crack the conundrum."[14] Maren's point is that cracking the conundrum of African famine requires a redirection of attention away from the wide-eyed starving children themselves and away from the easy, shallow commitment of donations toward food relief. Only by coming to understand and grapple with the *political* causes of suffering on display, Maren insists, can citizens of rich Western countries demonstrate "moral commitment on a higher level than writing a check." The first necessity is to realize how moral responses are shaped by media imagery and then to take responsibility for redirecting sympathy into more effective forms of action:

> The problem of commitment starts with our images of hunger. The face of famine in Sudan should not be that of a starving child. It should be the faces of the country's leaders, rebel leader John Garang and President Omar al-Bashir. And it should be the faces of the men in Washington and Tehran who have backed opposite sides in the SPLA's fight against the Islamic fundamentalist government in Khartoum. The faces of famine should not inspire pity, they should inspire anger and indignation. . . . And if these are the faces of famine, perhaps our first reaction should not be to reach for a checkbook, but to take to the streets or at least phone Washington.[15]

Maren's critique of humanitarianism and its misdirection by media imagery attacks familiar assumptions in several disturbing ways. First and foremost there is the shock of hearing that in humanitarian crises the good intentions of sympathetic Westerners are not enough. Where mass suffering is caused and perpetuated by politically motivated violence, donations for humanitarian relief may help some victims but only at the expense of continuing the conflict that victimizes many others. In these contexts, a purported act of care goes badly awry through donors' failure to realize the consequences of their actions. Beyond exposing the malignant consequences of food relief, Maren also poses a scathing critique of the manipulability and shallow moral engagement manifested by well-intentioned Western donors. In their susceptibility to what he calls "the pornography of African suffering,"[16] donors focus their reactions on victims while overlooking perpetrators. In embracing the easy and comforting fiction that their money can directly benefit the suffering persons whose images strike their conscience, donors fail to manifest a "higher level" moral commitment that would agitate politically to change the economic and diplomatic circumstances encouraging the Sudanese conflict to continue. In this state of affairs there is a failure of would-be caring to proceed as it should.

Given the human lives at stake in the success or failure of practical intervention in humanitarian crises, it is important to reflect further on what goes wrong in the cases of compassionate giving that Maren criticizes. What is discovered about these matters will also have wider implications for ethical theory and practice. Thus, we need to consider the *intrinsic* failure of moral perception and commitment that might inform misguided humanitarianism and the various *consequentialist* issues that also arise.

MORAL GRAPHICS AND POLITICAL CARE

In her article "Unnecessary Identities: Representational Practices and Moral Recognition," Margaret Urban Walker discusses ways in which stereotypes of social groups lead to misrepresentations of these groups that in turn reinforce patterns of oppression. *Pace* contemporary normative theories, she argues, more than just a systematically justified ideal of practical reasoning is required for an adequate philosophical grasp of the barriers to ethically sound social recognition. In many cases, failures of recognition arise out of ways in which groups of human beings are culturally represented and thereby become objects of moral (mis)perception: "Some picturing practices representationally 'ensoul'—personify, subjectify—some people for others in morally disturbing or vicious ways, whether as 'objects,' as diminished subjects, or as disqualified (or peculiarly qualified) agents."[17] Walker assigns the term *moral graphics* to picturing practices (such as racial stereotypes or pornography) that share the characteristic of impeding social recognition of certain persons as moral subjects and agents. Only by paying attention "to analysis of constructions of social identity," she contends, can philosophers' understanding of societal bias and prejudice advance beyond an overly narrow focus on "what or how individuals think in discrete episodes of explicitly moral reflection."[18]

While Walker's discussion focuses mostly on the social misrecognition informing contemporary types of oppression, she also objects to certain moral graphics that are less directly implicated in social malaise. What she identifies as "necrography" (i.e., imagery of death) appears in culturally familiar depictions of Nazi concentration camp victims as cadaverous, passive, and effectively "unsouled" or dehumanized in their absence of standard human subjectivity.[19] The problem here is that in blocking contemporary viewers' appreciation of the victims' robust humanity, these images foreclose morally appropriate reactions to the victims' fate. Walker extends this notion of "necrography" to the sort of media imagery that, as seen above, is criticized by Michael Maren. Walker expresses her own critique as follows:

In recent postwar decades, a disturbingly similar pattern of imagery has become familiar to the point of everydayness, the iconography of "starving Africa." In affluent Western countries we have seen so many of these images—of the emaciated, listless, empty-eyed, (and especially where a child, usually naked) "African"—that they amount to a picture-type, an icon. Alongside pictures of violence, these images are parts of another iconography of the helpless and hopeless, a kind of people doomed one way or another, either by starvation, plagues, or political chaos. While images of starvation have evoked outpourings of concern and money, the effects of this repetitive imagery occlude the actors, African, European, and American, and the histories and political complicities, that figure in the explanations of why these particular actual people are starving or dying at this particular place and time. At least the concentration camp imagery unambiguously signals specifically moral monstrosity, not only the obscene fate of victims but the culpability of a particular set of perpetrators.[20]

Walker's point is not that the images of "starving Africa" block a compassionate response altogether, for she takes it that the "outpourings of concern and money" show otherwise. Rather, her objection is that these compassionate donations are not accompanied by donors' recognition of famine victims as persons situated in a particular historical-political context. The implication is that such a failure of recognition is not *consequentially* but *intrinsically* ethically deficient. Notwithstanding the images' success in producing a salutary emotional and practical response, it is grounds for ethical criticism of the images that they foster a cognitive failure of recognition.[21]

However, there is reason to think that more than just intrinsically regrettable misrecognitions are at stake in the "necrography" or the "pornography" (as Maren calls it)[22] of African suffering. In certain extreme cases such as the Sudan, much practical harm is produced when compassionate donations embody a cognitive failure to look behind media imagery in order to discover political realities behind the suffering on display. These facts complicate any blanket assertion that care is embodied in donors' responses to the sufferings of distant strangers. As noted at the outset of this chapter, some advocates of a political version of care ethics contend that the reality of political care is shown in the fact that Westerners readily open their wallets in response to images of starving children. Yet, in light of the consequences of such donations in contexts in which food relief actually perpetuates warfare and famine, the purported caring has clearly gone wrong.

Are there resources in existing formulations of care ethics that could address these issues? Joan Tronto's distinction between modes of caring is useful in such an analysis. While care as such embodies a willingness "to work, to sacrifice, to spend money, to show emotional concern, and to expend energy toward the object of care," Tronto notes that forms of care differ with respect to the nature of their objects. Caring *about* someone or something "refers to less concrete objects" and "is characterized by a more general form of commitment," whereas caring *for* someone or something "implies a specific, particular object that is the focus of caring" and "involves responding to the particular, concrete, physical, spiritual, intellectual, psychic, and emotional needs of others."[23] To cite Tronto's example of this distinction, the Red Cross cares directly *for* earthquake victims, whereas private individuals may care *about* the earthquake victims by extending financial and other forms of support to the Red Cross efforts. Implicit in this example is the presumption that these two forms of engagement use appropriate means and succeed in meeting at least some of the needs of some of the victims. As Tronto elsewhere observes, however, the process of caring may be successful to varying degrees with respect to its methods and its goals. It is a practice that can be done well or poorly, and it may fail altogether.[24] Because caring well requires adequate knowledge of a given situation and wise deliberation about conflicting priorities and demands, in complex social situations caring may be "filled with inner contradictions, conflict, and frustration."[25]

Tronto's distinction between kinds of caring and her reminder that caring may be carried out in better or worse ways permit a clearer analysis of what can go wrong when Western donors respond to media images of starving children by sending off checks to the relief agencies that implore viewers to "show that they care." A first potential for failure in ethical response consists in an uncritical acceptance of the notion that through the intermediary of relief workers one is magically capable of caring *for* the particular starving children in the charities' ads. As critics of humanitarian relief note, donors cannot ensure that their money benefits the general class of persons they intend to help, much less those particular children whose plight so moves them. In delegating agencies to do the direct "caring-*for*" work, what donors do is manifest a "caring-*about*" the starving. Of course, delegating the task of caring-for is not intrinsically ethically problematic; when an earthquake strikes far-off countries, the best response possible for compassionate Westerners might well be a donation to relief efforts. Yet, in light of recent critiques of humanitarianism, it is clear that the delegation of caring-for becomes ethically problematic in circumstances such as the funding of famine relief in the Sudan. In such a case, the mode of caring-about that donors choose embodies a failure to grasp the political context of the famine and the role of relief resources in prolonging the civil conflict. Persons who donate in ignorance of the economic and political situation thus tacitly endorse the misleading media representation of the suffering on display as being caused simply by a lack of food that donations can allay. To put the point in Walker's terminology, care fails in this case because donors unthinkingly accept the moral graphics of "starving Africa" that occlude the political origins of famine and the fact of its necessarily political solution. The failure of care here can also be glossed with reference to Maren's critique: caring that embodies a susceptibility to misleading imagery and a cognitive ignorance of political realities reflects a distinctly low-level sort of moral commitment. In the case of the Sudan, he implies, it constitutes a sort of gullibility that produces morally worse results than total inaction.

The upshot of these considerations is that if caring about suffering is to be genuinely political, it not only must extend itself beyond parochialism to the wider world of strangers but must also be responsibly aware of realities of power as well as realities of need. In a world in which all famines are caused by drought, flood, earthquakes, and other natural catastrophes, it would be relatively simple to formulate ethically sound forms of response.[26] In such a world, an ethic of care would readily lead us to donate money for the relief of those in need. In the actual world, in which acute needs are created not just by natural disaster but by human evil as well, a concern for suffering must sometimes be expressed through modified kinds of ethical response.[27] Sometimes it is impossible to give direct relief to suffering persons without simultaneously aiding those responsible, advancing their causes, and perpetuating the status quo. Philip Gourevitch underlines this point in his criticism of humanitarianism in the aftermath of the 1994 Rwandan genocide, when Hutu forces fled the country to relief camps where a massive provision of foreign aid enabled the militias to regroup and to continue their genocidal campaign against the Tutsis. Decrying the naïveté that allowed this to happen, Gourevitch argues that because "it is impossible to act in or on a political situation without having a political effect," humanitarian aid that ignores this reality "becomes a smoke screen to cover political effects it actually creates."[28] In a situation in which large-scale misery will continue as long as certain agents' political agendas are being pursued, the necessary form of response will have to be a *political* one aimed at defeating the agendas in question rather than a *humanitarian* one aimed directly at the misery these agendas cause. Both Gourevitch and Maren recognize how agonizing it is to make such political judgments if one is an aid worker looking into the faces of the starving. Still, as they both contend, it is unconscionable to dodge these judgments when it is clear that such a refusal effectively supports the perpetrators of evil and enlarges the suffering they produce. For this reason Maren urges Western consumers of media imagery to realize that we ourselves are in an ethical situation analogous to that of the aid workers whose conundrum he describes. When we are in possession of salient facts about situations such as the Sudan, we should manifest a high enough degree of moral commitment to turn our attention away from the faces of individual victims in order to focus on the faces of those responsible for their suffering.

This argument does not presume that all humanitarian crises are like that in the Sudan. In many cases emergency relief efforts can be constructive in short-term crises (though again, an ongoing moral commitment to the affected regions will generally mandate activism aimed at changing political and economic circumstances as well). To say that addressing humanitarian crises ultimately involves the promotion of victims' economic security and the democratization of their political regimes highlights the fact that a discourse of justice is appropriate to bring to these matters as a complement to a discourse of care. What recent critiques of humanitarianism make clear above all is that being an agent committed to alleviating the suffering of distant strangers requires being media savvy, well informed, and capable of engaging with complex ethical and political realities. It is a daunting set of responsibilities.

CONSEQUENTIALIST CONSIDERATIONS

At this juncture we face a host of questions. Given the multitude of mass media appeals for donations toward humanitarian causes, it is hardly possible for most people to do detailed research on the facts of each crisis in order to determine the relative merits of donation versus activism. What is the value of pointing out pitfalls of impulsive humanitarian donations when it would seem to be a superhuman task to be fully informed about all of the international contexts in which we are called on to care for others? Moreover, is it even realistic to think that the shocked compassion produced by moral graphics of "starving Africa" can be "intellectualized" in a way that produces the motivation for information gathering and political activism? Would it not be more helpful on the whole to encourage Westerners' sympathies to flow freely in response to fund-raising pleas, rather than to risk alienating potential donors by a rehearsal of political complexities?

These questions seem largely unresolvable with respect to their empirical dimensions.[29] There are two competing schools of thought on the question of whether more consequential good than harm would be produced by encouraging popular scrutiny of the moral graphics in the news and in fund-raising ads for humanitarian relief. One view is that such imagery has obviously been hugely successful in motivating Westerners to donate money in face of urgent humanitarian crises and that they hold out a promise of ongoing success that less emotionally gripping and more intellectually complex calls for political engagement may well lack. In Margaret Walker's view, "The 'humanitarian' impulse is there to be tapped, while the motivation to political analysis and appropriate action is, for most people, not readily there to be tapped."[30] From this perspective, the desirability of relying on media imagery to create empathy with suffering strangers must come first in order to sustain the flow of aid, with criticism of media imagery a secondary priority.[31] On the other hand, it is also possible that an increasing saturation of public consciousness with images of and allusions to global suffering (not only in newscasts and charitable appeals but in Benneton ads and the like) will eventually have a deadening effect on viewers' emotional response.

Journalist and human rights scholar Samantha Power notes that the wide-spread use of Holocaust references and imagery by activists seeking to gal-vanize popular concern for contemporary crises does sometimes succeed in grabbing public attention; but in the long run, she warns, this tactic risks pro-ducing banality and disengagement.[32] Similarly, Michael Ignatieff decries the way in which Western mass media coverage of humanitarian crises courts short-term attention at the cost of long-term commitment. When television bathes "typical" individual victims in its sentimental humanitarian spotlight, he contends, it creates an empathetic identification between viewer and vic-tim that is "intense but shallow"; for "television personalizes, humanizes, but also depoliticizes moral relations, . . . it weakens the understanding on which sustained empathy—and moral commitment—depend."[33] Echoing other crit-ics of humanitarianism, Ignatieff notes that aid agencies' pragmatic interests in fund-raising and maintaining political neutrality often lead them to collude with the media in fostering depoliticized, sentimentalized stories of victims. Yet in so doing, he argues, agencies collaborate in "deny[ing] the audience the deeper understanding—bitter, contradictory, political, complex—on which a durable commitment depends."[34] This perspective suggests that be-cause the moral graphics of decontextualized victimhood will inevitably lose their motivating power with repeated exposure, the pressing task ought to be to generate a long-term commitment to politically informed activism.[35]

These competing perspectives show the difficulty of reaching a purely con-sequentialist assessment of how shocking imagery should be optimally used for humanitarian purposes. Ideally, a balanced kind of engagement could be fos-tered by modes of representation that both humanize and personalize suffering victims (thus engendering empathy and immediate financial commitment) and also convey intellectually complex information about the various circumstances (thus fostering a long-term commitment to changing the factors responsible for suffering). Indeterminacy also hangs over the consequentialist question of what degree of suspiciousness would best be cultivated in public consciousness with respect to the moral graphics of distant strangers' suffering. For all of the wrenching cases like the Sudan, in which relief supplies exacerbate the sources of suffering, there are plenty of other foreign and domestic causes in which do-nations as well as political activism are genuinely helpful. The trade-off be-tween fostering short-term donations and long-term political commitment to a cause—if indeed such a trade-off is inevitable—simply cannot be calculated in such a way as to direct a definitively optimal critique of the media.

Apart from these thorny consequentialist problems, however, there is much to be said for the intrinsic ethical value of responding to moral graph-ics of distant suffering with a degree of analytical detachment. Detachment is not incompatible with continuing to feel shock and compassion, but it must be sufficiently present to enable reflection on the ways in which, as Nancy Sherman says, "our private imaginations are fed by public images and narratives."[36] The desideratum that agents strive for transparency with respect to the workings of moral graphics on their own responses requires that emotions be reflectively scrutinized. As mentioned at the outset of this essay, such a demand for reflection on habitual patterns of emotion has characterized existing critiques of "feminine" patterns of emotion and practical judgment in intimate relations. A parallel line of critique, one premised on the fallibility of unreflective emotional responses to humanitarian appeals, may improve the theory and practice of care in the political sphere as well.

CARE AND THE CRITIQUE OF COMPASSION

Care ethics draws on a moral psychology in which emotions of love, compassion, and empathy are salient in motivating an attentive orientation to others' welfare. Critics of care as an ethos of intimate personal relationships have noted how the construction of feminine subjectivity under conditions of gender oppression is likely to introduce ethical liabilities into women's caring. Their criticisms show that not all impulses and actions oriented to satisfying others' needs should be considered infallible touchstones of ethical goodness or health. Elizabeth Spelman has extended this line of critique into an argument that care ethics must come to grips with the reality of women's egregious failures to care for other women. Citing social contexts such as Nazi Germany, American slavery, and the contemporary U.S. workplace, Spelman shows concretely how women can both misdirect their caring in problematic ways and fail to care at all.[37] As she argues, any effort to understand these phenomena must note that care and compassion are structured through a "political economy of attention" that gives emotion its cognitive content and direction. "As we sift through and try to make sense of the suffering to which we are called on to respond," she notes, "we implicitly and explicitly sort out, measure, and give shape to it."[38] Echoing the critiques made by Maren and Walker, Spelman contends that certain forms of attending to suffering are morally and politically problematic in the ways in which they direct attention, in the emotions they summon up, and in the narratives or paradigms of meaning they deploy. Contrary to naive assumptions about the intrinsic goodness and perceptiveness of emotions associated with care, the emotion of compassion is particularly susceptible to being problematic as a form of attention to suffering. For instance, insofar as white women in nineteenth-century America responded to slave narratives with compassion, their interpretations of the meaning of slaves' suffering occluded the possibility of directing politically significant outrage against those responsible for sustaining slaveholding society. Spelman takes such examples to show that, "like other forms of caring," compassion may "reinforce the very patterns of economic and political subordination responsible for such suffering."[39]

To understand compassionate attention as being structured by judgments, evaluations, narrative schemas, and interpretations presupposes a cognitive view of emotions. In the cognitive view, emotions are not brute passions that exist either in some "primal" form or not at all; to the contrary, because emotions are informed by knowledge and interpretation, they can stand in need of and be capable of adjustment.[40] It is possible to criticize forms of attention to suffering precisely because emotion-inflected responses such as compassion or outrage embody cognitive assessments that can be corrected by reflection and fuller information. In a cognitive view of emotion it follows that agents are responsible for scrutinizing the ethical appropriateness of how they react effectively (and hence practically) to others' suffering. An analysis of what it means for individuals and societies to take responsibility for the direction and content of care must be part of any satisfactory political ethic of care.

Recognition of the cognitive content and corrigibility of emotions also allows us to see how John Stuart Mill's remarks about women's charity can serve a prophylactic role in the ongoing theorization of care as a political ethic. His claim is that women's charitable impulses are misdirected by a culturally formed "feminine" mind-set that has two main traits: first, it focuses on specific individuals as objects of sympathetic emotion; and second, it presumes that sympathetic feelings in themselves constitute a veridical guide to appropriate practical response. Given the continuities in Western feminine subjectivity over the past century and a half, it is quite plausible that this mind-set might creep into present-day understandings of care as an ethos of relationship among strangers as well as intimates. As noted at the outset of this chapter, some advocates of political care highlight humanitarian caring for strangers' suffering as a paradigmatic case of care in the public sphere. Yet, insofar as this form of caring is still understood to be an ethos arising out of women's experience, its articulation in theory and in practice might betray traces of the ethically flawed philanthropic mind-set that Mill identifies in women of his own day. A care-oriented sensibility might be prone to presuppose that the appropriateness of whatever course of action is immediately prompted by a perception of individuals' suffering; and it might resist looking beyond immediate perceptions of need toward a more reflective and synoptic assessment of circumstances.

Insofar as a putatively caring response is to take this form in the context of humanitarian need, it would be oblivious to Michael Maren's and Margaret Walker's appeals for scrutiny of the moral graphics that commonly incite humanitarian concern. These images of decontextualized sufferers are designed to incite an unreflective compassionate response and impulsive donation. They target precisely the mind-set that Mill sees in women of his day. The existence of especially difficult humanitarian crises such as the Sudan famine, in which the unreflectively compassionate response of donation may worsen the problem, shows the importance of submitting initial caring impulses to reflective critique. The relevance of this warning to contemporary care ethics may be judged by the passing invocations of humanitarian compassion as a mode of political caring. The very brevity of these claims tacitly implies that the feeling of compassion and the actions it prompts amount to paradigmatic and laudable instances of caring. For the sake of offsetting this easy (and misleading) equation, Maren's and Walker's critiques must be taken seriously.

The temptation to deny the cognitive, politically inflected, and highly fallible aspects of care is, of course, not confined to exponents or practitioners of care ethics. It extends to all inhabitants of prosperous Western nations who sometimes adopt a naive understanding of the concern they feel for the suffering of distant strangers. There are many motives for taking an apolitical and sentimentalist view of humanitarian concern; such a view allows the luxury of intellectual simplicity, political innocence, and self-congratulation.[41] Yet, in order to take responsibility for emotional and practical responses to strangers' suffering, it is crucial to keep in mind Michael Ignatieff's reminder that humanitarian sympathies always rest on complex cultural interpretations:

> We would prefer to suppose that the mere sight of suffering victims on television would be enough to rouse us to pity. In fact, there is nothing instinctive about the emotions stirred in us by television pictures of atrocity or suffering. Our pity is structured by history and culture. . . . When we do make the misfortunes, miseries, or injustices suffered by others into our business, some narrative is telling us why these strangers and their problems matter to us.[42]

Articulating these cognitive structurings of emotion may destroy a happy innocence about the sources of our concern for strangers' welfare. It may seem as if acknowledging the cultural structuring of our emotions robs them of their ethical goodness or diminishes their motivating power. To be sure, the knowledge that Ignatieff offers cannot restore the comforts of prepolitical innocence. There is no guarantee that fuller cognitive awareness will not sometimes overwhelm and paralyze agency. On the other hand, this knowledge holds out the hope that when culturally structured concerns do prompt action, these actions will embody greater intellectual integrity and a deeper level of ethical commitment. Ultimately, such actions would surely be more effective in securing a lasting alleviation of human suffering.

NOTES

For valuable comments on an earlier version of this essay, I am grateful to the audience at the Feminist Ethics Revisited Conference in September 1999. I particularly want to thank those who read the essay and discussed it with me at length: Ruth Abbey, Simone Chambers, Ann Garry, Jean Keller, Eva Feder Kittay, Margaret Urban Walker, and Julie White. I also thank the editors of this volume for useful suggestions.

1. John Stuart Mill, "The Subjection of Women," in John Stuart Mill and Harriet Taylor Mill, *Essays on Sex Equality,* ed. Alice S. Rossi (Chicago: University of Chicago Press, 1970), 227. I am indebted to Ruth Abbey for bringing this passage to my attention.

2. Mill, "The Subjection of Women," 227.

3. See Claudia Card, "Gender and Moral Luck," in *Identity, Character, and Morality,* ed. Owen Flanagan and Amelie Rorty (Cambridge: MIT Press, 1990); and Sandra Bartky, *Femininity and Domination* (New York: Routledge, 1990).

4. Mary Wollstonecraft, *A Vindication of the Rights of Woman* (Harmondsworth, U.K.: Penguin, 1982). This critique is most evident in the character of Mrs. Ramsay in Virginia Woolf's *To the Lighthouse* (Harmondsworth, U.K.: Penguin, 1971), as well as in Woolf's critique of the "Angel in the House" in the essay "Professions for Women," in her *Women and Writing,* ed. Michele Barrett (New York: Harcourt Brace Jovanovich, 1980).

5. See, for example, Claudia Card, "Caring, Justice, and Evils," in her *The Unnatural Lottery* (Philadelphia: Temple University Press, 1996), 72–96. The assumption that principles of justice are a necessary complement to care is evident in Eva Feder Kittay's writings on the public dimensions of dependency and dependency work; see Kittay, *Love's Labor: Essays on Women, Equality, and Dependency* (New York: Routledge, 1999).

6. Marilyn Friedman, "Beyond Caring: The De-Moralization of Gender," in *Feminist Social Thought,* ed. Diana Tietjens Meyers (New York: Routledge, 1997), 671–72.

7. Virginia Held, "Feminist Transformations of Moral Theory," in *Ethics: History, Theory, and Contemporary Issues,* ed. Steven M. Cahn and Peter Markie (New York: Oxford University Press, 1998), 689–90.

8. Mill, "The Subjection of Women," 227.

9. See, for example, Michael Maren, *The Road to Hell: The Ravaging Effects of Foreign Aid and International Charity* (New York: Free Press, 1997); Alex de Waal, *Famine Crimes: Politics and the Disaster Relief Industry* (Bloomington: Indiana University Press, 1998); Michael Ignatieff, *The Warrior's Honor: Ethnic War and the Modern Conscience* (New York: Metropolitan Books, 1997), 109–63; Jonathan Moore, ed., *Hard Choices: Moral Dilemmas in Humanitarian Intervention* (Lanham, Md.: Rowman and Littlefield, 1999); Raymond Bonner, "Aid for Sudan's Hungry Keeps War Well Fed," *New York Times,* 11 October 1998; and Lewis Meixler, "Food Becomes a Weapon in Sudan," *Hartford Courant,* 9 August 1998.

10. Paul Lewis, "Humanitarians Worry That a Helping Hand Can Hurt," *New York Times,* 27 February 1999.

11. Michael Maren, "The Faces of Famine," *Newsweek,* 27 July 1998: 12.

12. Maren, "The Faces of Famine," 12.

13. Maren, "The Faces of Famine," 13.

14. Maren, "The Faces of Famine," 13.

15. Maren, "The Faces of Famine," 13.

16. Maren, "The Faces of Famine," 12.

17. Margaret Urban Walker, *Moral Understandings* (New York: Routledge, 1998), 178.

18. Walker, *Moral Understandings,* 180.

19. Walker, *Moral Understandings,* 191.

20. Walker, *Moral Understandings,* 191.

21. Nancy Sherman touches on similar issues in noting that "our private imaginations are fed by public images and narratives" and in citing the consequent "responsibility of

a democratic citizenry to be critical rather than passive consumers of the media and its manipulation" ("Empathy, Respect, and Humanitarian Intervention," *Ethics and International Affairs* 12 [1998], 114).

22. Maren, "The Faces of Famine," 12.

23. Joan C. Tronto, "What Can Feminists Learn about Morality from Caring?" in *Ethics: The Big Questions,* ed. James P. Sterba (Oxford: Blackwell, 1998), 347.

24. Joan C. Tronto, "Care as a Political Concept," in *Revisioning the Political,* ed. Nancy J. Hirschmann and Christine Di Stefano (Boulder: Westview Press, 1996), 146–47.

25. Tronto, "Care as a Political Concept," 143.

26. Even where famine has identifiably natural causes, however, it is further caused by governmental failures to distribute available resources effectively. As Amartya Sen has long argued, alleviating famine in Third World countries requires political reform toward a democratic system in which government is accountable to the people for maintaining adequate distributions of food resources. See Sen, *Development as Freedom* (New York: Knopf, 1999); also see de Waal, *Famine Crimes.*

27. This point has been eloquently argued within a Kantian paradigm by Christine Korsgaard in "The Right to Lie: Kant on Dealing with Evil," *Philosophy and Public Affairs* 15 (1986): 325–49.

28. Philip Gourevitch, *We Wish to Inform You that Tomorrow We Will be Killed with Our Families: Stories from Rwanda* (New York: Farrar, Straus and Giroux, 1998), 268–69.

29. I am grateful to Beryl Lang for discussion of this point.

30. Margaret Urban Walker, personal communication, 10 October 1999.

31. For an argument about empathy and humanitarian concern that suggests such a prioritization, see Nancy Sherman, "Empathy, Respect, and Humanitarian Intervention," *Ethics and International Affairs* 12 (1988): 103–19.

32. Samantha Power, "To *Suffer* by Comparison?" *Daedalus* (Spring 1999): 31–66.

33. Michael Ignatieff, "The Stories We Tell: Television and Humanitarian Aid," in *Hard Choices: Moral Dilemmas in Humanitarian Intervention,* ed. Jonathan Moore (Lanham, Md.: Rowman and Littlefield, 1998), 295.

34. Ignatieff, "The Stories We Tell," 296.

35. For a discussion of the purported phenomenon of "compassion fatigue" (emphasizing its origins in media excess), see Susanne Moeller, *Compassion Fatigue: How the Media Sell Disease, Famine, War and Death* (New York: Routledge, 1999).

36. Sherman, "Empathy, Respect, and Humanitarian Intervention," 114.

37. Elizabeth V. Spelman, *Fruits of Sorrow: Framing Our Attention to Suffering* (Boston: Beacon Press, 1997), 90–112.

38. Spelman, *Fruits of Sorrow,* 1.

39. Spelman, *Fruits of Sorrow,* 7.

40. Spelman, *Fruits of Sorrow,* 85.

41. As Luc Boltanski notes in his book *Distant Suffering: Morality, Media and Politics* (Cambridge: Cambridge University Press, 1999), centuries of European commentators have also ascribed darker psychological motives to the purportedly ethical interest that people take in others' suffering.

42. Ignatieff, "The Stories We Tell," 287–88.

14

Taking Responsibility
for Community Violence

Alison Bailey

The increasing visibility of hate crimes in the United States raises important moral questions about how we, as community members, might conceive of our responsibilities for violence occurring in the communities where we live and work.[1] Since World War II a substantial literature on collective responsibility has arisen that explores the possibility that groups might be held accountable for harms perpetuated by their members. Most of this literature simply extends the premises of individual responsibility to cover nations, corporations, associations, clubs, and random collectives. Feminists, communitarians, existentialists, and virtue theorists, however, find that such accounts are unhelpful when it comes to explaining how citizens might be required to take responsibility for the hate crimes in their communities. Efforts to extend standard observations about individual responsibility to collectives frames responsibility too narrowly. The tendency to understand acts of violence either individually or as the product of loose aggregates of individuals, they argue, prevents us from addressing the social and systemic dimensions of violence that permit hate crimes to flourish.

In this chapter I use the case of Bridesburg, Pennsylvania, to explore the limitations of traditional accounts of responsibility as well as recent alternatives to these views. I begin by explaining why traditional liberal approaches often offer superficial answers to questions about community responsibility. Next, I examine Larry May's social existentialist alternative. Although I argue that "shared responsibility" offers a more complete account of community responsibility than its predecessors, I conclude that this view is constrained by a traditional framework May inherits from earlier postwar discussions on collective responsibility. As a result, shared responsibility is constructed in ways that weaken the moral agency of those harmed either by excluding their voices from discussion or by having dominant voices represent the victim's concerns. Shared responsibility frames questions of accountability in ways that make it difficult for those harmed to enter the dialogue on their own terms. To avoid the possibilities of exclusion I suggest working toward a more open-ended notion of shared "respond-ability" that reframes collective accountability as a forward-looking process attentive to the ways in which group members see, understand, and interact with one another.

A PHILADELPHIA STORY

On Friday, 29 March 1996, Bridget Ward trudged her family's belongings into the row house she had just rented in the 2700 block of Eddington Street.[2] The thirty-two-year-old African American single mother's move to Bridesburg was a step up for her and her daughters, who had been living in West Philadelphia for six years. Ward wanted a safer place to raise her children and was delighted when she found Section Eight housing in the neighborhood. Bridesburg is a remote parochial suburb described by residents as one of "Philadelphia's best kept secrets." Families, mostly of Polish descent, have lived there for generations. Children live around the corner from their parents, and it is not uncommon for properties to be passed from one generation to the next. In 1980 the U.S. census recorded one African American living in this historically working-class white neighborhood. By 1990 there were three, making it a 99 percent white suburb in a city where blacks make up 39 percent of the population.

On the night of her move, Ward heard young people marching up and down her street yelling, "Burn motherfucker, burn!" Saturday morning, she awoke to find "Nigger Leave Now" scrawled on her house and sidewalk, as well as ketchup and motor oil splattered on her walk and steps. After the vandalism was discovered, her sister called the local news station and the police; within an hour reporters arrived to get the residents' reactions to the incident. The majority of the media's attention focused on hostile neighbors who viewed Ward's arrival as a threat to the safety they associated with this part of town, where "everybody knew everyone else." They feared that Bridesburg would soon go the way of other suburbs that "went down the toilet" when "people like Bridget" moved in. Many residents blamed Ward for the hostilities following her move; they held *her* responsible for the bad press the community was receiving. While not directly hostile, other community members positioned themselves as silent onlookers who feared that they might have problems if they supported Ward's family. Only a few residents supported Ward's decision to remain on the block. They apologized for their neighbor's ignorance and tried to convince her that Bridesburg did not condone the violence directed at her.

Two weeks later, Ward received an anonymous letter saying, "We fire-bombed the lady on Thompson Street, and we will firebomb your house too. We'll get your daughters, you better keep them inside."[3] In the end, the police protection and support from City Hall, local churches, the NAACP, the mayor's office, and a handful of community members were not enough. On 2 May Ward came down her steps, threw her hands into the air, and said, "Yes, I'm going to move. Y'all got your neighborhood. You can have it."

WHY TRADITIONAL LIBERAL VIEWS FRAME RESPONSIBILITY FOR HATE CRIMES TOO NARROWLY

In a series of interviews in *Philadelphia Daily News,* Bridesburgers pressed police "to find those responsible for the crimes against Bridget and make *them* accountable for their actions." Residents prefaced their responses to reporters' questions by insisting that *they* were not racists, that the crimes were the product of a few bad apples in the community, and that "the community [did not like] *to be blamed as a whole* for what happened."[4] The tenor of these responses is in keeping with the basic elements of accountability in the liberal tradition that casts individual and collective responsibility in the language of liability, praise, and blame. These discussions have historically taken place at the level of the individual. To say that Person P is morally responsible for wrongful action A usually is taken to mean that a particular individual intended to do A. Similarly, to claim that Person P is morally responsible for Result R means simply that this person in some way contributed to, caused, or intended the result, perhaps with the qualification that these action(s) were done voluntarily, that less harmful alternatives were available and rejected, or that there was some awareness that the individual was contributing to *this* particular result and not another one. Without departing radically from this general picture, individualist premises have been extended to explain collective responsibility—that is, the problem of how nations, random collectives, clubs, corporations, and other aggregates might be understood to be held accountable for a particular state of affairs. These approaches focus primarily on the relationships among individuals in groups and the causal contributions each makes to a particular state of affairs. To say that group member G is, in part, morally responsible for wrongful action A usually is taken to mean that a particular individual shares an intention with others to do A. Similarly, to claim that group member G is morally responsible for Result R suggests that this person contributed to, caused, or intended R, perhaps with the qualification that the action(s) were done voluntarily, that less harmful alternatives were available and rejected, or that there was some awareness that the individuals were contributing to result R1 and not R2. Both accounts vary in subtle and interesting ways, but there is a predominant tendency among such approaches to examine these states of affairs from a perspective that looks downward and back. In addition, as I will argue, such approaches frame responsibility in a way that foregrounds the actions and intentions of harm causers, making the victim's voice difficult to hear.

Few challenge the idea that individual moral agents are the primary bearers of responsibility. The parties guilty of terrorizing Ward's family should be held accountable for their actions; this much is clear. The strength of individual-focused approaches lies in their ability to redress harms simply and quickly. Despite their immediate usefulness, these approaches frame responsibility for hate crimes in ways that maintain the invisibility of the systemic nature of racism. Reducing the crimes against the Ward family to the level of a child's tale of good neighbors rewarded for their kindness and bad neighbors paying for their hatefulness with a moral about the virtues of tolerance treats hate crimes as if they were no different from nonracially motivated crimes. Burglary, car jacking, and armed robbery, for instance, are normally understood as isolated incidents. Victims are picked because they are easy targets; race and gender are often incidental to these crimes. Find the perpetrator, solve the crime, and usually that series of crimes stop. Rape, gay bashing, and racially motivated hate crimes, however, presuppose the conscious choice of female, gay/lesbian, or racial/ethnic minority targets. The identity of the victim is not incidental to the crime. Thus, catching perpetrators is no guarantee that the next "minority" family moving to Bridesburg will not have the same thing happen.

On the surface liberal views recognize that hate crimes deserve urgent attention in a way that random burglaries do not. What I find curious is that these approaches fail to explore what most feminists see as the obvious differences between burglaries and gay bashings. Homogenized approaches to responsibility overlook the important political and cultural fact that hate crimes have systemic backing.[5] To fully address the harms resulting from practices such as rape, gay bashing, and racially motivated violence, our notion of responsibility must look beyond the moral moment of the crime itself. If we understand racism as a complex system of domination that is systemically created and culturally nourished (and irreducible to the attitudes and actions of a few bad people), then it makes sense to frame responsibility in ways that not only hold individual perpetrators responsible but also take into account the systemic dimensions of injustice and the role that communities play in keeping these systems in place. The main complaint against the way liberal theory frames responsibility, then, is that it fails to capture the systemic dimensions of harms associated with (hetero)sexism, racism, and anti-Semitism because it focuses too narrowly on isolated intentions and actions of harm producers and ignores the ways in which complex systems of domination institutionalize practices that increase the likelihood of hate crimes.

The habit of focusing on individual actions and not institutionalized practices reveals an interesting wrinkle in standard conceptions of responsibility. It has been suggested that "downward and back" moral perspectives are epistemically the products of race, gender, and class privilege.[6] Privileged standpoints foreground punishment and reward and the pressing desire to bring guilty parties to justice. This asymmetrical approach is concerned primarily with assigning responsibility for past wrongful actions rather than with preventing future ones. As Claudia Card explains, "The backward-looking orientation embodies a perspective of observation—what Williams calls the 'view from there' as opposed to the 'view from here.' The 'view from there' is characteristic of the administrator, and to some extent, of the teacher or therapist. It is basically a third-person perspective, although we can learn to take this perspective on ourselves."[7] Minnie Bruce Pratt's "view from there" observations about her identity as a southern white woman illustrate Card's claim nicely: "I was taught to be the *judge* of moral responsibility and of punishment only in relation to *my* ethical system; was taught to be the *martyr,* to take all the responsibility for change, *and* the glory, to expect others to do nothing; was taught to be a *peacemaker,* to meditate, negotiate between opposing sides because *I* knew the right way; was taught to be a *preacher,* to point out wrongs and tell others what to do."[8]

Card's and Pratt's descriptions demonstrate how individualist and collective views of responsibility position deliberating agents—the administrator, the judge, the scientist, practitioners of noblesse oblige—as disembodied assigners of praise and blame. I do not mean to dismiss these perspectives altogether. In some cases they are useful. My worry is that privileged perspectives come with epistemic "blind spots." Those with race privilege, for example, will find it difficult to understand why people of color cannot just work harder to get ahead like their parents did. And gender privilege makes it difficult for most men to understand and to take seriously women's constant charges of discrimination and harassment on the job. If liberal views of responsibility are constructed in ways that foreground the concerns of those in positions of privilege (the view from there), it will be more difficult to engage the standpoints of those harmed.

LARRY MAY'S ALTERNATIVE: SHARED RESPONSIBILITY

Larry May's social existentialist account of shared responsibility offers a promising alternative to earlier liberal views. His basic argument is that community members ought to conceive of their moral and political responsibilities as shared; that is, we should learn to see ourselves as being partially responsible for harms perpetuated by or occurring in the groups of which we are members. In *Shared Responsibility,* he describes how community members' racist attitudes might increase the odds that hate crimes will occur in a community. Shared responsibility has two dimensions. As May notes, "Responsibility, like justice, is sometimes backward-looking, concerning the harms that one has caused or the harms one could have prevented. But, responsibility, like virtue, is also forward-looking, concerning character traits, attitudes, and dispositions that one needs to develop to minimize future harm."[9] In the backward-looking sense, the word *sharing* is synonymous with *dividing, parceling out, allotting,* or *apportioning.* Some feminists reject divisive approaches, arguing that they presuppose the existence of a few knowledgeable authorities capable of doing the dividing. This makes assigning responsibility amount to an exercise in control and encourages antagonism among individuals.[10]

The most promising feature of shared responsibility is found in May's forward-looking discussion of how individuals are responsible for those character-based attitudes and dispositions that increase the risks of harm. This approach distinguishes itself from earlier views because it expands responsibility beyond actions and intentions to cover *affective states.* This extension distresses traditional theorists who argue that holding people accountable for their attitudes stretches responsibility to the point of meaninglessness.[11] Nevertheless, May's argument is very convincing. In some instances, he thinks, community member's shared attitudes (e.g., the attitude that "Bridesburg is Philadelphia's best kept secret") contribute to a climate that increases the risks of harm in a community.[12] In his section "Racist Attitudes and Risks," he explains,

> In discussing harmful attitudes, I am not interested in what may be described as *mere* thoughts. Attitudes are not mere cognitive states, but they are also affective states in which a person is, under normal circumstances, moved to behave in various ways as a result of having a particular attitude. . . . Certain cultural attitudes such as racism, can have an effect similar to that produced by the careless parent. Those who have racist attitudes, as opposed to those who do not, create a climate of attitudes in which harm is more likely to occur.[13]

Affective attitudes, such as stereotyping, are morally problematic because they make us insensitive to the needs and feelings of those we perceive to be most unlike us. Bridesburgers who understand African American single mothers to be lazy, promiscuous, or "welfare queens" were more likely to act unneighborly toward Bridget Ward. By maintaining an attitudinal climate that fears having people of color as neighbors, residents share agency for harms to which they may indirectly contribute.

Unlike the earlier divisive connotations of *sharing* that feminists find so worrisome, May's forward-looking usage has a positive participatory meaning. By holding the attitude that newcomers of color are to be regarded with suspicion, Bridesburgers participate in something analogous to a joint venture that increases the likelihood that the next "minority" family moving into the area will be greeted violently. Bridesburgers' role in this "joint venture" is not straightforwardly causal. In some cases, attitudinal climates can be the direct cause of hate crimes; but normally people who hold racist attitudes do not actively *do* anything that can be said to stand in the causal chain leading to violence. Insofar as the residents of Bridesburg make no effort to decrease chances of such violence, by acknowledging or changing their attitudes, May argues that they demonstrate a kind of moral recklessness.[14] However, if communities begin to think in terms of sharing responsibility, May thinks that they will be motivated to be more concerned about the interests of others in their communities. Understanding responsibility as shared leads to an increased sensitivity to the role that community members can and ought to play in the prevention of harms. This sensitivity involves an awareness of and appropriate response to the needs and feelings of others. Reconceiving responsibility as shared, then, aids in the development of sensitivity to the point at which group members will feel ashamed or tainted by their association with the harm and will try to reconcile differences in the future.

SOME CHALLENGES TO MAY'S FORWARD-LOOKING VIEW

The forward-looking account of shared responsibility is a promising resource for those interested in addressing questions of how communities might begin considering questions of moral responsibility. Because May extends responsibility to cover attitudes, the social existentialist account has greater explanatory power than earlier liberal approaches. And, like feminist approaches, May's work helps us to understand how simple emotions can in fact be a socially effective means of maintaining systems of domination: personal attitudes and social mores often have a political function and a political genesis.

Yet I think that shared responsibility suffers from a number of difficulties that weaken it as a resource for feminists concerned with community responsibility. First, although May addresses questions of responsibility from a social existentialist perspective, he still buys into the liberal problem space shaped largely by the language of individual and collective responsibility. This in and of itself is not unusual. Philosophical projects setting out to explore traditional topics anew almost always engage philosophical problems as they have been addressed in the earlier literature. In so doing, such projects may unknowingly inherit the frameworks and epistemic standpoints shaped by earlier conversations. When this happens, the alternative views they propose may be initially more reformative than liberatory. That is, their departures will either shift existing variables within traditional frameworks or introduce new variables into those frameworks. Rarely do they change, challenge, or reinvent those frameworks.

Starting a new conversation in a traditional problem space is not without political consequences. The difficulty with shared responsibility is this: Like earlier views, it has an asymmetrical character that focuses almost exclusively on the behaviors and attitudes of community members who *contribute* to harms while paying less attention to—and sometimes distorting—the attitudes of those harmed. This alone is not problematic: responsibility, on some level, requires linking individual contributions to concrete states of affairs. Problems arise, however, when shared attitudes—and thus shared responsibility—are connected directly to shared agency. This conjunction makes it sound as if only harm-contributing Bridesburgers have moral agency—that only those residents who are aware of their contributions to a racist climate are able to act in ways that stop the hate crimes in their suburb. As May remarks, "There is a sharing in the responsibility for harm by all those who share in potentially harm-producing attitudes"; "the shared risk of being a harm producer is the element which links the members to the harm caused by other members."[15] If shared agency is cast in terms of *contributions* to harm, then how can we address the anger, fear, and concerns of Bridget Ward and her family? When Ward's voice becomes background noise in conversations on responsibility or when white Bridesburgers' speak for her, the dialogue between black families who live in Bridesburg and in the surrounding areas and the larger white community is one-sided: white Bridesburgers do the talking, and those harmed listen. Understanding responsibility in this way makes it easy to explore the interactions between harm producers (e.g., the vandals that terrorized Ward's family) and harm contributors (e.g., white Bridesburgers who stood by without helping Ward or who shared racist attitudes), but it also makes it difficult to explore the interactions between harm contributors and those harmed (e.g., the Ward family and families of color in the surrounding areas). When it comes to explaining responsibility across racial differences, shared responsibility is just as noninteractive as its collectivist predecessors. By framing the conversation in terms of the connections among an agent's attitudes, actions, and harms, shared responsibility obscures an important piece of the community dynamic. It foregrounds the moral agency of harm producers and harm contributors; yet the concerns of those harmed are either obscured or made visible only through the observations and reactions of the harm contributors. Responsibility focuses on and responds to the shame and taint that white Bridesburgers feel, without addressing the fear, frustration, and anger that Ward's family experiences. When this happens, motivation for preventing further harms may be driven more by shame than by genuine concern.

Again, Claudia Card's observations on oppression and responsibility point to what I understand to be the basic sticking point here. Card suggests that what it means to take responsibility might vary with one's social location. To understand this she asks us to consider "what emerges when we look forward and up, toward the future and from the standpoint of those [like Bridget] struggling to put their lives together."[16] For members of oppressed groups, responsibility is often complicated by the moral damage they have sustained through the constant wear and tear of daily injustices. One reason that May's framework makes it difficult to address Bridget's anger and fear is that—despite its forward-looking character—it still looks down! Although May makes a clean epistemic shift away from the "view from there," there is still a sense in which the epistemic perspective underlying shared responsibility is privileged—that is, constructed by white Bridesburgers who frame their observations about responsibility from a privileged downward-looking "here" that can be characterized by feeling "at home" in their suburb.

The nature of the privileged "here" is best described in Maria Lugones's language of "world" travel.[17] Anyone who "world travels" will experience being "at ease" in worlds populated by people who share their experiences and histories. They will share being "ill at ease" in worlds where arrogant perception constructs them in ways that they do not recognize. Although both privileged and oppressed groups can and do world travel, the experience for each is different. One feature of oppression is having to world travel out of necessity. Members of marginalized groups are often required to leave their worlds to work, shop, attend classes, or find safe housing in "worlds" that perceive them arrogantly. This experience gives oppressed peoples the skills they need to interact safely with members of dominant groups on a regular basis. Members of privileged groups rarely world travel out of necessity. Part of what it means to have race privilege is to be "at ease" in most "worlds" most of the time. I am convinced that the individualist undertones in most of the responsibility literature are due, in part, to the fact that the authors addressing these issues have constructed responsibility from worlds in which they are at ease. This alone is not problematic. Most of us write from the space of "worlds" in which we are at ease. Difficulties arise only when we insist that constructions of philosophical concepts, such as responsibility, are *not* world dependent or that traditional constructions of these concepts can be easily extended to cover the experiences of persons who are ill at ease in the worlds in which we are comfortable and that, by doing so, these views can be reimagined as interactive.

Shared responsibility is "world" dependent in the sense that its perspective mirrors more closely the experiences of those who feel "at home" or "at ease" in a community than it does those of residents, like the Ward family, who are perceived arrogantly as outsiders. Two themes in May's early work suggest this. First, when applied to the case of Bridesburg, shared responsibility automatically foregrounds the actions of those residents who either directly and indirectly contribute to harms. This centers our attention on the agency of dominant group members and explores how that might take responsibility for any harms to which they might contribute. Because outsiders do not share responsibility for the ways they are constructed in worlds where they are ill at ease, Bridget's concerns can only be engaged indirectly through discussions of how white Bridesburgers might become sensitive to the effects of *their* attitudes and actions on others. If this is the focus, Ward and her family become the subject of the conversation rather than discussants. This is not just another wrinkle in the old problem of how to divide responsibility: it raises important issues about who gets to speak.

Next, May's discussion of moral sensitivity to harms seems to be constructed from what Marilyn Frye might call a "whitely" here.[18] Shared responsibility is world dependent because it requires white Bridesburgers to be critical of their attitudes and dispositions and to understand how their affective states work with those of other community members to increase risk. The difficulty here is not with cultivating sensitivity to harms per se; rather, it is with the unidirectional nature of the sensitivity. This requires more than simple attentiveness to how others are harmed by our actions or how we might learn to become sensitive to the needs of others. White Bridesburgers are said to share responsibility for harms when, upon examining their own attitudes, they discover that they hold harmful stereotypes about black single mothers and that these stereotypes shape the way they see the Ward family. However, shared responsibility has no provisions encouraging white Bridesburgers to explore how Bridget might see them—how she might be angered by their self-focused efforts to take responsibility for potentially harmful attitudes and character traits. To avoid charges of reasserting dominance, the morally sensitive person must be critical of this dynamic. "Responsibility," as Linda Bell suggests, "extends to the way in which one is seen by others and to one's being as an inert presence in the world."[19] But understanding responsibility in these terms requires a great deal of work, and it is easier for those in positions of privilege to engage and critique their own attitudes without leaving the worlds in which they are at ease than it is for them to engage "outsiders within," like Ward, in ways that challenge their very character and identity. Sensitivity to the pain or anger others might feel is cultivated not only by an awareness of one's attitudes but also by learning to see oneself as others see one; and world travel is an essential means of cultivating this form of bifurcated consciousness. When our examination of moral sensitivity is unidirectional, possibilities for dialogue are limited; Bridget, again, becomes the subject of conversation rather than a participant.

Now, there is nothing about May's view that would exclude him from discussing how white Bridesburgers are seen by people of color in the community. But his failure to explore the details of interactions between harm contributors and those harmed suggests that dominant group members' worlds are what shape the "view from here." And again, this has political consequences. As Lugones explains,

You [whites/Anglos] are inattentive to our interactions. You are not keenly attentive to what our interactions might reveal.

You block identification with that self because knowing us in the way necessary to know that self would reveal to you that we are also more than one and that not all the selves we are make you important. . . . Being central, being a being in the foreground is important to our being integrated as one responsible decision-maker. Your sense of responsibility and decision making are tied to being able to say exactly who it is that did what, and that person must be one and have a will in good working order. And you are very keen on seeing yourself as a decision-maker, a responsible being: It gives you substance.[20]

The forward-looking dimensions of shared responsibility are, I think, restricted by the "desire to see ourselves as decision makers" and our failure as decision makers to be "keenly attentive to what our interactions might reveal." White Bridesburgers' examination of community dynamics takes place within the worlds, texts, laws, conceptual frameworks, and vocabulary of responsibility with which they feel at ease. May's suggestion that we examine those habits and attitudes that increase the likelihood of harm does not address the importance of white Bridesburgers getting out of their worlds—and thus seeing themselves as plural selves—as a way of understanding those harms from the perspective of the harmed. It does not emphasize the links between most traditional constructions of responsibility and the failure of most dominant group members to examine the nature of their interactions with members of marginalized communities.[21]

SHARED "RESPOND-ABILITY"

The alternative [moral] epistemology . . . will not be one of individuals standing singly before the impersonal dicta of Morality, but one of human beings connected in various ways and at various depths responding to each other by engaging together in a search for shareable interpretations of their responsibilities, and/or bearable resolutions to their moral binds.

—Margaret Urban Walker[22]

I want to preserve the participatory use of *sharing* that May highlights in his forward-looking description of responsibility, but I wish to do so without embracing the noninteractive baggage he inherits from earlier collectivist views. To overcome this limitation, I suggest rethinking shared responsibility in ways that allow us to problematize the downward-looking nature of this world-dependent view. Although I cannot offer a full-blown alternative theory at this point, I can offer a few suggestions about the kinds of issues we should be attentive to when addressing questions of accountability for community violence. I do have a few suggestions as to how we might proceed. I can also encourage scholars and activists to begin thinking about how to reframe responsibility in ways that avoid the pitfalls of downward-looking epistemic standpoints. I recognize that this is difficult. Hearing from the oppressed is just what people in privilege have historically refused to do. So the process of making the concerns I have raised visible to members of privileged groups is a long and difficult one.

Feminists' interest in questions of responsibility should extend beyond a simple intellectual curiosity that can be satisfied by achieving accurate moral judgments regarding the party or parties responsible for harmful states of affairs. Instead, it should seek out something that Margaret Walker describes as "shareable interpretations and bearable resolutions to our moral binds."[23] To an extent this means giving up seeing ourselves as responsible beings—in the sense that being responsible means focusing exclusively on short-term fixes *for* those harmed. Instead, all community members need to dialogue *with* those harmed to prevent future harms. In this way responsible action becomes more a matter of "acting with" than of "acting for."

We need a more open-ended account of responsible action that constructs responsible action in terms of how a community should *respond* to harms regardless of each member's contributions. The worry that responsibility continues to be crafted as an ethics of control is one reason why some feminists have traded the language of responsibility for one of responsiveness.[24] What is needed here might be called shared *respond-ability:* a way of thinking about accountability that reframes our approach to harm along noncausal forward-looking lines. A shared respond-ability would emphasize how community members can take a practical interest in determining not only how they might respond to the "guilty parties" but also how they should support those harmed. Respond-ability will also leave room to address how the community as a whole might strategize ways of preventing future harms. Harriet Goldhor Lerner captures this sentiment when she expresses her desire not to discuss responsibility in terms of causality or self-blame and instead speaks of "the ability to observe ourselves and others in interaction and to respond to a familiar situation in a new and different way."[25]

The case of Billings, Montana, nicely illustrates what Lerner means about responding to a familiar situation in a new way and different way.[26] Billings is a town of about 84,000 residents bordering the Crow Indian Reservation in south-central Montana. In the early 1990s the town experienced a wave of hate crimes later attributed to Aryan Nation groups whose literature made it clear that that they would, by any means, racially "purify" the Northwest. Their threats were followed by a series of violent incidents. "Nuke Israel" posters appeared in Synagogues, Ku Klux Klan flyers were stuffed into local newspapers, Jewish gravesites were desecrated, a local African Methodist Episcopal (AME) church was defaced, the home of Dawn Fasthorse was vandalized, and a brick was thrown through the window of the Schnitzer home where a Chanukah menorah was displayed.

After the first few incidents, members of the Human Rights Commission and groups of concerned citizens held a meeting to strategize possible responses to the events. They decided that doing nothing was the moral equivalent to creating an environment in which harms would only escalate, so they encouraged all community members to visibly demonstrate support for them. When the AME church was visited by skinheads, citizens who did not normally attend the church showed up in record numbers the following week, as if to say, "If you want to harm this congregation, you will have to harm us as well." When the Fasthorse home was vandalized with anti-Indian graffiti, the local painters' union donated time and paint to restore the home. When the Schnitzer home was attacked, the *Billings Gazette* ran the story on the front page, printed a full-page color menorah, and encouraged all citizens to hang the reproduction in their windows. A few days later six homes and one church displaying the image were vandalized, but the town redoubled its efforts, and by the end of the next week 10,000 homes displayed the menorah and the crimes stopped.

Billings's population is less homogeneous than that of Bridesburg, and perhaps this contributes to the unified success there. I present the case of Billings not to suggest that it might be a template for tolerance that will work for all towns. It will not. Instead, I offer it as a clear illustration of how one community came to understand the importance of respond-ability. Unlike Bridesburg residents, they took risks and came up with a bearable solution to their moral binds by acting with and not for those harmed. Shared respond-ability does not end with acknowledging one's role in community harms; it extends to strategizing about how to make future threats unsuccessful. In the Ward case, the goal is not just to find the guilty parties and move on; shared respond-ability also has the long-term goal of making the community safe for the next black family that moves in. To acknowledge and engage the forward and up moral perspective, shared respond-ability must have an active, persistent, collaborative dimension: sharing must be sharing across worlds. The point is not only to change the attitudes, actions, and practices of individual community members but to do so successfully with long-term changes in mind. Sharon Welch describes this as creating a "matrix of further resistance."[27]

The extent to which an action is an appropriate response to the needs of others is constituted as much by the possibilities it creates as by its immediate results. Responsible action does not mean one individual resolving the problems of others. It is, rather, participation in communal work, laying the groundwork for creative response of people in the present and in the future. Responsible action means changing what can be altered in the present even though a problem is not completely resolved. Responsible action provides partial resolutions and the inspiration and conditions for further partial resolutions by others. It is sustained and enabled by participation in a community of resistance.[28]

Shared respond-ability, then, requires a more elastic view that ties action not only to individual contributions but also to community responses that creatively lay the groundwork for long-lasting social change. What if the Ward family had moved into a community with this view of responsibility firmly in place?

NOTES

1. I have in mind here recent events such as the kidnapping, beating, and murder of Matthew Shepard in Laramie, Wyoming, and Benjamin Smith's two-state rampage against Jews, blacks, and Asian Americans on 4 July 1998 that resulted in two deaths and nine woundings in Illinois and Indiana.

2. This incident was covered on ABC's *Nightline* on 20 May 1996. For accounts of racial harassment against Bridget Ward and her family, see Suzette Parmley, "This Stuff Won't Come Off: Newcomer to Bridesburg Shaken by Slurs but Digs In," *Philadelphia Inquirer,* 1 April 1996: B01; Nicole Weisensee, "Racism Hits Bridesburg; But Some in Neighborhood Deplore Hatred," *Philadelphia Daily News,* 1 April 1996: 03; Murray Dubin, "Bridesburg Residents Reflect Racist Welcome," *Philadelphia Inquirer,* 3 April 1996: B01; Suzanne Sataline, "Bridesburg's Enemy? To Many It's Change," *Philadelphia Inquirer,* 7 April 1996: B01; Jeff Gelles, "Black Family Fleeing Bridesburg after Death Threat," *Philadelphia Inquirer,* 2 May 1996: B01; and Lea Stilton, "Leaving Bridesburg: 'You Can Have It,'" *Philadelphia Inquirer,* 3 May 1996: A01.

3. The crimes against Ward were not unique to Bridesburg and other Philadelphia neighborhoods during the mid-1990s. A year earlier an Arab family opened a pizza parlor in Bridesburg and endured a summer of taunts, vandalism, and fights. That same summer a black family moved into a house on Thompson Street but moved a month later after their house was spray painted with insults and an M-80 exploded in front of their door. In South Philadelphia, Arnold Bickerstaff, an African American man, also received a threatening letter when he tried to move into the mostly white neighborhood. On 8 June, Samantha Starnes's rental house was ransacked and vandalized a week before she planned to move in. In November, the Daggett family, who had been living in the mostly white community of Mayfair, received the first of several anonymous threatening letters. See Myung Oak Kim, "Philly Housing Rate Climbing," *Philadelphia Daily News,* 18 June 1996: 04; Sataline, "Bridesburg's Enemy?" B01; Peter Nicholas, "Pastor Leads Crusade against Racism: Northeast Philadelphia Has Had Some Incidents," *Philadelphia Inquirer,* 29 December 1997: A01; and Nicholas, "Voice of Tolerance Arrested as Bigot," *Philadelphia Inquirer,* 14 June 1996: B01.

4. Myung Oak Kim, "Bridesburg Don't Smear Us," *Philadelphia Daily News,* 10 April 1996: 6, emphasis added.

5. For a discussion of the institutional nature of hate crimes, see Claudia Card, "Rape Terrorism," in her *The Unnatural Lottery: Character and Moral Luck* (Philadelphia: Temple University Press, 1996), 97–117.

6. See Claudia Card, *The Unnatural Lottery: Character and Moral Luck* (Philadelphia: Temple University Press, 1996), 22–48; and Naomi Scheman, *Engenderings: Constructions of Knowledge, Authority, and Privilege* (New York: Routledge, 1993), 229–39.

7. Card, *The Unnatural Lottery,* 25–26.

8. Minnie Bruce Pratt, "Identity: Skin, Blood, Heart," in *Yours in Struggle: Three Feminist Perspectives on Anti-Semitism and Racism,* ed. Elly Bulkin, Minnie Bruce Pratt, and Barbara Smith (Ithaca: Firebrand Books, 1984), 14–15.

9. Larry May, *Sharing Responsibility* (Chicago: University of Chicago Press, 1991), 34.

10. For a discussion, see Sarah Hoagland, *Lesbian Ethics: Toward New Value* (Palo Alto, Calif.: Institute for Lesbian Studies, 1988), 256; and Sharon Welch, *A Feminist Ethic of Risk* (Minneapolis, Minn.: Fortress Press, 1990), 23–24.

11. The clearest expression of this view can be found in H. D. Lewis, "Collective Responsibility," *Philosophy: The Journal of the Royal Institute of Philosophy* 23 (1948): 3–18. Susan Wolf addresses this worry indirectly when she asserts that it is a mistake to set moral requirements too high; see her "Moral Saints," *Journal of Philosophy* 79, no. 8 (August 1982): 419–39.

12. Iris Marion Young and Linda Bell also suggest that subtle behaviors and dispositions that reproduce oppression ought to be subject to moral evaluation. See Young, *Justice and the Politics of Difference* (Princeton, N.J.: Princeton University Press, 1990), 122–55; and Bell, *Rethinking Ethics in the Midst of Violence: A Feminist Approach to Freedom* (Lanham, Md.: Rowman & Littlefield, 1993), 10.

13. May, *Sharing Responsibility,* 46.

14. This view is not as demanding as it sounds. Expanding agency to include attitudes and dispositions likely to increase harm does not require that we assign responsibility for those attitudes not completely under the control of our will. May's claim is weaker: persons are responsible for attitudes that can partially change, and he argues that it is reasonable to think that they should change. Following Jean-Paul Sartre, he claims that individuals cannot be excused from responsibility for their attitudes merely because they did not choose to be aware of those attitudes and reflect on them: "Pre-reflective awareness of an attitude is sufficient for supporting the claim that a person could have chosen to reject that attitude, since the person could have begun such a process by first bringing the attitude before reflective awareness" (Larry May and Stacy Hoffman, eds., *Collective Responsibility: Five Decades of Debate in Theoretical and Applied Ethics* [Lanham, Md.: Rowman & Littlefield, 1993]).

15. May, *Sharing Responsibility,* 48, 51.

16. Card, *The Unnatural Lottery,* 23.

17. Maria Lugones, "Playfulness, 'World'-Travelling, and Loving Perception," *Hypatia* 2, no. 2 (Summer 1987): 3–21.

18. Marilyn Frye, "White Woman Feminist," in her *Willful Virgin: Essays in Feminism* (Freedom, Calif.: The Crossing Press, 1992), 147–69.

19. Bell, *Rethinking Ethics in the Midst of Violence,* 214.

20. Maria Lugones, "On the Logic of Pluralist Feminism," in *Feminist Ethics,* ed. Claudia Card (Lawrence: University of Kansas Press, 1991), 35–44.

21. May's later work does a better job at addressing community interactions across difference; see Larry May, *The Socially Responsive Self: Social Theory and Professional Ethics* (Chicago: University of Chicago Press, 1996), 86–102. However, I would argue that even his revised account constructs responsiveness to people outside of the worlds in which we are comfortable in ways that fail to address the importance of selves getting out of the worlds in which we are comfortable and attempting to understand how those harmed see us.

22. Margaret Urban Walker, "Moral Understandings: Alternative 'Epistemology' for Feminist Ethics," *Hypatia* 4, no. 2 (Summer 1989): 15–28.

23. Walker, "Moral Understandings," 20.

24. See, for example, Hoagland, *Lesbian Ethics,* and Welch, *A Feminist Ethic of Risk.*

25. Harriet Goldhor Lerhner, *The Dance of Anger: A Woman's Guide to Changing the Patterns of Intimate Relationships* (New York: Harper and Row, 1985), 14.

26. This case is chronicled in the California Working Group's video production *Not in Our Town* (California Working Group, P. O. Box 10326, Oakland, Calif. 94610).

27. Welch, *A Feminist Ethics of Risk,* 29.

28. Welch, *A Feminist Ethics of Risk,* 74–75.

Index

Abel, Elizabeth, 43n11
Adorno, Theodor, 125, 126
African American, xxvi, 23, 24, 26, 27,
    31n12, 39, 43n1, 224; care,
    cooperation, and interdependence,
    121; damage imagery of, 88, 89;
    families, 87–88; feminists, 42;
    identity, construction of, 38, 39; men,
    21, 35; Moynihan report, 87–89; in
    Philadelphia, 220, 232n3; women,
    21, 123, 224, 232n14. *See also* Black
    Americans, cut-off category
agency, 233n14; female, 124; individual,
    222; inequality and oppression, xi;
    moral, xii, xiii, xvii, 50, 52, 55, 56, 60;
    counterstory, 58; identity, 45; love,
    130; responsibility, 85, 221, 222;
    understanding, 6; free, 51, 54;
    oppression, 85
agent, moral, 125, 154; abstract and
    isolated, 106; competent, 57;
    embodied, 105; forgiveness, 139;
    ideal, 120; social and political, 110
Alcoff, Linda, 43n2
Allison, Dorothy, xix, 135
Amelung, Heike, 116n34
Andrew, Barbara, xv, xvii–xix

Angel in the House, xvii, xviii, xxixn8,
    129, 130; care ethics' *telos,* 120, 122,
    124; expectation of women, 119;
    purity of, 123
Anglo-European men, 10, 11
Anglos, 39
Anita Hill/Clarence Thomas hearings, 27
Anscombe, G. E. M., 74n6
anti-individualism, 173; emotions, 174;
    mental phenomena, 170, 176–78. *See
    also* Scheman, Naomi
Appiah, K. Anthony, 35, 37
Arendt, Hannah, xiv, 65–68, 70–72,
    75n22; action, 71, 74n8; democracy,
    74n17; ethics and politics, 67, 68,
    74n9; objection to feminism,
    75nn29,30; power, 66, 74n13; racism,
    75n19; violence, 65, 66, 74n6,14,16,
    75n34
Aristotle, xv, 104, 110, 165n3; good life,
    82, 93; the mean, 147, 148; virtue, 79,
    81, 105, 112
Asian American, 26
Austen, Jane, xxii, xxiii, 167–68, 170–74,
    176, 179, 181, 183n28
autonomy, xi, xvii, 120; basic goods,
    121; ideal, 125; justice, xviii; learned

About the Contributors

Barbara S. Andrew is an assistant professor of philosophy at the University of Oregon. She has published articles in *Philosophy Today* and *Hypatia* and is currently working on a book on love and freedom in feminist ethics.

Alison Bailey is an associate professor at Illinois State University, where she teaches philosophy and women's studies. She is the author of *Posterity and Strategic Policy: A Moral Assessment of U.S. Strategic Weapons Options* (Unwin-Hyman, 1989) and several articles on feminist peace politics. Her current research explores moral questions addressing whether members of privileged groups have responsibilities to use privilege to dismantle complex systems of domination. Her work appears in *Hypatia, The Journal of Social Philosophy, Whiteness: Feminist Philosophical Narratives,* and *Decentering the Center: Philosophy for a Multicultural, Postcolonial and Feminist World.* Her current obsession is Iyengar-style yoga.

Bat-Ami Bar On teaches philosophy and women's studies at the State University of New York at Binghamton. Her primary theoretical and activist interests are in violence, though she escapes them (often?) by pursuing other themes. She is the editor of *Daring to Be Good: Essays in Feminist Ethico-Politics* with Ann Ferguson (Routledge, 1998), "Women and Violence: A Special Issue of *Hypatia*" (Fall 1996), *Engendering Origins: Critical Feminist Readings of Plato and Aristotle,* and *Modern Engenderings: Critical Feminist Readings in the History of Modern Western Philosophy* (both State University of New York, 1994).

Natalie Brender, an assistant professor of philosophy at Wesleyan University, writes and teaches in the areas of ethics, feminist philosophy, philosophy and literature, and political philosophy. Her current projects focus on Kantian moral agency and on problems of cosmopolitanism and international ethics.

Peggy DesAutels is an assistant professor of philosophy at the University of Dayton. She is the coauthor with Margaret Pabst Battin and Larry May of *Praying for a Cure: When Medical and Religious Practices Conflict.* She has published in such areas as feminist bioethics, moral psychology, and the philosophy of mind. She is currently writing a book on moral perception.

Margaret A. McLaren is an associate professor of philosophy at Rollins College in Winter Park, Florida, where she teaches philosophy and women's studies. She received her Ph.D. from Northwestern University in 1991. Her research interests are in feminist theory, contemporary Continental philosophy, social and political theory, and ethics. She has published articles on communitarian ethics, the social construction of gender, and feminism and Foucault. Currently she is working on a book entitled *Foucault, Feminism and Embodied Subjectivity* (State University of New York Press, in press).

Diana Tietjens Meyers is a professor of philosophy and women's studies at the University of Connecticut at Storrs. She is the author of *Self, Society, and Personal Choice* (Columbia University Press, 1989) and *Subjection and Subjectivity: Psychoanalytic Feminism and Moral Philosophy* (Routledge, 1994). *Feminists Rethink the Self* (Westview Press, 1997) and *Feminist Social Thought: A Reader* (Routledge, 1997) are her most recent edited collections. She is currently at work on a new monograph—*Gender in the Mirror: Imagery that Confounds Us* (Oxford University Press, in press).

Uma Narayan is an associate professor of philosophy and the director of the Women's Studies Program at Vassar College. She is the author of *Dislocating Cultures: Identities, Traditions and Third World Feminism* (Routledge, 1997), which was awarded the American Political Science Association's 1998 Victoria Schuck Award for the best book on women and politics. She coedited *Reconstructing Political Theory: Feminist Perspectives* (Pennsylvania State University Press, 1997) with Mary Lyndon Shanley; *Having and Raising Children: Unconventional Families, Hard Choices and the Social Good* (Pennsylvania State University Press, 1999) with Julia Bartkowiak; and *Decentering the Center: Philosophy for a Multicultural, Postcolonial and Feminist World* (Indiana University Press, 2000) with Sandra Harding.

Hilde Lindemann Nelson is an associate professor in the Philosophy Department at Michigan State University. She is the coauthor, with James Lindemann Nelson, of *The Patient in the Family* (Routledge, 1995) and *Alzheimer's: Answers to Hard Questions for Families* (Doubleday, 1996). She has edited two collections—*Feminism and Families* and *Stories and Their Limits: Narrative Approaches to Bioethics* (both Routledge, 1997)— and coedited *Meaning and Medicine: A Reader in the Philosophy of Health Care* (Routledge, 1999). Her articles in feminist ethics have appeared in *Hypatia* and a number of edited collections. She coedits the Reflective Bioethics Series for Routledge and the Feminist Constructions Series for Rowman & Littlefield. Her most recent book is *Injured Identities, Narrative Repair* (Cornell University Press, 2001).

James Lindemann Nelson is a professor of philosophy at Michigan State University, where he teaches and writes on topics in bioethics and moral theory. He has coauthored two books and coedited an anthology; essays on feminist themes have appeared in *Hypatia, The Kennedy Institute of Ethics Journal, The Hastings Center Report,* and *Theoretical Medicine,* as well as in several collections, including *Feminism and Bioethics: Beyond Reproduction,* edited by Susan Wolf, and *Mother Time: Women, Aging and Ethics,* edited by Margaret Walker (Rowman & Littlefield, 1999).

Nancy Potter received her Ph.D. in philosophy and feminist studies from the University of Minnesota and is now an assistant professor at the University of Louisville. Her primary interests are in ethics and social and political philosophy, including philosophies of peace. Her latest research concerns the philosophical implications of teaching empathy to sex offenders in the state prison system. She is also writing a book on trustworthiness as a virtue.

Phyllis Rooney is an associate professor of philosophy at Oakland University in Michigan. Much of her work is in feminist and naturalized epistemology (including moral epistemology), with a special focus on the reason question in feminism. She has published articles in *Hypatia, American Philosophical Quarterly, Philosophical Forum, Metaphilosophy, Proceedings of the Philosophy of Science Association,* and *Epistemology: The Big Questions,* edited by Linda Martín Alcoff (Blackwell). She is preparing a book with the working title *Reason and Gender.*

Lisa Tessman is an assistant professor of philosophy and women's studies at the State University of New York at Binghamton. She is currently working on a book that critically examines the possible uses of virtue ethics for communities involved in liberatory struggles, such as feminist communities and communities of people of color; the project aims to provide tools for communities to be reflective about the moral significance of both their own internal structures and their strategies of political resistance.

Joan C. Tronto is a professor of political science and women's studies at Hunter College and the Graduate School, City University of New York. She has written on care in feminist theory, publishing *Moral Boundaries: A Political Argument for an Ethic of Care* in 1993. She coedited (with Kathy Jones and Cathy Cohen) *Women Transforming Politics: An Alternative Reader* in 1997 (New York University Press, 1997). She is currently writing on the political dimensions of unequal caring in society.

Margaret Urban Walker is a professor of philosophy at Fordham University. Author of *Moral Understandings: A Feminist Study in Ethics* (Routledge, 1998) and editor of *Mother Time: Women, Aging, and Ethics* (Rowman and Littlefield, 1999), she writes on moral judgment, epistemology, and responsibility. Her current project is a book on "moral repair," the practices we use to respond to wrongdoing and the effects of those practices on moral relations, and the beliefs and feelings that sustain them.

Joanne Waugh is an associate professor of philosophy at the University of South Florida in Tampa. From 1995 to 1998 she was one of the editors of *Hypatia: A Journal of Feminist Philosophy*. She has published articles in *The Journal of Aesthetics and Art Criticism, The Monist,* and *The Journal of Aesthetic Education,* as well as chapters in a number of collections on Greek philosophy. She is currently writing a book on why Plato wrote dialogues.